D1585184

THE DICTIONARY OF NATIONAL CELEBRITY

THE DICTIONARY OF
NATIONAL
CELEBRITY

HERMIONE EYRE &
WILLIAM DONALDSON

WEIDENFELD & NICOLSON
LONDON

First published in Great Britain in 2005
by Weidenfeld & Nicolson

1 2 3 4 5 6 7 8 9 10

A CIP catalogue record for this book is available from the British
Library.

ISBN-13 9 780304 368051
ISBN-10 0 304 6805 9

Design by www.carrstudio.co.uk

Printed in Great Britain by Clays Ltd, St Ives plc

Weidenfeld & Nicolson

The Orion Publishing Group Ltd
Orion House
5 Upper Saint Martin's Lane
London, WC2H 9EA
www.orionbooks.co.uk

The Orion Publishing Group's policy is to use papers that are natural, renewable and
recyclable products and made from wood grown in sustainable forests. The logging and
manufacturing processes are expected to conform to the environmental regulations of the
country of origin.

FOREWORD

Willie Donaldson and I started working together in late 2003. He was 69, a renowned satirist, sybarite and recluse. I was 23, and just settling into my first job in journalism. Fascinated by his reputation, I used a feature I was writing on "the joy of hangovers" as a pretext to interview him. No one was allowed to visit him at 139 Elm Park Mansions, the address familiar from the top of the Henry Root letters, so I telephoned him, nervously. He had nothing to say about hangovers, but he did want to talk about my job at the *Independent on Sunday*. "Do you write those naughty bits about celebrities?" I did. Willie made a noise somewhere between a gasp and a snort (his breathing, I noticed, was bad; in a year and a half, it was to kill him) and said he had an idea for a collaboration. It was to be a Devil's Dictionary of Celebrity, making fun of everyone who was famous for being famous. A few weeks later, we met for the first of our working lunches at Kettners, in Soho. We drafted entries, allocated topics and, while Willie had his brandy and cigar, decided which has-been celebrities deserved to be filed under "Maze at Longleat, Celebrities lost in the". Willie was always encouraging, and kind, and fun. After a period of happy collaboration we produced this strange little monster of a dictionary. We had just handed our final text in to the lawyer when Willie died unexpectedly in June 2005. (The last entry he wrote was "Ingredients, the best.") It is to my great sadness that Willie didn't live to see this book published.

Hermione Eyre, October 2005

The engraving bears the inscription:

ALBERT9
DVRER
NORICVS
FACIEBAT
AD·1504·

Adam and Eve (*c*.4031 BC–*c*.4004). The first Celebrity Couple – 'the Katie Price and Peter ANDRE of their day.' In a paper published in November 2004, a team of clinical psychologists at the University of Sussex argued that, 'had Adam and Eve been alive today they would have brought out a raunchy fitness video and their own range of saucy lingerie. Adam and Eve insiders would have reported that on holiday in the Caribbean the loved-up twosome couldn't keep their hands off one another. It is open to speculation as to whether, on returning to Heathrow looking tanned and relaxed, Eve would have announced an ambition to star as Roxy in *Chicago*, a West End musical. Certainly, the once distinguished house of HarperCollins would have offered her a seven-figure sum for her no-holds-barred autiobiography' (Salter, Horrocks-Taylor and De Santos, *The Celebrity Syndrome: Notes Towards a Diagnosis*, Sussex University Press, 2004).

Adam Ant, properly **Stuart Leslie Goddard** (b.1954). Rock-and-roll musician. After graduating from art school, Goddard changed his name to Ant and formed a band. His distinctive appearance (fancy dress and a white striped face) and self-named 'antmusic' – uninhibited theatrics and a tribal drum sound – ensured that he was soon at the forefront of the 'New Romantic' movement. The band issued several hit singles, most notably 'Dick Wear White Sox', 'Stand and Deliver' and 'Goody Two Shoes'. It is to Goddard's credit that when his popularity dwindled he didn't, in Tom Sutcliffe's construction, reveal himself to be merely a 'spike-haired opportunist', palling up with orang-utans in their natural setting

and, in the company of soap-opera actress Tamzin Outhwaite, swimming with dolphins for the benefit of daytime-television viewers. Rather, he continued to display an eccentric personality. In 2002 he was arrested in the Prince of Wales public house in South London for assault and possession of a firearm. Other customers had laughed at his clothing ensemble and he had threatened them with a starting pistol. For this offence he received a one-year supervision order. When last heard of, he was examining his priorities in a Celebrity Clinic.

Adams, Helen (b.1979). Welsh hairdresser employed by the Classy Cutz Salon, Newport, before participating in *Big Brother 2* in 2001. Her observations on the human condition endeared her to the nation, as did her bubbly personality, her frequent references to Cwmbran, which was her birthplace rather than a breakfast cereal, and catchphrases such as 'I'm really into blinking, me'. This turned out to be a local euphemism for experimental fumblings under the duvet with other housemates. Her refreshing performance earned her a place in the South East Wales Hall of Fame – something of an honour bearing in mind that only two other residents of this area have been thus elevated: Mr Howard Winston, the former world champion boxer in the featherweight division, and Mr Sion Morgan, a fan of Miss Dorothy Squires, the accident-prone cabaret singer. Miss Squires's final years were spent in a flat above a fish-and-chip shop loaned to her by Mr Morgan. When the mother of Voice-of-an-Angel soprano, Charlotte CHURCH, asked Mr Morgan whether the flat might be available in the near future for her daughter, he was obliged to tell her that he was keeping it for Miss Geri HALLIWELL. After her eviction from *Big Brother 2*, Helen enjoyed a brief moment of Celebrity, appearing as a cosmetics expert on Sky TV's short-lived *Lorraine Kelly Show*. A video of her naked on the *Big Brother* set has surfaced on the internet (www.celebrityoops.com).

Adolescence. Post-pubescent condition enjoyed by the majority between the ages of 13 and 18, but not by soccer players until their late twenties.

Adult content. Under Mark Thompson, CHANNEL 4 took over from Channel 5 as the natural home for programmes containing adult content. It is customary to warn the audience in advance: 'The documentary which follows, *Ruislip: Behind Closed Curtains*, contains adult material which some viewers may find disturbing.' There follow scenes in which elderly fat women in thongs discipline professional men in leather restraining pouches. With a back catalogue such as this, Thompson was the natural choice to succeed Greg Dyke as director general of the BBC in 2003. At Channel 4, Thompson was succeeded by Kevin LYGO, previously director of programmes at Channel 5.

See also TELEVISION WE DESERVE, THE.

Adultery, Celebrities taken in. *See* BONKING BORIS; EDWINA, COUNTESS MOUNTBATTEN (*under* 'HUTCH'); ELLIOTT, GRACE DALRYMPLE; HENRY VIII; LANCELOT AND GUINEVERE; PARKER BOWLES, CAMILLA.

Adultery, Celebrities allegedly taken in. *See* BECKHAM, DAVID (*under* BECKHAM, VICTORIA).

Advertisements, ill-judged appearances by Celebrities in. Michael Winner selling motor-car insurance dressed in a ballerina's tutu. Johnny Vaughan dressed as Little Bo Peep puffing his Breakfast radio show on Capital FM. Cartoon versions of former England cricketers Ian Botham and Allan Lamb punningly appearing on behalf of British lamb. Vicki Walberg, a former Miss UK, appearing as Fern Britton's body in a commercial for Ryvita Minis.

Affair. Always 'sordid', unless conducted behind his wife's back by the representative of a global 'brand', in which circumstance merely 'alleged'. To protect the value of the brand it is customary for the betrayed wife to 'stand by' her husband, to draw attention to the pressure he's been under, to wear his children in public and, in her fashionable stilettos, to teeter around South America on a swift compassion visit to a jungle clearing. For all this, she is commended by the tabloids, who round on the foreign temptress like a pack of funnel-faced attack dogs, though with less finesse.

Afternoon viewing on BBC2, your. 'At 3.30 the Pillock family from Warrington will open a fish-and-chip shop in the Languedoc region of France! And then, at 4.30, Ainsley's back!' Who's Ainsley? The viewing public should be informed. Not everyone is glued to BBC2 in the afternoon like an incontinent pensioner waiting to be bin-bagged with the household refuse. Some daytime viewers have already switched over to Channel 5, hoping to catch an episode from the late period of the 1970s classic, *Charlie's Angels,* by which time the excellent Tanya Roberts (Victoria Blum) had replaced the stern-faced Kate Jackson.

See also AINSLEY!; ROBERTS, TANYA.

Ainsley! properly **Ainsley Harriott** (b.1957). For Ainsley, food and fun just go together. He's been on intimate terms with the nation's grannies ever since he first urged them on *Good Morning with Anne and Nick* to 'shake your thing!' and 'rattle those pots and pans!' – occasions on which he wore a paper hat and blew Christmas-cracker whistles into the old folks' faces. He may have inherited his flamboyant style from his father, Chester Harriott, a pianist and singer in the manner of the cocktail-bar baritone, Leslie T. Hutchinson, colloquially known as 'HUTCH'.

Air, Donna Marie Theresa (b.1979). Saucy Geordette who married beneath her. Her husband Damian Aspinall is the heir to the gambling dynasty founded by his father, John Aspinall, the right-wing oaf famous for his friendship with Lord Lucan, and for his intimate associations with tigers and gorillas. Donna is a bit of a tart, but at least she doesn't invite people to lose their family, car and savings on red 18, straight up. She acted in *Byker Grove*, did a fair bit of scantily clad mooching around, and was a moderately successful TV presenter. The highlights of her career included her asking the family group The CORRS how they had met. Jokes about her surname and the contents of her head are unnecessary.

Airey, Dawn (b.1961). Since Dawn's arrival at Sky One as chief executive, broadcasting standards have noticeably improved, albeit at Channel 5, where she had previously been director of pro-grammes. There, she had delivered unexpected profits by sticking to her notorious formula: 'Films, football and fucking'. Her arrival at Sky One immediately yielded a sharp downturn in the ratings, obliging Dawn to rethink her scheduling philosophy. In August 2004 she announced that 'Sun, sand and shagging is [sic] not what it is all about. I think you will see us steering clear of programmes with an ADULT CONTENT towards a more thoughtful output.' Examples of Dawn's re-think include *Celebrity Fear Factor*, in which Tania DO-NASCIMENTO, a leggy *Big Bruv* reject, was to be seen upside down on a rope in her knickers, transferring live crabs from one bucket to another by means of her mouth, and *Celebrity Snatch*, which, disappointingly, turned out to be a straight rip-off of MTV's *Punked!*, where Celebrities are set up for some Jeremy Beadle-style humiliation.

Aitken girls, the (b.1979). Alexandra and Victoria, identical twin daughters of Jonathan Aitken by his first wife, Lolicia. Aly poses for gentlemen's periodicals in her underwear, in other people's underwear, and with underwear on top of her head. Her Celebrity

reached its apogee in 2003 when she played the part of a Polish au pair in the feature film *Enduring Love.* She only had two words to deliver ('refrigerator magnet') but she gave them her all. Victoria, a well-built young woman, wants to be a hip-hop rap star – an unusual ambition, given her background on the playing fields of Rugby (where she shone as a crash-tackling centre three-quarter) and at a Swiss finishing school. 'I'm like J-Lo, but in reverse. I've gone from riches to rags. I'm just Vicky from the yacht, yah?'

See also OPTICAL ILLUSIONS.

Alcohol abuse. *See passim.*

Alfred the Great (849–99). Anglo-Saxon king of Wessex and wannabe Celebrity chef. Like certain other historical figures (Robert the Bruce, King CANUTE), his name has become attached in legend to just one – in all probability apocryphal – incident. Although a promoter of education, the father of the English navy, a patron of the arts and widely travelled (as a child he was a guest at the Frankish court of Charles the Bald (r.843–877)), Alfred is now celebrated only in humorous newspaper columns, whose composers amusingly refer to 'his singular lack of culinary skills!' It is possible that Stephen FRY deploys the same agreeable construction in after-dinner speeches. Once, when participating in a theatrical skit, Fry had the line, 'Pass the sick-bag, Alice.' He insisted on changing this to 'Pass the disgorgement receptacle, Alice.'

Album, working on material for a new. Shoe shopping in Bond Street; alternatively, in a meeting at the Priory Clinic, Roehampton. 'It's not my fault. It's a disease.' Hocus pocus and group hugs.

Allen, Ray (b.1925), a ventriloquist, and **Lord Charles** (b.1963), his puppet. Lord Charles impersonated a curmudgeonly drunk in the manner of the American comedian, W.C. Fields. Allen and Lord Charles, who were very close, eventually settled in BOURNEMOUTH, where they were able to keep in touch with Lord Charles's best friend in the business, Archie ANDREWS. A friend of Allen's, Cardew Robinson, had also retired to Bournemouth. Mr Robinson (1923–92) was a tall, skinny vaudeville comedian. His act was as an elderly schoolboy known as Cardew 'The Cad' at a school called St Fanny's.

Allsopp, Kirstie (b.1974). Plummy TV property finder, who presents *Location, Location, Location, Relocation, Relocation, Relocation* and *Location, Location, Location Revisited.* As a child at Bedales, a co-educational school in the independent sector, she wore velvet Alice bands. She now has TV-friendly swishing dark hair, but, spiritually the Alice band is still in place. Hearty and no-nonsense, Kirstie always knows where to find things (especially houses). When scandalized tabloids claimed that she had stolen a schoolfriend's husband, Kirstie rebutted the accusations convincingly and came out of the affair smelling like, well, a rather good egg.

Almada, Nadia, originally **Almada, Carlos** (b.1977). Sex-change bank clerk born in Portugal but later resident in Surrey. While working in Allders in Woking she was driven to depression after persistent teasing from members of staff. Dubbed 'the Portugeezer' by the tabloids when participating in *Big Brother 5*, she emerged victorious. For a transsexual, she isn't very pretty. Indeed, she could easily be mistaken for a woman. When last heard of she was playing a mermaid in panto at Southampton and touting herself as a reality TV travel rep, but she may have been paid a seven-figure sum to write a book for HarperCollins. Her triumph in *Big Bruv* was widely taken as proof that the British public has at last become accustomed to accepting 'the other'. As has been observed, albeit in a different context, 'every block of stone contains a statue'. An interesting idea, but not one to live your life by.

Alpha *Mail*. A person who is more paranoid and right-wing than would seem possible but who argues that he or she is merely speaking up for Middle England.

See also REAL WORLD, THE.

Americans. It is generally supposed that Americans have no interest in – indeed have probably never heard of – any British Celebrities. This is not always the case. In December 2002, a Christmas fancy-dress party was held for patients at the St Luke's Insane Asylum in Washington D.C. Among the guests, 87 came as potatoes and 22 as Baroness Thatcher.

Amstell, Simon (b.1979). Clownish daytime-TV presenter. He made his mark on *Popworld*, when he suggested to Britney Spears that she had gone 'a bit crazy recently'. He then asked Mutya from the Sugababes if her new hairdo was inspired by a wet spaniel. Both perfectly sensible questions, but the two little madams flounced off. 'Britney didn't even say goodbye,' Simon complains. Girls Aloud have called him 'a right horrible bitchy queen that needs his hair cutting'.

Amy, Susie (b.1980). Steely-faced actress who came to prominence as Chardonnay Lane in the popular TV series, *Footballers' Wives* (commonly abbreviated to *Swives*). When she left the series in order to pursue a career in film, her character was killed off slowly with anorexia. Amy went on to star in the film *La Femme Musketeer* (2004), helped in this demanding role by her training in dramatic studies at Strode's College, Egham. 'Experimental drama was a bit of a challenge [for her],' says a former teacher, 'but she was always enthusiastic.' Amy lives in Virginia Water, Surrey, and claims to eat approximately one bar of chocolate per day.

Anagrams, Celebrity. *See* BECKHAM, VICTORIA; CANUTE, KING; CLARKSON, JEREMY; HERVEY, LADY ISABELLA; PALMER-TOMKINSON, TARA.

Anderson, Dougie (b.1981). Slotting comfortably into Channel 5's freak-show scheduling is its new gossip progamme, *That's So … Last Week*, presented by Dougie Anderson, a cheeky Scotch twerp. 'Your one-stop shop for all things Celebrity' is how Dougie describes it. Dougie is joined by a posse of cocky twentysomethings whose job it is to come up with gross-out 'witty' one-liners. 'Like Barbara Cartland's clitoris' was how one of these unpleasant children described the dissected skin he'd seen on a recent anatomy show. The flight of fancy is so startlingly unamusing it is assumed in some quarters that Stephen Fry has already attributed it to Peter Cook.

Anderton, Sophie (b.1978). The former Gossard bra-beauty's been to hell and back. After her 18-month affair with soccer hooligan and coke fiend Mark Bosnich, Sophie has found sanctuary as the girlfriend of Mark Alexiou (29), the proprietor of Pangaea, a fashionable night club in London's West End. Mark is determined that Sophie won't return to her former bad habits. When she visits the lavatory at Pangaea he has her followed by a 22-stone bodyguard who is obliged to line up with the other ladies while Sophie has a wazz.

Andre, Peter (b.1974). Born in Harrow, North London, of an English mother and a Greek Cypriot father. Real name Andrea, a circumstance that caused him some embarrassment when the family relocated to Sydney, Australia, when Peter was ten. Not

realizing that he had arrived in the gay capital of the world, he quite unnecessarily dropped the 'a' and built up a formidable six-pack. It was this feature, rather than his vocal abilities, that accounted for his immediate success when he decided to become a pop singer. His biggest hit was 'Mysterious Girl', released in 1996. Shortly after this, he moved to Cyprus, where he pursued a life of quiet contemplation. In 2004, he suddenly cropped up in the British Reality TV Show, *I'm A Celebrity, Get Me Out Of Here.* In this, he won the public's admiration for the sensitive way in which he courted fellow jungle-mate, the busty glamour model, Jordan (32FF). In long, whispered, night-time philosophical discussions, Andre persuaded her that it was not 'Jordan' the silicone-enhanced sex-pot with whom he had fallen in love, but Katie Price, the unspoilt country girl who longed to live in Sussex and keep a pony. The bosomy sex-bomb was impressed enough to return Andre's feelings and to announce that 'Jordan' was now officially dead. Henceforth, she wished to be known as Katie Price. On the strength of their blossoming relationship, Andre's catchy 1996 single, 'Mysterious Girl', was re-released. Thousands of fans disguised in hockey-masks bought the record at self-service checkouts. The unmanned facilities are normally used by embarrassed shoppers buying banana-flavoured prophylactics and the complete *Star Wars* series on DVD. While there is something undeniably repellent about Andre's looks, it cannot be argued that he's actually hurting anyone. He just pops up every ten years with a horrible record.

See also ADAM AND EVE.

Andrews, Eamonn (1926–87). Irish broadcaster best known as the original Man with the Red Book. 'Big Hearted Arthur Askey! This is Your Life!' he would shout. Cheerful Charlie Chester! Stanley Matthews! Fanny Cradock! Bomber Harris! Hermann Goering! Roy Hudd! He did them all. In his day, Celebrities were known as

Andy Pandy

'Personalities' – though a personality was precisely what they didn't have. (As the distinguished novelist Howard Jacobson has pointed out in his *Independent* column, 'In those days, discovering a personality in the family was a cause for shame, rather like an unwanted pregnancy, and the owner of one was immediately packed off to the nearest Butlin's Holiday Camp with a joke book and novelty costume.') Eamonn Andrews himself didn't have a personality. He was Michael ASPEL waiting to happen. As host of *What's My Line?*, the first of the family game shows that came to dominate the schedules, he is of some seminal interest. Unlike today's over-familiar frontpersons, Andrews was a reassuring presiding presence in a dinner jacket. The real star of the show was Gilbert Harding – not, as many assumed, a homosexual policeman in the Sussex force, but in fact a schoolteacher, and billed as 'the rudest man in Britain' (thus a forerunner of Simon COWELL). Alas, rage and disappointment brought on cardiac arrest at the age of 51, causing Harding to burst suddenly like a bag of crisps outside Broadcasting House. Another key member of the panel was Lady Isobel Barnett, a provincial magistrate with a locally styled hairdo who later disguised herself as a poacher's pocket and ran out of her local Leicestershire butcher with two sides of beef and a Christmas turkey. *What's My Line* was removed from the schedules after these mishaps, but its long shadow influences today's game shows in which mere Members of the General Public can briefly share the limelight with Chris, Brucie, Jim and Davina.

Andy Pandy (b.1950). As little has been heard for several decades of the star of BBC TV's *Watch with Mother*, he is presumed to be examining his priorities in a Celebrity Clinic.

Annis, Francesca. *See* CLEOPATRA; LANGTRY, LILLIE.

Ant and Dec, properly **Anthony David McPartlin** (b.1975) and **Declan Joseph Oliver Donnelly** (b.1975). Geordie jokers with but one personality between the two of them. Small wonder that a poll in January 2004 revealed that 87% of the population couldn't tell one from the other. Even their own mothers don't know which is which. Does it matter? It seems unlikely. Posh Spice and Chris Eubank? Eddie Izzard and Clare Balding? Vanessa Feltz and Michael Winner? Can anyone tell one from the other? Certainly not. And yet they prosper. As do Ant and Dec.

Apologies. It is customary on Reality TV shows for housemates to apologize to one another every few minutes. These apologies are instantly accepted:

'You showed disrespect then, man.'

'Whoa! Whoa! Back off, man. You've, like, invaded my space.'

'But you dished up dinner while I was sat on the toilet. I didn't get any sprouts.'

'You're right. I did. I dished up dinner while you was sat on the toilet. You didn't get any sprouts. That was disrespectful. I apologize.'

'Apology accepted.'

'Group hug everyone?'

You'd think these young people were attending an AA meeting.

See also SINCERE REGRET, EXPRESSING.

Appleton, Natalie (b.1973) and her sister **Nicole** (b.1974). Formerly of Sylvia Young's Academy and the girl band, All Saints. The name of the band refers to the road on which the girls grew up in West London. The girls spent their early youth in Canada and retain that country's accent. Their songs are laid-back pop, catchy, soulful and incoherent: 'Thoughts and vocabulary run right through me…' (from 'Never Ever', 1998). The sisters are entirely responsible for the women's street-fashion style that became prevalent in 1998 (hoodies, fleeces, low-slung baggy combat trousers), a contribution to society for which they are not to be thanked. The sisters share a sporting interest in famous men. Their scores are as follows:

Nat: Jamie Theakston
Nic: Jonny Lee Miller
One all
Nic: Robbie Williams
Nat: —

One–love to Nic
The game concludes with a deuce of marriages:
Nat: Liam Howlett of The Prodigy
Nic: Liam Gallagher of Oasis.

After the acrimonious split of All Saints, neither of the sisters spoke to former bandmates Shaznay Lewis or Mel Blatt. (Mel says of a chance meeting on board a plane: 'They kept calling over at me. But I suddenly became really absorbed with my daughter Lily, like, "Of course I'll read you a story, darling." Eventually they got the hint.') The sisters formed a duo, called Appleton, but this was ill-fated: its first single, 'Aloud', was released on the same day as the girl band Girls Aloud hit the charts and was renamed, bafflingly, 'Everything's Eventual'.

In 2004, Natalie appeared on the show *I'm a Celebrity, Get Me Out of Here*. She failed to distinguish herself, disintegrating like fly-blown fruit in front of the cameras as the public voted to torture her with jungle trials. These included the Bushtucker dinner, in which she was challenged to eat Jungle Oysters (kangaroo testicles) but only managed to swallow a Vomit Fruit. Having been nominated for five trials in a row, Natalie stormed off the set, weeping. You wouldn't have thought that spending time with her and her sister was once described by Jamie Theakston as 'like hanging out with a pack of wolves'.

During the 1990s, the All Saints Road was known as 'The Front Line'. Upper-class crack whackos could buy what they needed at point of sale rather than wait for an unreliable dealer to set off on his milk-round.

Aristocrats. No longer invited even to C-list functions, unless they've been to prison, in which case they are welcome as retarded toffs on Reality TV shows (*see* BROCKET, CHARLES RONALD GEORGE NALL-CAIN, 3rd BARON) or are clearly bonkers, in which case they are filmed in afternoon documentaries on BBC2 wandering round their estates looking like a bad night at the Chelsea Arts Club

April Celebrity *Faux Pas*

On *The Weakest Link* (BBC2), **Anne Robinson** asks a Liverpool schoolteacher whether she takes classes in shoplifting. She is invited to apologize to the people of Liverpool, but declines. Anne drops five rungs on the Celebrity *Faux Pas* Ladder.

Liz Hurley takes language lessons so that she will be able to make her wedding vows to Arun Nayer in Hindi. During the ceremony, she gets her phrases confused and orders a chicken biryani.

To promote his latest television series, **Dr David Starkey** takes part in the London Marathon dressed as Anne Boleyn.

Jayne Middlemiss interviews J.D. Salinger. She asks him what shoe size he takes.

The royal family spends the Easter holiday at Windsor Castle, having told the **Duchess of York** that they've gone to Sandringham (it works every year). After dinner, the Duke of Edinburgh suggests they play the 'Which Celebrity Would You Rather?' game.

'Janet Street-Porter or Johnny Rotten?

'Michael Winner or Vanessa Feltz?'

'Peter Stringfellow or Raine Spencer?'

'Amanda Platell or Neil 'Razor' Ruddock?'

'Hulk' Hogan' or Mr T?'

'No, no, *no*, Edward! You *still* haven't understood the game!' **Prince Edward** drops ten rungs on the Celebrity *Faux Pas* Ladder.

(*see* BATH, ALEXANDER THYNN, 7th MARQUESS OF). Lord Charles, formerly the partner of ventriloquist Ray ALLEN, might still be welcome at A-list functions but is reluctant at his age to leave the comfort of BOURNEMOUTH and its many facilities.

Army officers, dodgy ex-. *See* HEWITT, MAJOR JAMES; INGRAM, MAJOR CHARLES.

Arrangements with the media. It is rumoured that in its arrangements with the media the Priory Clinic, Roehampton, will henceforth be represented by PR guru Max Clifford. If the rumours turn out to be true, troubled Celebrities seeking help will be referred in the first instance to the Priory's marketing department. If their credit ratings and stock portfolios meet the Priory's exacting requirements, they will then be passed on to the head of the addiction unit, a Mr Bacon, who has a certificate in addiction disorders and is trained in reality therapy.

See also KATONA, KERRY.

Arthur, King (*c.*500 AD). The son of Uther Pendragon and Igraine of Cornwall, he is the celebrated figure at the heart of the Arthurian legend.

See also LEGEND, THE ARTHURIAN.

Art, a 1st-class degree in the History of Fine. A reasonable qualification, though wannabes have found it to be less profitable in the short term than coming fourth in *Big Brother* and thereafter appearing on the cover of *Loaded* in their knickers.

See also JUBIN, SHELL.

As ever. 'As ever, we at Channel 5 News want to know *your* views on the key issues of the moment. Here is the result of yesterday's talking point – "Do you want to see this country swamped by illegal asylum seekers and their scarred fighting women?" 57% of you said "Yes". 43% of you said "No". And here's today's topic: "Can Michelle Heaton's skirts get any shorter?" For "Yes" dial 0901 890 2900. For "No" dial 0901 890 2901. Calls cost just 25p from a BT landline. For text messages the number is 76544, and remember to put the words "Tyneside twat" before your message. In the meantime, join me, Kirsty, after the break, for more Real News, Real Stories about Real People...'

Ash in the mouth. *See* ASH, LESLIE.

Ash, Leslie (b.1960). Actress who soldiers on. The ultimate trooper. Trained at Italia Conti, where she probably learnt her 'smile though your heart is breaking' routine. Forever being rushed into intensive care with broken ribs and a punctured lung after a saucy sex romp has gone wrong, she is another Celebrity who would rather be thought of as eroto-kink-monster than as victim. Leslie, who came to prominence as the lusted-after girl upstairs in the sit-com *Men Behaving Badly,* is married to former Leeds United striker, Lee Chapman. (Coincidentally, *The Meaning of Cantona,* Gallimard, 1996, a collection of philosophical *pensées* by Eric Cantona, the French soccer player who joined Leeds United in 1991, contains the following entry: '73. There is growing unease in Cantona's relationship with Chappo, the big striker. Increasingly, they invade each other's space. In Cantona's view, Chappo is leaving him exposed in the box. "I'm getting all the knocks," he says. "So I gather," retorts Chappo. They are like two stags, disputing the same reviving water-hole. Cantona reflects. What is the price of victory if it is gained at a team-mate's expense? When a player has to leave a famous football club because he has fallen out with his colleague in the box, what is he left with? Ash in the mouth.' Many commentators have tried to tease out the meaning of this passage but none has succeeded.) Leslie is famous for having introduced the phrase 'trout pout' into the lexicon. It's what people spontaneously shouted at her in the street after lip-enhancement surgery resulted in a mouth like an inflatable rubber ring.

See also BRYSON, DR KIT.

Aspel, Michael (b.1933). Is the forever youthful Aspel the Dorian Grey of his generation? The thinking woman's Cliff Richard? Aspel began his career as a radio actor in Cardiff in 1954, then via newsreading, he hit Celebrity status presenting such shows as *Crackerjack*, *This Is Your Life* and *Antiques Roadshow*. On this last programme, the patina of age barely discernible beneath the pink pancake, he is frequently expected to reach as much as five hundred pounds at auction, although you really ought to insure him for nearer a thousand. After all, he's a national treasure, an heirloom passed down from mother to daughter for centuries.

For other Celebrity Antiques, albeit in poorer condition, *see* CLARK, ALAN; DICKINSON, DAVID.

Asylum seekers in the shrubbery. *See* REAL WORLD, THE.

Atkins, Dr Robert (1932–2003). Clinically obese diet guru. When he suffered his fatal heart attack, he weighed 25 stone and his massively bloated body had to be winched from a sixth-floor window to the waiting hearse by a system of blocks and pulleys.

See also HUMPTY DUMPTY.

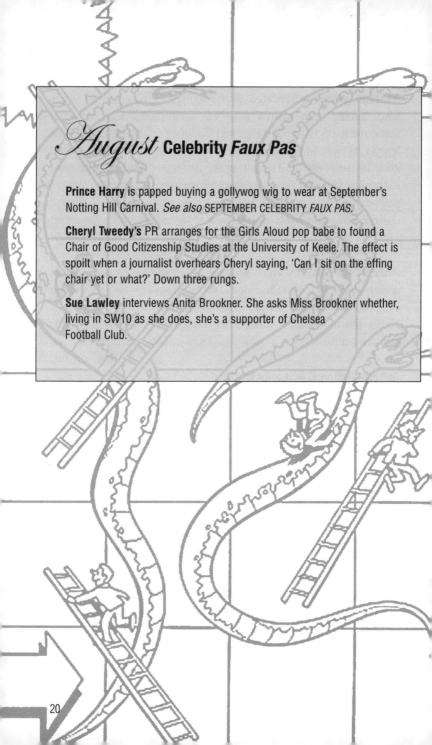

August Celebrity *Faux Pas*

Prince Harry is papped buying a gollywog wig to wear at September's Notting Hill Carnival. *See also* SEPTEMBER CELEBRITY *FAUX PAS*.

Cheryl Tweedy's PR arranges for the Girls Aloud pop babe to found a Chair of Good Citizenship Studies at the University of Keele. The effect is spoilt when a journalist overhears Cheryl saying, 'Can I sit on the effing chair yet or what?' Down three rungs.

Sue Lawley interviews Anita Brookner. She asks Miss Brookner whether, living in SW10 as she does, she's a supporter of Chelsea Football Club.

At large, still. The reported circumstances of two working girls who, having been invited to a wayward soccer legend's hotel suite, made off with his wallet and cufflinks. The wayward soccer legend, by way of retaliation, head-butted his wife and broke her nose in three places. He is thought not to be still at large, but examining his priorities in a Celebrity Clinic. (According to tabloid newspapers such as the *Daily Mail,* miscreant working girls are customarily 'at large'; murderous aristocrats – such as Lord Lucan – are merely 'missing'.)

Attheendoftheday. A term used by celebrated sports people in post-match analyses. It has no relationship to any actual 24-hour period. For example, 'What I'm saying is, John, when you get up at six in the morning to train, attheendoftheday you've got to be focused on the job.'

Autobiographies, Celebrity warts 'n' all. Mostly ghosted bollocks.

- ✎ *A Northern Soul* by Jimmy Nail
- ✎ *A Royal Duty* by Paul Burrell
- ✎ *Being Jordan* by Jordan
- ✎ *Call Me Charlie* by Lord Brocket
- ✎ *I Don't Mean to be Rude But* by Simon Cowell
- ✎ *Feel* by Robbie Williams
- ✎ *Gazza: My Story* by Paul Gascoigne
- ✎ *Geri* by Geri Halliwell
- ✎ *Honest* by Ulrika Jonsson
- ✎ *Learning to Fly* by Victoria Beckham
- ✎ *My Side* by David Beckham
- ✎ *So Me* by Graham Norton
- ✎ *Winner Takes All* by Michael Winner

See also CELEBRITY PUBLISHING.

Autumn. November paranoia sets in. Celebrities can't go out because they think they look like Jade GOODY. It's worse. They look like Nell McANDREW.

Award for Orangeness Sponsored by Terry's Chocolate Orange. Celebrities nominated in January 2005 for most indiscriminate use of fake tanning aids include:

- ✉ Cat Deeley
- ✉ Robert Kilroy-Silk
- ✉ Benito Mussolini
- ✉ Dale Winton
- ✉ Jodie Marsh
- ✉ Sir Trevor McDonald
- ✉ Hiawatha
- ✉ Alex Best
- ✉ David Dickinson
- ✉ Donatella Versace
- ✉ Richie Benaud
- ✉ Peter Andre
- ✉ Richard Madeley
- ✉ Judith Chalmers
- ✉ Atomic Kitten
- ✉ Des O'Connor
- ✉ Silvio Berlusconi
- ✉ and the 2006 winner Gavin Henson,
  the conceited Welsh rugby union three-quarter.

B

Babies' names, shocking Celebrity: Simply de rigeur nowadays. 'Ooh, that's a cracker!', says Suzanne Shaw. Little De Rigeur was born to Suzanne Shaw and Darren DAY in December 2004. It's good, but not quite barmy enough. For real Celebrity status, you need something more like:

- **Anais** (Meg Matthews and Noel Gallagher)
- **Apple** (Gwyneth Paltrow and Chris Martin)
- **Audio Science** (Shannyn Sossamon and Dallas Clayton)
- **Banjo** (Rachel Griffiths and Andrew Taylor)
- **Daisy Boo** (Jules and Jamie Oliver)
- **Dweezil** (Gail and Frank Zappa)
- **Fifi Trixabelle** (Paula Yates and Bob Geldof)
- **Heavenly Hirani Tiger Lily** (Paula Yates and Michael Hutchence)
- **Lennon** (Patsy Kensit and Liam Gallagher)
- **Lourdes** (Madonna and Guy Ritchie)
- **Martha Sky** (Ulrika Jonsson and Gerard Wright)
- **Moon Unit** (Gail and Frank Zappa)
- **Nell Marmalade** (Helen Baxendale and David Eliot)
- **Peaches Honeyblossom** (Paula Yates and Bob Geldof)
- **Pilot Inspektor** (Jason Lee and Beth Riesgraf)
- **Phoenix Chi** (Mel B and Jimmy Gulzar)
- **Poppy Honey** (Jules and Jamie Oliver)
- **Rocco** (Madonna and Guy Ritchie)
- **Zowie** (Angie and David Bowie)
- **Cruz** (David and Victoria Beckham)

Regarding the name Cruz, Lola Oria, a Spanish language tutor at Oxford University, said: 'They will have problems in Spain because it will be seen as a name for girls. It is an old-fashioned girl's name and also it is quite clearly Spanish and difficult to pronounce for an English-speaking person. It is quite a strange thing to do to a little boy.'

Back in the nut-house within a week. *See* ALBUM, WORKING ON MATERIAL FOR A NEW; DIVAS, POP; NATURAL TALENT, A SUBLIME.

Backlash against elitism, the. The retreat from paternalism has now shaped a popular culture defined by its accessibility. Anyone who thinks this culture is moronic is dubbed a snob. Paradoxically, a person who actually embodies it is immediately, and snobbishly, ridiculed as a 'chav' – a term coined by those of a superior, and sarcastic, disposition, to describe a young, lower-class person with little education and no dress sense. Just as Channel 4 smuggles prurient material on board by pretending to criticize it (*see* ADULT CONTENT), so do wine-bar liberals pass on chav jokes as examples of how snobbish wine-bar liberals are. For this, they have rightly been chided by other wine-bar liberals. Typical 'chav' jokes:

1. When out driving, you see a chav on a bicycle.
   Should you run him over?
   No. It's probably your bicycle.

2. What do you call a chavette in a white tracksuit?
   The bride.

3. You pass two chavs in a car without any music.
   Who's driving?
   The police.

Back-street hooker, fellated on Sunset Boulevard by a. *See* GRANT, HUGH.

Baked beans, flatulence-free. *See* GREAT TELEVISION.

Balfour, Lady Shrimpy (b.1985). One to watch. At present only a teenage twinkle in the eye of London society. But Shrimpy has legs. Long legs. And she'll be walkin' on 'em, just you wait.

Ballet. Once described by playwright John Osborne (1929–94) as '19th-century poofs' football'. Against Osborne, it could be argued that a virtuoso male dancer in one of the great classical variations can display a pleasing athleticism and musicality. Some enthusiasts like to look at Darcey Bussell's legs through naval binoculars, but on the whole it is advisable, when it is the ballerina's turn, to join late arrivals and queer-brigade majors in the Floral Hall. Since balletic expertise can only be achieved by natural talent combined with arduous training it would not in any case be an attractive career option for today's wannabes.

Bang 'em up! According to its feisty editor, Rebekah Wade, the *Sun* and its readers have a very simple approach to law and order. 'Bang 'em up!' ran an editorial on 15 February 2005: 'If you're doing time, you can't commit more crime.' On page 13 of the same edition it reported that 'Britain's most notorious drugs baron, Curtis Warren, has been able to mastermind a £125 million drug operation while serving a 12-year prison sentence.' Rebekah Wade is married to the bald soap actor, Ross Kemp.

Bardsley, Lizzie (b.1973). Celebrity yob. In November 2004, Lizzie's hectic telly schedule prevented her from making an appearance before magistrates in Rochdale, Lancashire. The mother-of-eight and foul-mouthed wife-swap sponger was unable to attend the hearing because she was filming a new series for Channel 4. *Bed and Bardsley* will feature Lizzie and her husband running a B&B where surprise Celebrities drop in. The magistrates in Rochdale had a grasp of what makes 'GREAT TELEVISION' and told a

Channel 4 representative that Lizzie could turn up when her hectic schedule permitted.

Barefoot Doctor, the, properly **Stephen Russell** (b.1974). Mystical salesman. He flogs enlightenment, shower gel, funky CDs, his own-brand fruit juice and inner peace. Allegations that he is a habitual shoe-wearer with anger-management issues are entirely wide of the mark.

Barker, Linda (b.1961). Farmgirl from Yorkshire who recognized the untapped mileage in doing potato prints on furniture. She is to sofas what Captain Birdseye is to fish fingers, but with noticeably less sex appeal. Basically the homely older sister of the girl next door. After modest success on *Changing Rooms*, where she was somewhat overshadowed by the pomp of Laurence LLEWELLYN BOWEN, Linda's career was kick-started when she appeared on *I'm a Celebrity, Get Me Out of Here*, running around the Australian Outback in an unbecoming bikini, accompanied by a chef, a cricketer, a DJ in a wig and a queer from the old days. She cleared an estimated £2.5 million in the ensuing months.

Bassey, Shirley (b.1935). Brassy Welsh belter aspiring to the condition of a second-rate drag act.

Bateman, 'Nasty' Nick (b.1965). But for Nick's behaviour in *Big Brother 1* the show would not have been the ratings winner for Channel 4 that it has since become. That, at least, is the view advanced by Nick himself. He was the only contestant, he argues, who realized that he was taking part in what was essentially a *game*; further, that it followed from this insight that cheating was built into the formula. You don't have to be Kurt Gödel to spot the logical error. A game could indeed be defined as the sum of its rules. It doesn't follow, however, that a contestant is thereby obliged to break them. Nick's blunder may be accounted for by the fact that, like many members of the British royal family, he was educated at Gordonstoun, an independent school in Scotland founded by a madman. At Gordonstoun, success in outdoor sporting activities of a homoerotic nature is rated more highly than academic distinction. Since his moment of notoriety, Nick has made a living from panto appearances, his King Rat in *Jack and the Beanstalk* at the Theatre Royal, Lincoln in 2002 winning praise from the local critics.

Battleaxes, Celebrity. *See* BRADDOCK, BESSIE; CRADOCK, FANNY; HAMILTON, CHRISTINE; IFAN, MARGED FERCH.

Bazalgette, Joseph William (1835–1901). Civil engineer. On 11 May 2002, a ceramic bust of Bazalgette was unveiled at Crossness Engines in Bexley. It was commissioned by Mike Dunmow of Crossness Engines Trust and executed by his one-time colleague, and long-term friend, Harold Stevenson (Steve). Working from photographs, Steve, an amateur sculptor, had executed an excellent likeness of the Victorian engineer responsible for London's sewage system. The unveiling was performed by Bazalgette's great-great-grandson, Peter Bazalgette, in the presence of the Mayor of Bexley, Councillor Colin Wright, and members of the trust. Invited guests included Mr Arthur Green and Peter Bazalgette's two small children, who took a keen interest in how effluence can be distributed at maximum profit while giving minimum offence.

See also CHANNEL 4.

Bazalgette, Peter (b.1958). Chairman of Endemol UK, one of Britain's most powerful television production companies. In addition to *Big Brother* and *The Salon* (which is set in a barber's shop), Bazalgette has created *Food and Drink* for BBC2 and a number of other equally innovative shows including *Ready, Steady, Cook, Changing Rooms* and *Ground Force*. *Changing Rooms* was the first

programme to be commissioned by Mark Thompson, now director general of the BBC (*see* ADULT CONTENT). *Ground Force* featured Alan Titchmarsh (five times winner of *The Literary Review*'s 'Bad Sex in Fiction Award') and Charlie DIMMOCK, the burly gardener. Alan Titchmarsh is properly Alan Marsh. As a child, he was so small that his schoolmates nicknamed him 'Titch'. He was referred to so often as Alan 'Titch' Marsh that he began to believe that it was his real name.

See also BAZALGETTE, JOSEPH WILLIAM; CHANNEL 4.

BBC's news bulletins, the. When he took over as director general of the BBC in January 2004, one of Mark Thompson's first initiatives was to announce that in future the Corporation's news bulletins would follow Channel 5's example and become more accessible to Ordinary People (a.k.a. REAL PEOPLE).

Henceforth the newscaster would open the bulletin with a simple game for the whole family: 'Good evening. The time is 10 o'clock and I'm Huw Edwards. Before the first news story tonight, here is a short quiz. What is the name of Marge Simpson's husband in the hit comedy show *The Simpsons*? O.J. Simpson? Homer Simpson? Edward and Mrs Simpson? Phone your answer to 0900800724, or text it to 76943, remembering to start with the words 'Scouse Git'. Here are tonight's main stories. Of the Celebrity Couples who recently split – Kerry and Brian, Jade and Jeff, Chris and Billie – the most likely to get back together are thought to be...'

Beautiful boys, the exploitation of. According to Germaine Greer ('A woman who has views on everything, all of them ridiculous' – Professor Camille Paglia, *Vamps and Tramps*, 1994), 'Boys are permanently erect and can produce sperm like a running tap' (*Beautiful Boys*, 2000). Some might argue that by publishing more pictures of naked adolescent boys than can be found on the internet after the most strenuous and devoted search, Professor

Greer is guilty of depersonalizing the human body and exploiting lonely homosexuals, sentencing them to a lifetime of self-abuse in the lavatories of mainline railway stations.

See also ILL-JUDGED ATTEMPTS TO BECOME CELEBRITIES BY SUPPOSEDLY SERIOUS PEOPLE.

Beaversnatchclit, Fanny. *See* CHECKING INTO HOTELS.

Beckham, David (b.1975). Soccer player and Celebrity Father.

See also ADULTERY, CELEBRITIES ALLEGEDLY TAKEN IN; BABIES' NAMES, SHOCKING CELEBRITY; BECKHAM, VICTORIA; BROOKLYN BRIDGE, THE.

Beckham, Victoria (b.1974). Beverley Hills meets Streatham High Road; formerly Posh Spice of a girl band popular in the 1990s. The daughter of a successful Essex builder, she was ferried to school in a Rolls Royce, sallied into assembly in her neatly pressed uniform, with a cheery 'Morning Miss!' Then the other girls beat her up. Not to encourage mindless violence or anything, but who wouldn't want to punch her? Her career's in the doldrums, although she's better known in the USA than her husband, the footballer David Beckham, but that's only because soccer's

a girls' game there. They assume that Posh is the soccer player and David her lesbian baggage handler. Victoria understood the importance of branding even as a toddler. At the age of five she announced that she wanted to be as famous as Persil Automatic – an appropriate choice since some claim that Persil Automatic doesn't work either. It has recently been discovered that 'David and Victoria Beckham' form the anagram 'Bravo! Victim and dickhead'.

For references to other Celebrity Anagrams, *see* ANAGRAMS, CELEBRITY.

See also CLITORIS, VICTORIA BECKHAM'S.

Beckinsale, Kate (b.1973). Prim-looking Hollywood star. Daughter of British actor Richard Beckinsale, who died of a heart attack at 31 when Kate was 5. Kate studied some Russian at Oxford University before struggling with anorexia and then leaving to distinguish herself as Flora Poste in the TV film of Stella Gibbons's *Cold Comfort Farm.* She then achieved Celebrity status by appearing in a string of terrible US blockbusters: *Pearl Harbor, Van Helsing, Underworld...* (It was in the last of these that she ditched her co-star and partner of seven years, Michael Sheen – no relation to Charlie or Martin – and took up with the director of the film, Len Wiseman. This must have made for some embarrassing silences over the breakfast bagels prior to the day's shooting.)

If Beckinsale hadn't appeared in these stonker blockbusters, she would just be a respected actress. As it is, she's a tabloid banquet. '*Heat* magazine are constantly trying to get a picture of me picking my nose,' she says. And using telephoto lenses to photograph the bikini she wore on her honeymoon, studded with her new marital name 'Mrs Wiseman'. And door-stepping her personal waxer, and claiming that her breasts slip over her collarbones when she bends down. Perhaps Kate would have been better off with the RSC.

Beckwith, Tamara (b.1970). She looks like a boiled egg with eyebrows painted on, yet she is still Britain's most invited party girl. All credit to her, frankly. She started off at Cheltenham Ladies College, where she left after getting preggers before she'd even sat her cookery 'O' Level (or, more significantly, her biology 'O' Level). 'The best thing I ever did was have my daughter Anouska,' she says. Anouska is now training to be an actress in New York, while her mother continues to attend daily photo shoots, openings,

press calls and chat shows. For all her industry, Tamara Beckwith is almost impossible to categorize. To say she was an actress would be to gloss over her outstanding ability to pose for hours holding a dead fish, if required. To say she is a party animal would be to forget the brilliant tin rattling she does for charity. To define her most accurately, simply prefix her name with 'celebrity'.

Bedingfield, Daniel (b.1979). Squinty singer with a sprouty chin and a penchant for natty beanie hats. His irritating garage numbers are as catchy as a cold sore. He claims on his recent hit – a departure into a more soulful sound – that 'Nothing Hurts Like Love'. Perhaps a really firm headlock might change his mind on that.

Bedingfield, Natasha (b.1981). Over-styled sister of David (no-one needs that much lip gloss). She emerged onto the pop scene in 2003 with the hit 'These Words Are Mine'. However, given the fact that her debut album credits nine different songwriters as well as Natasha, a more accurate title would be 'One Or Two Of These Words Might Be Mine'. She would be a perfectly reasonable popstrel, if it weren't for her clammy ambition to be thought of as a talented songwriter. And don't deactivate your Bedingfield firewall

yet. There's another sibling, Nikola, currently being groomed in the family hit factory. Forewarned is forearmed.

Bedtime for Bonzo. Light-hearted Hollywood comedy (1949) co-starring Ronald Reagan and a monkey. Often referred to by Greg Dyke when, as director general of the BBC, an idea was submitted that he judged to be too elitist for the market. 'Remember this,' he'd say. 'In *Bedtime for Bonzo* the monkey stole the notices but Ronald Reagan became President of the United States. So much for notices. Next!'

B, Emma, properly **Emma Broughton** (b.1971). The disc jockey with a voice like a tea-cosy is ever-ready with the radio hugs. She presents the Radio 1 agony programme, *The Sunday Surgery*. When Emma B moved home, it was reported thus: 'Emma B is the latest minor addition to the galaxy of stars that call Hampstead home. She's spent £300,000 on a three-bedroom flat near the Heath. That means she'll have somewhere to walk her black and white cocker spaniel and her boyfriend Damien, who is a radio producer.' Emma has a tattoo of a pair of angel wings across her back and she's no good at drinking beer because it gives her terrible wind.

See also JUST LIKE YOU AND ME.

befuddle.co.uk. Extremely rude website featuring Celebrities who look drunk or nude or both. Highly recommended.

See also DALY, TESS; HERVEY, LADY VICTORIA FREDERICA; MARSH, JODIE.

Benaud, Richie. *See* GODIVA, LADY.

Berlin, Sir Isaiah (1907–97). Historian of ideas who customarily held tutorials at the Ritz Hotel, London (*see* CELEBRITY HAIRDRESSERS).

Best, Calum (b.1979). Son of the wayward soccer legend, George Best. The totally fit stud muffin is said to have set his sights on Lady Isabella Hervey, the younger sister of Lady Victoria Hervey. Lady Isabella surprised everyone when, in 2003, she emerged victorious in the Channel 5 reality show, *The Games*, proving too quick over the high hurdles for her rivals, who included gorgeous, pouting topless model Jodie MARSH (32DD), Charlie DIMMOCK, the beefy gardener, Major Charles INGRAM (the Coughing Major) and Jarrod Batchelor (Mr Gay UK). Miss Dimmock won the wrestling when she secured Mr Gay UK in a head-scissors. He was unconscious for six days, but recovered.

Best Celebrity Haircuts. *See* BRYLCREEM AWARDS, THE.

Bez, properly **Mark Berry** (b.1960). Formerly a novelty dancer and maraca player with the Mancunian pop group Happy Mondays. In January 2005, and in the company of, among others, Caprice, the underwear model, Brigitte Nielsen, a battle-scarred actress, Miss Nielsen's former mother-in-law, Jackie Stallone (the mother of Sylvester Stallone), John McCririck, the racing tipster, and Professor Germaine Greer, Bez participated in *Celebrity Big Brother 3*. Professor Greer disappointed her admirers by announcing on her arrival that 'I don't do anal.' Some viewers felt that the programme had thus got off to a start that was unfortunate even by Channel 4's new standards. Although Bez emerged victorious from what must have been a most unpleasant ordeal, his performance was judged to be a poor advertisement for Celebrities who have a cannabis habit. Equally, it could be argued that the behaviour of the other participants was an even worse advertisement for Celebrities who don't have a cannabis habit. Bez, who has never before sung, recently announced that he will be doing the vocals on an album to be released in April 2005.

Big Brother contestants. Ten points off their IQs and you'd have to water them once a week.

Biggins, Christopher (b.1956). Waddling fat walker to decrepit former film stars.

Big pants, Bridget Jones's. *See* ICONIC, SO.

Big time, troubled Celebrity back in the. Confused ex-boxer turns on Christmas illuminations in Chertsey.

Bits, Germaine Greer talking about her. 'Sounds like one for us, Kevin.'

See also ADULT CONTENT; CHANNEL 4; LYGO, KEVIN; TELEVISION WE DESERVE, THE.

Birley, Mark (b.1932). 1960s man-about-town who founded the nightclub Annabel's, named after his wife, Lady Annabel Vane-Tempest-Stewart, daughter of the 8th Marquess of Londonderry. The couple, who married at London's Caxton Hall in 1954, had three children, Rupert, Robin and India Jane. In 1964 Lady Annabel started an affair with the entrepreneur James Goldsmith, whom she had first met at Annabel's. She left Birley and married Sir James in 1978. By 2004 Birley had branched out into gentlemen's cosmetics. Escentual – The UK's Premier Beauty Destination for Skin Care, Fragrances, Bath Salts and Perfumes – was able to announce on www.escentual.co.uk that 'The words distinguished, elegant and civilized not only describe Mark Birley himself, they describe "Mark Birley's Scent For Men".' Other Birley products include 'Mark Birley Energizing Aftershave' and the 'Mark Birley Deodorant Stick'.

Björk (b.1976). Icelandic pop star whose voice has been likened to the sound of a cat being neutered. Björk's behaviour can be unreliable. Arriving in Bangkok airport for a series of pop concerts, she beat up a reporter. Perhaps one should try to see the incident from Björk's point of view. She is suddenly greeted by a Chinese woman with the words:

恩　永　命　清　慈　英　信　氣-明
'Wang　ton　hui　ping　djin　fo　li　lung-mien'.

For all Björk knew her interlocutor might have been saying, 'We think you're a crap singer.' Small wonder she got a slapping.

Black, Cilla (b.1941). 'Our Cilla'. Raucous and copiously toothed TV hostess and former pop singer in the Gracie Fields mode. Dionne Warwick, whose recordings Our Cilla consistently emulated, likened her voice 'to labour pains set to music'. To which she would undoubtedly respond: 'Worra lorra nonsense.' As a TV presenter she has been called the natural successor to Wilfred PICKLES.

Blacker, Terence. *See* BRYSON, DR KIT; CELEBRITY PUBLISHING.

Blair, Anthony Charles Lynton (b.1953). Britain's first Celebrity Prime Minister, the Triumph of Style over Substance – or *Il trionfo dello stilo sopra la sostanzia*, as Blair's associate, Italian entrepreneur Silvio Berlusconi, would say. Among the prime minister's other Celebrity Friends is fellow Christ-insider Cliff Richard, at whose Barbados villa the Blairs have spent quality time (like all Celebrities, they never pay for their own holidays). Then there's the ex-minor-rock-star looks. The Fender. The Celebrity Baby. The orange tan. The slightly batty wife. The five-times-a-night sex habit. Where will it all end?

See also AWARD FOR ORANGENESS SPONSORED BY TERRY'S CHOCOLATE ORANGE.

Blair, Lionel (b.1932). Elderly tap dancer. A showbiz legend. The mere mention of his name in a seaside vaudeville venue can cause the same gales of laughter as greet 'knickers', 'Wigan' or 'Des O'Connor'.

Blatt, Melanie (b.1971). Singer-songwriter, married to Stuart Zender (formerly Jamiroquai's bassist) with whom she has a four-year-old daughter, Lily. With Shaznay Lewis she was the talented half of the girl group All Saints who released several hit records in the late 1990s. For her opinion of bandmates Nicole and Natalie, *see* the APPLETON sisters. To date, she has produced only one record as a solo artist, 'Do Me Wrong' (2001).

Blazing Squad. They look like an assortment of singing pickpockets. They are in fact to So Solid Crew what S-Club Juniors are to S-Club 7. That is to say, a juvenile knock-off designed to keep the franchise ticking over. One of their number, Kenzie, took a bath in a hot tub with cigarillo-toting feminist icon Germaine Greer during *Celebrity Big Brother 3*. Despite the professor's well-documented interest in young men (*see* BEAUTIFUL BOYS, THE EXPLOITATION OF), he emerged from the Jacuzzi undefiled. Far from possessing 'street cred', Kenzie is a nicely brought-up middle-class boy who still lives in Chingford with his mother, a librarian, and his father, who teaches English. This Middle England background accounts for the fact that when he speaks he sounds like a bad impression of Ali G.

Bloom, Orlando (b.1978). Elf who does a remarkably good impression of an actor. Born in Sevenoaks, Kent, he yet seems more comfortable wearing a velveteen jacket in LA. Many praised him for his performance as Legolas in the insanely boring trilogy *The Lord of the Rings*. Others admired his sensitive nostril-flaring as Paris in the turkey *Troy*. But his finest hour to date is his nimble turn in a Gap advert, in which he shows his mitten-wearing skills to be unrivalled. He strenuously denies that it was on the set of this advert that he met his former girlfriend, the toothsome US actress Kate Bosworth.

***Blue Peter* presenters.** Either shovelling cocaine up their noses or standing behind an elephant when it relieves itself. In the former circumstance, five-year-olds are suddenly confronted by a terrifying close-up image on their television screens of BBC1's stern-faced director of programmes. Having explained the dangers of five-year-olds taking cocaine, she issues a formal apology and confirms that the offending presenter has been sacked. The five-year-olds retire to bed in a state of confusion. The next day at playschool they say to each other, 'You sorted by any chance?'

See also ELEPHANTS.

Blum, Victoria. *See* ROBERTS, TANYA.

Bodyguards. A redundant accessory. Celebrities now realize that they don't need bodyguards unless, paradoxically, they already have bodyguards, since without bodyguards no one would know they were Celebrities, in which case bodyguards would not be needed. It is now recognized that the only people who need bodyguards are bodyguards themselves since they are forever being beaten up by their employers (*see* BRAZIER, JEFF; CAMPBELL, NAOMI).

Bodyguards, the Queen's. Forever filming themselves having group sex, often within a stone's throw of Buckingham Palace. In February 2005 the *Sun* was able to report that 'nine Life Guards troopers – members of the British Army's most senior regiment – staged a late-night orgy less than a mile from Buckingham Palace. They then distributed copies of the video among colleagues. A full-scale probe has been launched by commanding officer, Lt Col Valentine Wonka.' A prominent director of programmes and maker

of GREAT TELEVISION at Channel 4, is currently conceptualizing a show in which a platoon of Life Guards will compete in a ROASTING competition with a team of soccer players drawn from the Tyneside area. Colonel Wonka has agreed to act as referee. Up-for-it GEORDETTES have already formed a queue that stretches from Newcastle's Town Hall to St James's Park and back again. Problems may arise when it is discovered that it is the Geordettes who expect to roast the soccer players rather than vice versa.

Boleyn, Anne (1501–36). First co-respondent in a divorce case. The daughter of Thomas Boleyn and Elizabeth Howard, whose father was the Duke of Norfolk. Her many suitors included Henry Percy, the heir to the Earl of Northumberland, and King Henry VIII. Henry, who had already had an affair with Anne's sister, now showered favours on her father. Anne refused to respond until negotiations for Henry's divorce from Catherine of Aragon began, but, as these dragged on, her association with Henry became more open (some commentators have noticed interesting historical parallels here) and they were secretly married in January 1533. It was Henry's determination to end his marriage to Catherine that marked the turning-point in his reign. All Catherine's children, except Mary Tudor (later Mary I) had died in infancy and Henry professed to see in this the judgement of God on an unnatural alliance. However, Henry soon tired of his new bride, and had her charged with adultery, incest and witchcraft. Proof of her satanic liaisons was found in the form of an eleventh finger and a third nipple (the latter thought to have been a mole on her neck). The court brought in the required verdict, and Anne had her head cut off.

See also APRIL CELEBRITY *FAUX PAS*.

Boltholes, Celebrity.

✈ Leslie Ash – Calais

✈ Zoe Ball – Seychelles

✈ Sol Campbell – Assisi

✈ Charlotte Church – St Lucia's Le Sport

✈ Sara Cox – Ibiza

✈ Kate Moss – Mustique

✈ Posh and Becks – Courcheval

☠ Ian Hislop – Frinton-on-Sea

☠ Patsy Palmer – Romford caravan site

Bombshell, Curvy Kate's New Year. 'Good evening. The time is 10 o'clock and I'm Huw Edwards. Here is tonight's quiz for all the family. Which disguised Celebrity is Abi Titmuss romping with in the clip which follows:

A. Kriss Akabusi?

B. Richard Blackwood?

C. Kofi Annan?

Text your answer to 76953 remembering to put "Birmingham Bollock-Brain" before your message. And now for tonight's headlines. "I Quit *Corrie*!" Good gracious! Apparently, 27-year-old Kate Ford, who plays man-mad Tracy Barlow in the popular soap opera, is so keen to expand her career she intends to ask *Corrie* chiefs to release her early from her £70,000-a-year contract. A bombshell indeed. The feisty babe (forgive me – I just read this stuff out, I don't compose it) aims to make it big in movies – just like fellow soap star Anna Friel. Fat chance. Here in the BBC News Room we say, "Get real, Kate!" More about that later. The rest of the news now follows. This afternoon, former home secretary David

Blunkett visited a vet with his dog. "Do you want it neutered?" asked the vet. "Yes please," replied the dog. Excellent! 221,000 people, including more than 23 Brits, are now known to have died in the earthquake which recently rocked Asia.'

See also FRIEL, ANNA.

Bond (b.2001). Troupe of fiddling tarts trying to give classical music a bad name. First there was Vanessa-Mae, followed by the Mediaeval Baebes, and then Bond. Bond is made up of Tania, Gay-Yee, Haylie and Eos. That's a Pasty One straddling a cello as if it were a sex machine, a Brunette One who makes Zoe Lucker look classy, a Stripy One and a Scary One wearing rags. Strads out for the lads!

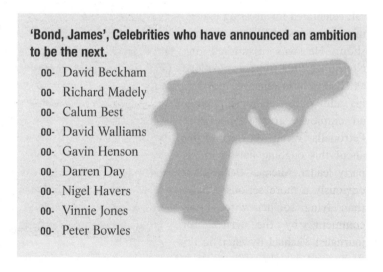

'Bond, James', Celebrities who have announced an ambition to be the next.
- 00- David Beckham
- 00- Richard Madely
- 00- Calum Best
- 00- David Walliams
- 00- Gavin Henson
- 00- Darren Day
- 00- Nigel Havers
- 00- Vinnie Jones
- 00- Peter Bowles

Bond, Jennie (b.1948). Royal correspondent, now retired. She was the connecting link between the late Princess of Wales and a nation in grief, or so she says. It's unclear what the claim amounts to, but it sells tickets for *Jennie Bond's Royals* – a stage-show that

Miss Bond performs in venues such as Basingstoke and Guildford. Appearing on *I'm a Celebrity, Get Me Out of Here* in 2004, she was shown to be so dependent on her make-up collection that when her fuchsia lipstick was confiscated she improvised with termite droppings. Her ingenuity endeared her to the general public in the UK. Abroad, Ms Bond is worshipped by a remote Philippine community, which believes her to be the deputy Queen of England.

Bonking Boris, properly **Alexander Boris de Pfeffel Johnson** (b.1965). Comic-opera Tory politician, editor of the *Spectator* and backbench love rat; celebrated for dressing like a man who's had a fit in a charity shop. He was dismissed in November 2004 from his position as shadow arts minister, not for his adulterous relationship with an employee at the *Spectator*, Petronella Wyatt, but for lying about this ongoing liaison to his party leader, Michael HOWARD – obviously a more serious offence than lying to his wife. Some comments by the writer and journalist Michael Bywater on this

fiasco, and on Johnson's earlier supposed *faux pas* involving the self-pitying people of Liverpool, are worth preserving. 'On what basis,' asked Bywater in the *Independent on Sunday* on 21 November 2004, 'did someone say to Michael Howard, "You can't have Boris being nasty about Liverpool and possibly, or possibly not, having a step-out with Petronella Wyatt. The electorate simply won't stand for it." Rubbish. We all know that Liverpool is a hellish, cold tip of a place populated by self-pitying scallies whose idea of a good time is weeing down a rolled-up copy of the *Echo* at a football match. Further, there's not a man living whose heart doesn't sing at the thought of Petsy getting a thoroughly rococo seeing-to, even if it's not something we'd have time to do ourselves.' Absolutely right. So why did Boris have to go? The debate continues.

Booker Prize, the. The official panel of judges – a Celebrity Historian with an award-winning haircut, a politician with the literary tastes of a country curate, the former editrice of an erotic magazine and David Baddiel – is comprehensively upstaged each year by Professor Hermione Lee who assembles an alternative panel of bruisingly clever novelists (Adam Mars-Jones in a collarless shirt, Peter Ackroyd in a moustache, Philip Hensher in punk braces), which offers a contemptuous televised critique of the chosen shortlist. The proceedings are hosted by Miss Cat DEELEY, who announces that 'This is the time of year when literature meets show business!' Having expressed the opinion that William Boyd is '*far* too good-looking to be a novelist!' she asks Julian Barnes what he intends to do with the money if he wins. Unfortunately, Mr Barnes is present merely as a guest and hasn't been shortlisted. Cat then asks Martin Amis, similarly ignored by the judges, to what extent his height has affected his prose style. He turns away, looking sardonic.

Borgia, Lucrezia (1480–1519). Italian noblewoman, said by some to be the Barbara Amiel or Alexis Carrington *de ses jours*. Born in Rome, the illegitimate daughter of Rodrigo Borgia, later Pope Alexander VI. She was married off three times by her father for political reasons: first, at the age of 12, to Giovanni Sforza, Lord of Pesaro, but the marriage was annulled by her father (1497); second, to Alfonso of Aragon, nephew of the king of Naples

(1498), but this marriage was ended (1500) when Alonso was strangled by her brother, Cesare Borgia; and third (1501), to Alfonso d'Este (1486–1534), the son of the Duke of Este. Alfonso inherited the duchy of Ferrara, where Lucrezia established a brilliant court of artists and writers. A patroness of art and education, she has, quite unfairly, become notorious in legend for wantonness, vice and crime, and a comic indicator for humorous columnists, who were able, before British Rail was privatized, to describe its caterers as 'the most notorious poisoners since Lucrezia Borgia!'

Bottle, Spin the. A variation on 'Truth or Dare', an after-lights-out dormitory game popular among fumbling adolescents. It is peculiarly unsettling when played by middle-aged Celebrities in Reality Television shows. 'Sounds like one for us, Kevin'.

See also ADULT CONTENT; CHANNEL 4; GREAT TELEVISION; LYGO, KEVIN; TELEVISION WE DESERVE, THE.

Boudicca (*fl.* AD 60). Barmy charioteer or feminist role model? The first female Celebrity or merely a curtain-raiser to the glorious parade that includes Lady GODIVA, Nell GWYNN and Fanny CRADOCK? The popular historian, Lady Antonia Fraser, is in no doubt: 'She stands aloft in her chariot, knives sprouting from its wheel. Hers is a gallant – and a savage – story' (*Boadicea's Chariot – A Study of Warrior Queens*, Weidenfeld & Nicolson, 1978). The *Sun* newspaper is equally convinced. Dubbing her an early version of Essex Woman, it suggests that Boudicca 'was an inspiring figure' whose example, like 'Margaret Thatcher, Wall's pork sausages and Denise Van Outen, makes one proud to be British'.

Bough, Frank (b.1935). Formerly a reassuring, Pringle-knitted front-person on television sports programmes, Frank is now missing, presumed disgraced, alternatively, shamed. Cocaine, suspender belts and lower-class women are rumoured to have been involved. If that is the case, Frank can console himself with the thought that, as the saying goes, such stories are yesterday's fish and chips. He was last seen driving through Conques, with his wife Nesta speechless at his side, checking out Route Nationale 140 for Arthur Eperon's *Traveller's France*. Perhaps he's prospered, acquiring a small property in the Dordogne – a most agreeable part of the world from all accounts, not least his own (*Dordogne & Lot*, 2nd edition).

Bournemouth. The preferred retirement locale for D-list Celebrities. The facilities include two ice rinks, an archery range, an aquarium (featuring Fang the Halibut) and *thés dansants* for waltzing old folk at the Winter Gardens Ball Room. On the award-winning beach, large corseted women tuck their skirts into their pink ballooning knickers and wade squealing into the sea. On the promenade, old men in deckchairs pass the day in thin continuous dreaming. Further inland, a fishy aroma of cod and chips, of dead crabs in buckets under boarding-house beds, hangs in the air. Rough local girls smelling like low tide on the Dogger Bank are turned away from discos by representatives of the Russian Mafia. Later, in a bus shelter, they receive a sexual hammering from visiting roustabouts. Cannon and Ball and Anita Harris star in the summer show at the Pavilion Theatre. Celebrated residents: Max Bygraves, Matthew Kelly, Archie Andrews, 'Whispering' Ted Lowe ('The Voice of Snooker'), Ray ALLEN and Lord Charles.

Boy bands. A good slapping and two years National Service wouldn't hurt.

Braddock, 'Battling' Bessie (1899–1970). Belligerent Labour MP for Liverpool Exchange. Built like a First World War battle-cruiser, she had a bosom that could break pack ice. A role model for heavyweight rude women. Anecdotes abound. On one occasion she was confronted by Winston Churchill in the House of Commons. Churchill took an alarmed step back. 'By God, you're ugly!' he proclaimed. 'And you're drunk, Mr Churchill!' replied Mrs Braddock. 'Yes? Yes? Is that so?' said Churchill. 'You want to make something of it? You think you can take me? Is that it? You want a bit of me? Put 'em up! Here's one! Oooof! Is that it? Is that all you've got? Try another! Jumping Jesus! What was that? Have a care, woman! Ow! Ow! You horrible old cow! Get off, I say! Help! Guards! *Guards!*'

Branson, Sir Richard (b.1950). Thatcherism in a friendly cardigan, a black hole of dynamic suburban niceness into which the strangeness of life around him disappears without trace.

'Bravo! Victim and dickhead.' An anagram of 'David and Victoria Beckham'. For references to other Celebrity Anagrams, *see* ANAGRAMS, CELEBRITY.

Brazier, Jeff (b.1979). Baby-faced former soccer player with Leyton Orient FC and abused partner of *Big Brother* megastar and chav role model, Jade GOODY. Unusually for a soccer player, it was Jeff who got the worst of it in domestic punch-ups and the couple separated in September 2004. Mr Brazier may count himself more fortunate than Mr M'Hammed Soumayah, Miss Liza Minnelli's 26-stone, $130,000-a-year personal bodyguard. In November 2004 it was announced that Mr Soumayah was suing Miss Minnelli for £55 million, claiming that she beat him up on a regular basis and forced him to have sex with her. Minnelli has subsequently counter-sued him for breach of contract. It is not known whether Mr Soumayah plans to bring out his own range of gentlemen's lingerie.

See also BODYGUARDS.

Brigitte warms the toilet seat for her mother-in-law, Jackie Stallone. 'Sounds like one for us, Kevin'.

See also ADULT CONTENT; CHANNEL 4; GREAT TELEVISION; LYGO, KEVIN; TELEVISION WE DESERVE, THE.

British intellectuals. *See* FRY, STEPHEN; PHILISTINISM, BRITISH.

Britton, Fern (b.1960). Daytime television Celebrity who, in spite of her considerable popularity, has remained thoroughly down-to-earth. In November 2004 her head was featured in a TV commercial for Ryvita Minis with former Miss UK, Vicki Walberg, appearing as her body. Fern's agent, Geraldine Wood, was able to confirm that the size-16 TV star doesn't 'take herself too seriously'. Fern and Vicki met for the first time when the commercial was being filmed and hit it off immediately. 'The two of them had a great time on the shoot,' revealed Geraldine, 'and even though they both had hectic schedules they managed to have a cup of tea and a girlie chat.' Fern, whose partner is Phil Vickery (the daytime chef, not the English tight-head prop of the same name) is the daughter of the actor, Tony Britton. Miss Walberg, now a successful lingerie model, is busy writing her first book for HarperCollins, after which she hopes to star in a West End musical.

Brocket, Charles Ronald George Nall-Cain, 3rd Baron (b.1952). After Eton, Brocket trained as an architect, but never practised. Instead, he devised various schemes to turn his inherited ancestral seat, Brocket Hall, into a profit centre. This necessitated an overhaul of the plumbing system, which required Brocket to flush plastic of different colours down the lavatories ('damn good fun').

When his scheme to relaunch the hall as a venue for business conferences failed, he assembled a collection of classic cars with several million pounds borrowed from a bank. This failed too, so he concocted an insurance fraud, burying the cars underground but claiming that they had been stolen. His disaffected wife, Tia, an American who now lives in Costa Rica, informed on him to the

police, and Brocket served two years of a seven-year prison sentence. In accordance with the prevailing *zeitgeist*, he now possessed the qualifications to become a Celebrity, and in January 2004 he obligingly filled the role of goofy upper-class bra-twanger on *I'm a Celebrity, Get Me Out of Here*. Amusingly dubbed 'Lewd Brocket' by his jungle pals, he achieved notoriety by buffing Alex Best's bottom as if chamois-leathering one of the Ferraris in his fraudulently disposed-of car museum. Alex Best is the ex-wife of the troubled soccer legend, George Best.

See also ARISTOCRATS.

Brooklyn Bridge, The. *See* POSITIONS, CELEBRITIES' FAVOURITE SEXUAL.

Brosnan, Pierce (b.1953). According to *Time* magazine (1996), one of 'The World's Fifty Most Beautiful People'. In fact, he is an ageing catalogue model from County Meath, a needy-looking poseur with hooded eyes. Rather fancies himself, which is just as well because nobody else does. The eponymous hero of four James Bond films, he was sacked from the franchise in September 2004.

Brummel, Beau, properly **George Bryan Brummel** (1778–1840). Known as 'Buck' at Eton, Brummel was the Rupert Everett of his day. A Regency dandy who possessed all the hallmarks of a Celebrity:

He had a catchphrase: 'Who's your fat friend?' He said this loudly and was then informed that 'the fat friend' was in fact the Prince of Wales.

He was a consumer trendsetter who got everyone, including the Duke of Wellington, wearing his special foot-hugging trousers. He was thus responsible for 'leggins', the modern wardrobe item popular with fat people in the early 1990s .

He was a figure of curious sexuality (Was he or wasn't he? Or was he both?).

He suffered a demise that was pitiful and could be greatly enjoyed, therefore, by Ordinary People. He died penniless and insane in Northern France.

Most importantly, he came from humble stock and rose to the greatest social height.

It is figures like Beau Brummel who did most to help Britain avoid a bloody revolution, since he would never have stood for the mischief it might have done his trousers.

For other dandies, *see* CHRISTIAN, FLETCHER; HORSLEY, SEBASTIAN.

Brylcreem Awards, the. 'Good evening. The time is 10 o'clock and I'm Huw Edwards. First, here is the answer to last night's quiz question – Which celebrity autobiography was recently described by Matthew Norman as "the product of a stupefyingly repugnant and degenerate mind" The correct answer is *So Me* by Graham Norton. Norton has just been signed up by the BBC in a £5 million golden handcuff deal. How embarrassing is that? Not in the least in fact. These people are unembarrassable. And here is tonight's quiz for all the family. Which former newspaper editor is one of the seven heterosexual male journalists in Britain never rumoured to have had relations with *Spectator* publisher, Kimberley Quinn? Text your answer to 76923 remembering to start with the words "Liverpool Layabout". Now for tonight's headlines: "*X Factor* Lads Triumph in Showbiz Hair Vote!" Big deal! *X Factor* runners-up, G4, are winners at last, apparently – for having the best Celebrity Haircuts. You couldn't parody this stuff, could you? If you want to complain, write to the director general, Mark Thompson. Anyway, the group, made up of pals Matthew Stiff (24), Ben Thapa (22), Jonathan Ansell (22) and Mike Christie (23), beat off competition from stars such as David

Beckham (30), Charlie Simpson (19) from the pop group Busted (it says here) and Prince Harry (21) to win the title of Brylcreem Best Male Celebrity Hairstyle 2004. Now for the good news. The holidaymakers held hostage for three days in an Athens bus have all been released. It turned out that their captors weren't carrying a bomb, merely a bag of croissants. Have you noticed that one of the G4 lads is the spitting image of the Greek Bloke who runs Easy Jet? Well, there you are.'

Bryson, Dr Kit (1935–2005). Former sociology Lecturer at Keele University, and Emeritus Professor of Red Carpet studies and Warden of Rehab College, Kent. Bryson was co-editor (with Selina Fitzherbert and Jean-Luc Legris) of *The Complete Naff Guide* (1983) and co-editor (with Terence Blacker) of *The Meaning of Cantona: Meditations on Life, Art and Perfectly Weighted Balls* (1997). Dr Bryson moved among the followers of Eric CANTONA – the so-called Cantonistes – collecting aphorisms, reflections and snatches of changing-room badinage to produce a book that reflects the contradictory essence of this simple, yet complex, character: artist and man of action; team leader and solitary maverick.

See also ASH, LESLIE; ROOT, HENRY.

Bubbly. Plain but cheerful (*see* ADAMS, HELEN; ELLISON, JENNIFER).

Bucephalus. Even conservative historians now agree that Bucephalus was hung like a horse. For other Celebrity Horses, *see* RED RUM; SHERGAR.

Bull, John. A personification of England, or of the English people, in so far as the national character is marked by a kind of bovine stupidity (*see* CLARKSON, JEREMY; LITTLEJOHN, RICHARD; MADELY, RICHARD). He derives from a character personifying England in *The History of John Bull* (1712) by John Arbuthnot (1667–1735), an English physician and man of letters. He is not to be confused with John Bull (*c.*1562–1628), an English composer and organist who wrote mainly for voices and the keyboard. The attribution to Bull of the British national anthem is disputed. In most works of reference the fictional John Bull's entry falls between 'bulky' (taking up a lot of room – *see* BRITTON, FERN) and 'bull' (an uncastrated male of the ox or buffalo family; the male of certain other large animals – for instance, the whale, elephant, elk or moose; on the stock exchange, a person buying shares as a speculation in the hope that prices will rise; 'bull in a china shop' – a person who is destructive or clumsy in a situation requiring tact and delicacy; *see* STREET-PORTER, JANET, *née* BULL).

Bumbling English prats, chaps who make a living out of portraying. *See* CHARLES, PRINCE; GRANT, HUGH.

Bunton, Emma (b.1976). A.k.a. Baby Spice. Bermondsey-born daughter of a fitness instructor and a milkman. She starred in beauty pageants as a child and appeared, age 11, in a British Rail advert wearing a pink tracksuit and long blonde bunches. She has stuck to this look ever since, in a sad case of arrested intellectual development. While her fellow bandmates in the Spice Girls were famous for being posh or scary, Emma's distinguishing characteristic was a passion for doughnuts. The girls tended to introduce themselves as follows:

> 'Hi! I'm Mel C and I love jumping about in scuffed trainers.'
> 'Hi! I'm Victoria and I love Prada.'
> 'Hi! I'm Geri and when we're, like, recording and I need to have a pump, I leave the toilet door open.'
> 'Hi! I'm Mel B and I've snogged all the others except Geri.'
> 'Hi! I'm Emma and I love doughnuts.'

Later, when asked her favourite colour, Emma said, 'Pink icing on a doughnut.' When quizzed about her main ambition in life she replied 'to eat 100 doughnuts at one go'. When she launched her solo career her doughnutophilia had to be cured by airbrushing her thighs – a process so laborious it was rumoured to have cost £20,000. If Emma ever looks vacant on camera it's because she's trying to read a sign displayed by her travelling clinical psychologist. This reads, 'Don't mention doughnuts!' If her next album fails to make an impact, she might do well to join 'Back To Reality' – a lookalike entertainment agency representing Celebs whose careers have collapsed but who hope to make a comeback as REAL PEOPLE. Emma could expect to land a walk-on role in a reality show as a lardy girl from Luton on holiday in the wrong part of Ibiza.

Buñuel, Luis (1900–83). Revolutionary Spanish film director and life-long anti-Fascist who had the misfortune to die on the same day as David Niven, the author of *The Moon's a Balloon.* The BBC's *Nine O'Clock News* opened with an eight-minute tribute to the latter but made no mention of Buñuel. The Sunday papers commissioned articles about the moustachioed light comedian by people such as John Mortimer ('Our meetings were all about laughter') but Buñuel received only a three-line obituary in the *Guardian* and two lines in *The Times.* The BBC launched a season of Niven comedy films but showed only one of Buñuel's, after which he was dismissed on *Late Night Line-up* as 'a forerunner of the video-nasty boom'. 'At a time when the government is trying to introduce a bill to outlaw this sort of filth,' observed the British intellectual Malcolm Muggeridge, 'the BBC has devoted an hour and a half to it.'

Burrell, Paul (b.1959). Creepy former butler to Diana, Princess of Wales, self-advertised as her 'rock'. When both Burrell and Janet STREET-PORTER were named as participants in *I'm A Celebrity, Get Me Out Of Here* in November 2004, intellectual fireworks were predicted. The match-up would be interesting, it was thought, since Burrell and Street-Porter ('I'm not here to flout myself – you know J S-P!') seemed to be dialectical equals, more or less, with Burrell, perhaps, enjoying a slight advantage. He certainly has a better grasp of the Queen's English, though not, apparently, of the Queen's property.

Busted (2002–5). Boy band: eight top-ten hits, four number ones, three singing goons. Busted comprised Charlie Simpson (the pretty one) Matt Jay (the dark horse) and James Bourne (the nerdy one who picked his nose – actually, they all picked their noses but James was particularly enthusiastic in this regard). Busted dissolved shortly after playing at the Conservative Party Conference in Bournemouth. Their music was most popular with a discerning listening demographic aged ten years and under.

Busy filming. A stock excuse for not turning up to an awards ceremony. What it really means is 'Thanks, but I'd rather die than attend your tuppenny ha'penny backslap buffet.'

Byron, George Gordon, 6th Baron (1788–1824). Poet and celebrated philanderer, famously described by one of his many mistresses, Lady Caroline Lamb, as 'mad, bad and dangerous to know'. His childhood was unhappy. It has been suggested that his mother's violent changes of mood instilled in him a life-long hatred of women. At the age of nine he had his first sexual experiences, with a servant girl, Mary Gray. It was her habit to take a succession of lovers with the boy Byron looking on. He later attended Harrow school, where he was introduced to homosexuality. When he went up to Cambridge University he visited prostitutes with such regularity that even his French procuress advised him to be more selective (*see also* HORSLEY, SEBASTIAN). At this time he published his first poems, but these were judged to be so poor that he thought for a while of killing himself. Instead, he embarked on a tour of Europe. He returned to England in 1812, and in the same year John

Murray published *Childe Harold's Pilgrimage.* This dark and romantic poem brought him instant Celebrity. He was adored by young women, while young men imitated his brooding demeanour and dangerous silences. Before long, his louche behaviour dominated society gossip. To silence this, he made a suitable marriage to a prim heiress named Annabella Milbanke. The marriage was not a success and the circumstances of its collapse (Byron had continued his many affairs, including a prolonged relationship with his half-sister, Augusta, while consistently sodomizing his pregnant wife) caused Byron to become the most vilified man in London. The celebrated poet was suddenly un-welcome in fashionable drawing rooms. Rather than be snubbed, he left England in April 1816 and rented a palazzo in Venice. There, his orgiastic behaviour shocked even the normally debauched citizens of that city. After a few years, once more overwhelmed with *Byronic* discontent, the poet set off again, this time to free Greece from the tyrannical Turk. But, with a bathos not in keeping with the ideal Celebrity Career, he became poorly, took a turn for the worse and died before he could fire a single shot.

C

Callow, Simon (b.1949). Swaggering ham.

Campbell, Naomi (b.1970). Amazonian model of legendary lateness.
The Streatham-born daughter of a single mum, a tapdancer, Naomi is
of Somalian descent with a face and figure so stunningly beautiful
that people who see her in the flesh for the first time often
spontaneously laugh, cry or burp. She made up one of the original
Big Five (Cindy Crawford, Linda Evangelista, Christy Turlington and
Tatiana) who stalked the catwalk for Versace in 1990 and inspired
the coinage of the term 'supermodel'. How do you go from chewing
gum at the back of tap lessons at Italia Conti to being an adopted
granddaughter to Nelson Mandela? Naomi did it by way of catwalks
and ad campaigns; by being the first black woman on the cover of
Vogue, *US Vogue* and *Time* magazines. And along the way, it's not
surprising if you become a little testy. Naomi is so talented at being
very, very late (at her best, she can be several days late) that people
feel very let down indeed if she is punctual and polite. She rarely
disappoints, though. In 2004 she kept an *Evening Standard*
journalist waiting for three months. Although she beat the *Sun* in
a legal case, winning the right to attend meetings of Narcotics Anony-
mous without their taking photographs of her, she lost another case
in 1998, when her one-time PA Georgina Galanis took her to court
claiming Ms Campbell had twice hit her with a telephone. In
November 2004, a second PA, Annie Castaldo, said of Ms Campbell:
'She needs 100% to get help.'

See also BODYGUARDS.

Cantona, Eric (b.1966). French soccer player. Fancies himself as *un peu d'un philosophe*. As the Scottish footballer and cultural critic Gordon Strachan so rightly observed in 1995: 'If a Frenchman goes on about seagulls, trawlers and sardines, he's called a philosopher. I'd just be called a short Scottish bum talking BALLS.'

For more Cantonese, *see* ASH, LESLIE.

See also BRYSON, DR KIT.

Canute, King, properly **Knut Sveinsson** or **Cnut the Great** (*c*.995–1035). King of England, Denmark and Norway. When his name is rendered as Cnut, he provides perhaps the most satisfying of Celebrity Anagrams. Like many Celebrities, he is defined by one misleading anecdote, in which it is said that he thought he could hold back the incoming tide; in fact, he was  trying to demonstrate to his courtiers that only God can control the tide, not man. In 1015 Cnut invaded England, then ruled by Ethelred the Unready, gaining the whole country except London. When Ethelred died in 1016, Cnut defeated his son, Edmund Ironside, at the Battle of Assandune, thereafter concluding a treaty under which they shared the kingdom. When Ironside died a month later, Cnut became undisputed king of England. Ethelred the Unready is now believed to be promoting his own-brand range of gentlemen's lingerie; King Cnut, for his part, is bringing an intellectual property suit against the clothing company Fcuk.

Caplin, Carole (b.1963). The spirit of Rasputin trapped in the body of a Pan's People performer; a druid who shops at Molton Brown; a white witch with a column in the *Mail on Sunday* (nothing new there, then). She is a former glamour model, employee of the Exegesis Cult and serial lover of unsuitable men (former lovers include Adam ANT), but yet she still considers herself qualified to advise people on how to make 'life decisions'. Ms Caplin is living testament to the powers of nettle tea and crystals: they really can get you into Downing Street. For a spell in the first years of the new millennium, she was Cherie Blair's 'lifestyle guru' (more accurately, lipstick consultant, feng shui coordinator and crystal swinger) and Tony Blair's sometime masseuse. She used to feed the couple strawberry leaves grown within the electromagnetic field of a Neolithic circle, and she gave Cherie a 'BioElectric Shield' made of crystals. This arrangement ended when the 'Cheriegate' scandal broke. The prime minister's wife had to apologize officially for having bought her son a flat in Bristol with the help of Caplin's boyfriend, the established Australian conman, Peter Foster. Carole has had her all-access pass to Downing Street removed, although she is still thought to be Cherie's closest friend. During the scandal, Alastair Campbell said that he expected Ms Caplin would soon be selling her story to the *Mail on Sunday*. 'He is so misguided,' said Carole, 'I actually feel sorry for him.' Two weeks later, Ms Caplin sold her story to the *Mail on Sunday*.

Caprice, properly **Caprice Bourret** (b.1974). Underwear model. In January 2005, in the company of, among others, Professor Germaine Greer, Bez, Kenzie and Sylvester Stallone's mother, Jackie Stallone, she participated in *Celebrity Big Brother 3*. Asked by one of the housemates what was the most she had ever earned in a day, Caprice replied, 'Half a million pounds'. In 2001, she released an album (*Oh Yeah*) which failed to find a market. Her musical output is not to be confused with the sublime 'caprices' or 'capriccios' flowing from the pens of such modern masters as Stravinsky, Richard Strauss and Janáček.

Carman QC, George (1930–2000). Offensively short Celebrity Barrister. High-profile defendants who benefited from his melo-dramatic posturing and insulting manner in cross-examination included Jeremy Thorpe, Sir Elton John and the comedian Ken Dodd. One jury was so affronted by his discourtesy to prosecution witnesses that they suggested to His Lordship that he acquit Carman's client but sentence Carman to 380 days community service. The story may be apocryphal, but is significant for all that. *No Ordinary Man* (2002), a posthumous memoir by Carman's son Dominic, revealed that after he had won a case the troubled silk would gamble away his winnings in games of chance, thereafter returning home in a drunken rage. He would then beat up his wife before falling backwards into the fireplace, where he would spend the night.

Cartesian dualism. For a fuller discussion of this philosophical theory, *see* ANT AND DEC; CELEBRITY HAIRDRESSERS; DESCARTES, RENÉ.

Cartland, Barbara (1901–2000). Romantic novelist, nutritionist and Vision in Pink. Miss Cartland could be a formidable opponent. Asked by an interviewer on BBC Radio 4 whether social barriers had been greatly reduced during her lifetime, she replied: 'Of course. Why else would I be talking to you?' The rumour always was that Queen Elizabeth II would never abdicate, not because she enjoyed having two birthdays and in any case didn't consider Charles up to the job, but because she feared that by her connection with Diana, Princess of Wales, Miss Cartland would by some constitutional anomaly become Queen Mother.

Catchphrases, Celebrity.

    '*Cogito ergo sum*' – René Descartes.
    'Me crackers are killing me!' – Joe Pasquale.

Caveman, the, properly **Nicholas Edward Cave** (b.1957). Looking rather more chipper than the junkie pipe-cleaner of old, the Caveman is back on the scene with the spaghetti-punk Bad Seeds and some knife-lean songs from their new album, *Abattoir Blues / Lyre of Orpheus*. The hair is thinning, but clubbers can expect the air to thicken with howling tales of lusty soul, untamed passion and literate lamentation. Nick was raised as an Anglican, which may explain the apparent influence of religion on his work. His debut novel, *And the Ass Saw the Angel*, appeared in 1997. He is married to Susie Bick. Nick's mother, Dawn, was a librarian.

celebdaq.co.uk. Online stocks-and-shares star system; the ideal site for anyone who likes to undergo a little pain and pleasure in the afternoon. Log on to www.celebdaq.co.uk and you can watch young lovelies losing it and broken old bastards bouncing back. 'JOHNNY AND DENISE – Sell! Sell! Sell!' 'BRIAN AND DELTA – Buy! Buy! Buy!' 'MICHAEL HOWARD – Sell! Sell! Sell!' The team of clinical psychologists at Sussex University, referred to under ADAM AND EVE, has pointed out that 'This website usefully demonstrates the fact that it is the main function of the contemporary Celebrity to undergo public humiliation for the sadistic satisfaction of normal people. The normal person thus experiences a form of spiritual detoxification' (Salter, Horrocks-Taylor and De Santos, *The Celebrity Syndrome: Notes Towards a Diagnosis*, Sussex University Press, 2004).

Celebrated *faux pas* on Clapham Common. Welsh politician offering fellatio.

Celebrated street performers. In the summer of 2003, Instant Madness, a group of street performers who normally do their act in London's Covent Garden, were invited to take part in the North East Arts Festival of Music and Drama held every year in Newcastle. They ate fire, lay on nails and walked around with poles

on their heads. Janice Thompson, the leading lady, broke both wrists doing a handstand, Des Watson was bitten by an Alsatian and Ronnie Lott, dressed as a circus *august*, was knocked down by the driver of a Ford Fiesta, who drove on and then, feeling remorse, perhaps, drove back and knocked him down again. 'There hasn't been much to laugh about on Tyneside recently,' said Festival organizer, Tony Perry, 'so we've invited them back next year.'

See also GEORDETTES.

Celebrities, British. Out of every ten Celebrities who could keep the nation in fits of laughter by crapping in a bucket in a jungle setting, nine would be British. The French have Celebrities but they are inferior to ours. They have Catherine Deneuve; we have Susan Hampshire. They had Edith Piaf; we have Lulu. They have Sylvie Guillem; we have Una Stubbs. They have Olivier Martinez; we have Darren Day. They have St Tropez; we have BOURNEMOUTH. When Eric CANTONA, the French soccer player, arrived in Leeds to play for the local team, he stopped a policeman and said: 'Could you direct me to the best of your opera houses?' The policeman took an alarmed step back. 'Hullo hullo hullo – what have we here? A comedian, are we?' Leeds now has its own branch of Harvey Nichols selling flat caps and ferrets on the third floor and a restaurant on the fifth floor where networking landladies eat tripe and onions and talk to one another on their mobile phones.

Celebrities born in a stable. *See* RED RUM.

Celebrities famous for not being famous. *See* COSGRAVE, FRAN.

Celebrities vs Personalities: a brief discussion. *See* ANDREWS, EAMONN.

Celebrity Bond Girls. Celebrities who have expressed an ambition to star as the heroine of the next James Bond film and to this end are taking acting lessons from Liz Hurley over lunch at the San Lorenzo restaurant in Beauchamp Place, London:

- Victoria Beckham
- Kirsty Gallacher
- Tania Do-Nascimento
- Lisa Snowden
- Caprice
- Vanessa the Undresser (properly Vanessa Nimmo) from *Big Brother 5*
- Michelle Bass
- Vicki Walberg (formerly Miss UK)
- Dr David Starkey
- Nancy Sorrell
- Geri Halliwell
- Jennifer Ellison (properly, Our Jen)

See also SAN LORENZO.

Celebrity Accessories. In addition to yappy little dogs, *see also* BABIES' NAMES, SHOCKING CELEBRITY; BODYGUARDS; MUSOS.

Celebrity Air Rage. 'Would Mr Gallagher, currently urinating in the hand-basin in the Executive Class toilet, please return to his seat. The captain believes it would be inadvisable for the English football team still to be singing 'Come and have a go if you think you're hard enough!' when we land at Ankara. And would Ms Courtney Love kindly put her underwear back on before disembarking. Thank you.'

Celebrity Cannonballs. Rita Thunderbird (b.1959), the leading human cannonball of her day, performed her act in a gold lamé bikini. At Battersea in June 1977, a large and appreciative audience cheered as Miss Thunderbird climbed down the gun-barrel. There was a loud explosion. Miss Thunderbird remained lodged in the cannon while her knickers were blown across the Thames.

Celebrity chefs. Class of below-stairs menials. Over the years, some have been persuaded that their concoctions contain artistic merit, this delusion allowing their creators, when on television, to erupt into sudden schoolgirl tantrums. Coincidentally, in his excellent study *Rubicon: The Triumph and Tragedy of the Roman Republic* (Little, Brown, 2003), Tom Holland writes: 'Nothing was more scandalous to the Romans than a reputation for enjoying *haute cuisine*. Celebrity chefs had long been regarded as a particularly pernicious symptom of decadence.'

See also RAMSAY, GORDON; RHODES, GARY; STEIN, RICK.

Celebrity cricketers. Traditionally the preserve of haughty toffs, suburban accountants and Nottinghamshire miners, cricket made little impact before 2005. West Indian fast bowlers (Brightwell Baldwin, Curtley Ambrose, Newington Bagpath) were habitually confused with English village names, and most people thought that LBW was a radio station. Not until 2005, when the Lancashire fast bowler James Anderson revealed to the world, 'I always use a daily moisturizer,' did cricket impinge on the consciousness of REAL PEOPLE. Anderson's admission opened the floodgates: strapping Welsh fast bowler Simon Jones posed naked for a *Cosmopolitan* centrefold; burly all-rounder Andrew Flintoff and his wife appeared on the cover of *Hello!* magazine; England captain Michael Vaughan acquired a CELEBRITY BOLTHOLE in Barbados; skunk-haired batsman Kevin PIETERSEN was included in *ES* magazine's 'top ten Casanovas'; England's Ashes heroes were bombarded with thongs and phone numbers by admiring women as they paraded along the Strand in an open-top bus.

In September 2005 it was announced that the former England cricketer Darren GOUGH was to appear on *Strictly Come Dancing*, and would thus become, as Richie Benaud astutely observed, the first Yorkshire right-arm seam bowler to appear in a Reality TV show. 'Gough will be switching from king of seam to dancing queen,' commented bbc.co.uk/sport. 'The legendary "Plum" Warner (Oxford University, Middlesex and England) restricted his steps to *thés dansants* at the Criterion,' raged a *Telegraph* leader. 'Where will it all end?'

See also REVERSE SWING.

Celebrity Dwarfs. *See* McCRAY, RAYMOND.

Celebrity Fit Club (ITV, 9 p.m.). A tubful of morbidly obese Z-listers run around on jelly legs being shouted at by a bug-eyed American drill sergeant. Unless Jo Hicks was sitting next to you in a little skate skirt and hardly any underwear, you'd have had more fun watching retarded cattle running into brick walls.

See also FORDHAM, ANDY.

Celebrity Hairdressers. The idiosyncratic behaviour of the word 'Celebrity' continues to cause difficulties, as is evident in this construction: Are Celebrity Hairdressers Celebrities themselves, or merely hairdressers who specialize in cutting Celebrities' hair? An appeal to usage fails to provide an answer, since the rules, if there are any, seem to be extremely flexible. A turkey farmer is certainly a farmer rather than a turkey, so no confusion arises. But the term 'Celebrity Psychologist' is, like 'Celebrity Hairdresser', systematically ambiguous. It could refer to a particularly famous psychologist or to a psychologist who specializes in the study of 'Celebrity' as a condition. On the other hand, the construction 'Celebrity Historian' causes no difficulties. No one would take this to refer to an academic who has devoted his career to chronicling the lives of dead Celebrities; rather to an unbecomingly ambitious historian, who, by appearing on *The Parkinson Show*, has himself achieved some kind of transient notoriety. The same could be said of 'Celebrity Chef', a term which, in general usage, would not be taken as a reference to cannibalism. Nor would 'Celebrity Philosopher' be used to describe someone who works in the philosophy of Celebrity, since there is no such speciality. Rather, it would apply to the likes of Professor Roger Scruton, whose ginger locks do not infrequently grace our screens. J.L. Austin (1911–60), the ordinary-language philosopher, would have had a field day here, wishing to examine in depth, perhaps, constructions such as 'jewel thief', 'Celebrity Thief' (almost certainly not someone who swags Celebrities and makes off with them into the night, but a Celebrity himself), 'Celebrity Barrister' and 'criminal barrister' (ambiguous). Austin's colleague, Gilbert Ryle (1900–76), would have dubbed such constructions 'category mistakes', a term he coined in his attack, developed in the *Concept of Mind* (1949), on Cartesian dualism, and the French philosopher's celebrated slogan, *'Cogito ergo sum'*. Just as it would be a mistake, Ryle would have argued, to call a pair of shoes three things (a left shoe, a right shoe and the pair), so it would add yet another unnecessary entity to Quine's already 'bloated universe' (see *Two Dogmas of Empiricism*, William Van Orman Quine, 1951) to suggest that a Celebrity Hairdresser is two things: a Celebrity and a hairdresser. 'Imagine', Ryle might have said, 'that I invite you to a party. Hoping to persuade you to attend, I tell you that many Celebrities have promised to be there. I give you the names of a famous actor, a chart-topping pop singer, a currently dominant sportsman, an afternoon-TV chef, the most photographed of today's crop of Page 3 Stunners (for example, Jo Hicks) and so on and so forth. "Yes," you might say, "but which Celebrities are coming?" You would be making a category mistake. Alternatively,' Ryle, who liked to pile on the examples, might have continued, 'imagine that I am showing you round Cambridge University. I point out the colleges, the students, the Fitzwilliam Museum, the lecture rooms, King's College Chapel, the rooms in Trinity in which Wittgenstein famously attacked Popper with a poker. "Ah yes," you might say, 'but where is the university?" "I have just shown it to you," I would say. "Like a salad, a university has no existence above and beyond the sum of its parts *properly arranged.* Salads, universities, Celebrities (perhaps) are logical fictions. They are not in the same category as tomatoes, cucumbers, lecture rooms, colleges, Page 3 Corkers and so forth."' Ryle himself was a celebrated philistine. On one occasion, he and Isaiah Berlin both happened to be visiting Cambridge, Ryle to call on Wittgenstein, Berlin to attend a concert in King's College Chapel. They bumped into each other on King's Parade. 'You been listening to tunes again, Isaiah?' said Ryle.

Celebrity Horses. *See* BUCEPHALUS; RED RUM; SHERGAR.

Celebrity Hanged, Drawn and Quartered. It is believed that this Reality TV show, fronted by Dr David Starkey and inspired by the first Celebrity Conspirator of the Stuart Age, is already being conceptualized by Channel 4. The trial of Guy Fawkes will be reenacted and the viewers will then decide his fate. If guilty... *see* FAWKES, GUY.

Celebrity Labrador. When John Slater (b.1947), the driftwood artist, conducted a charity walk from John o'Groats to Land's End in his bare feet and wearing his pyjamas, he was accompanied by his Labrador, Guinness. Guinness was wearing suede shoes. When he got home, Slater appointed Guinness to a directorship of his tour-guide company.

Celebrity Laughter. Research scientists at Aberdeen University have recently discovered that the way Celebrities laugh reveals their innermost thoughts. They have been able to identify five main categories:

The Howler – Jade Goody (23). An uncontrollable bellow that frightens large dogs and small children. Tears and flailing limbs are part of the attention-seeking performance.

The Snorter – Sir Alex Ferguson (62). A difficult, short-tempered person who expels sudden loud bursts of air through his nostrils. Usually feels superior, but with no obvious reason, to those around him.

The Sniggerer – Graham Norton (41). Very unattractive. Displays an insensitive and dirty-minded character.

The Giggler – Cameron Diaz (32). The most flirtatious and sexual of the five categories. In all probability originated in Essex, though not in the case of Cameron Diaz.

The Cackler – Janet Street-Porter (57). Shrill, primate-style shrieks and guttural vocalizations unrelated to known speech and language patterns. Often found in pantomime villains.

Celebrity Mothers. 'Oh mum! What! She's *so* funny! I took her clubbing Friday. If I hadn't dragged her away she'd still be there! Imagine! She's, like, 39! She's brilliant, my mum!'

Celebrity Owls. *See* McCARTNEY, SIR PAUL.

Celebrity Publishing. The novelist Terence Blacker has argued in his *Independent* column (31 December 2004) that 'The experience of reading a book should be an intimate one; it should tangle with our inner lives. By contrast, the books which have turned our large bookshops into museums of contemporary Celebrityhood are as exterior as the authors' photographs on the covers. The words they contain are the least important part of the product and whether they have been compiled by ghost writers is of no consequence whatever. It is the object itself that matters. The very act of leaving it on a coffee table establishes the illusion of one-to-one contact with a famous person. This trend towards books which are bought but never read is bliss for the publishing business. Editors fantasize about acquiring projects that require little or no reading; sales managers dream of the title that can be marketed with the invocation of a single, magical name.' Among conglomerates, the Orion Publishing Group in general, and Weidenfeld & Nicolson in particular, are exceptions to this rule, continuing to operate according to the rigorous literary principles established by George Weidenfeld.

Celebrity Rakes. *See* CLARK, ALAN; DIMMOCK, CHARLIE.

Celebrity Spats. 'Good evening. The time is 10 o'clock and I'm Huw Edwards. We pride ourselves here on our consistency. 10 p.m. and we're up and running. On the dot. Every night. A very different story at ITN, I think you'll agree. They're all over the place. Like a mad woman's breakfast. One night at 10.30 p.m. The next at 11 p.m. It all depends on whether the soccer's finished. That's enough of that – onwards! Here is the answer to last night's quiz question for all the family – "Which former newspaper editor is one of the seven heterosexual male journalists in Britain never rumoured to have had an affair with *Spectator* publisher Kimberley Quinn?" The correct answer is Andrew Neil, amusingly dubbed Brillo Pad by the spoof magazine, *Private Eye.* Now for tonight's headlines. "Celebrity Spat!" Michael Winner has been banned from Antony Worrall Thompson's restaurant, Woz. No losers there, then. More about that later. Last night Mrs Edwards and I were watching *Who Wants To Be a Millionaire?* when, rather to my surprise, I got a telephone call from Chris Tarrant. "I'm here with David and Victoria Beckham," he said.

Christmas Celebrity *Faux Pas*

Lenny Henry pays compassion visit to land-locked country in Africa. Eats all their food. Drops ten rungs on Celebrity *Faux Pas* Ladder.

The **Duchess of York**, on skiing holiday in Colorado, tackles run beyond capacity and flattens unsuspecting chairlift queue. Down two rungs.

Jayne Middlemiss interviews the Archbishop of Canterbury. She asks him whether he'll be watching *Johnny and Denise's Christmas Party* on ITV.

The *Spectator* publishes a double Christmas issue. *Two* columns by **Taki**. Down ten rungs.

Sean Connery makes a misguided appearance in a Marks and Spencer mince pie advert, in which a false beard and capacious cloak cause him to be mistaken for Jeremy Beadle.

The people of Portsmouth invite **Christine Hamilton** to turn on their Christmas lights. This backfires spectacularly when she likes the place so much she decides to move there.

Embarrassed quiz masters (**Jeremy Paxman**, **Eamonn Holmes**, **Sir Trevor McDonald**) guest for low comedians on light entertainment television specials, swapping their suits for suspender belts and singing 'There's Nothing Like A Dame'.

The **Marquess of Blandford**, stocking up for Christmas, loots local chemist for heroin, loses his nerve, bursts out of Boots with a trolley-load of Night Nurse, Do-Do's, Otrivine and Lucozade.

At **David Furnish**'s and **Elton John**'s wedding, **Geri Halliwell** is chief bridesmaid and Sebastian Horsley the vicar. Unfortunately the best man, David Beckham, loses the ring. Another Celebrity Guest immediately produces a cock ring from her pocket. Horrified faces all round.

The Royal Family spends the holiday at Windsor Castle. After dinner, the **Duke of Edinburgh** suggests that they play the 'Which Celebrity would you rather?' game.

'Chris Evans or Geri Halliwell?'

'Michael Parkinson or Gloria Hunniford?'

'Jade Goody or Chris Moyles?'

'Rambo or the Terminator?'

'No, no, *no,* Edward. You *still* haven't understood the game!'

Prince Edward drops ten places on Celebrity Ladder. Prince Harry gets boisterous, doesn't know when to stop, goes too far with ice cubes and whoopee cushions, puts a corgi in a bagpipe, pulls chair from under old Lady Furness (101), causing her to have a heart attack. Prince Philip barks with laughter. 'That's my boy!'

"With your help we can get them up to £100." Now for the good news. The prime minister, Tony Blair, was able to inform the House of Commons today that gorgeous *Hollyoaks* babe, Ali Bastian, has not been a victim of the earthquake which has devastated Asia. What a relief! Flirty Ali, on holiday in Thailand, has phoned family and friends to let them know she's safe. Thank goodness for that. Tony Blair has kept in close touch with sexy Ali's mum and dad throughout their ordeal...'

Channel 4. Under Mark Thompson Channel 4 became the new Channel 5. His ratings winners included *Celebrity Stools,* in which a former contestant in the European Song Contest had the evacuated contents of her lower colon analysed on camera, *Disabled Gladiators* ('Gladiator Scrotum, you will go on my first whistle! Irritable Bowel Syndrome, you will go on my second whistle!') and *Anglotrash*, which featured a mad woman in a Bournemouth clinic claiming to cure baldness by manipulation of the sexual organs. His most admired scheduling initiative, before becoming director general of the BBC, was to broadcast *The Sopranos* at 2 a.m. on alternate Tuesdays; alternatively, and when viewers were least expecting it, at 3.30 a.m. on every third Wednesday. In his first interview as director general of the BBC, Thompson seized the opportunity to parade his scheduling policy. Having given his reasons for awarding *Fame Academy* a second series, he told a press conference: 'You can't stand there like a headmaster, saying we're not going to have anything like this. I try not to be elitist about any particular genre.' Howard Jacobson commented in *The Independent:* 'I have long given up expecting to hear anything either intelligent or intellectually courageous from anyone in television, particularly from anyone at Channel 4 or the BBC, and Mr Thompson, having laid waste to one, now presides over the other. But even by broadcasting's prevailing standards of egalitarian vacuousness, this is scraping the barrel. In fact, behind the pretence of open-mindedness the most ruthless selection is afoot. Try selling Mr Thompson a 20-part series on

Wittgenstein's *Tractatus* and you quickly come to the end of his careful avoidance of any particular genre. Some of the most exclusivist people I know are populists: they will kill to prevent the dissemination of anything else.'

See also ADULT CONTENT; GREAT TELEVISION; LYGO, KEVIN; TELEVISION WE DESERVE, THE.

Charles the Bald. *See* ALFRED THE GREAT.

Chat show legend. Smirking sales person; not so much an interviewer as a cog in the merchandizing process; Richard and Judy without the confrontational bite. Adopting a submissive posture, he lathers up and puts soft questions to product-placing show-offs. Sitting opposite an alpha male or Hollywood legend, he has been known to wet himself.

Cheap tat from Torremolinos. *See* McLOUGHLIN, COLLEEN.

Checking into hotels. Celebrities cannot be expected to check into hotels under their own names. That would be like inviting all their homicidal stalkers over for a slumber party. Instead, they have to find a pseudonym. And then change it as often as possible. Elton John has checked in as: Lillian Lollipop, Lord Choc Ice, Lord Elpus, Binky Poodleclip and, on one occasion in Sydney, Australia, the gay capital of the world, as Fanny Beaversnatchclit. ('Will Madam be wanting room service?' asked the bellhop hopefully.) Sir Elton has never yet used his real name, Reg Dwight. When Eminem stays in London, he is said to favour the name Mr Gun and to use the password Mr Poison. Light-hearted chappie, that one. The foregoing notwithstanding, a Celebrity who really wants to be ignored might do better to call himself Noel Edmonds.

Christian, Fletcher (1764–*c*.1794). Dandy and mutineer. In 1787 Christian was selected by Captain William Bligh as first mate on the *Bounty*, sailing to Tahiti to collect breadfruit plants. Bligh was an officer steeped in the navy's finest traditions: he understood the benefits of being lashed abaft by the bosun's mate while secured to the for'ard bollards. Mr Christian could speak French and danced the gavotte with his toes turned out, so he and Bligh were bound to clash. Unable to hack it on a diet of weevils and ship's biscuits, the foppish Christian seized control of the *Bounty*, cast the heroic Captain Bligh adrift in an open boat and took refuge with his associate ne'er-do-wells on Pitcairn Island. Here he founded a settlement of degenerates, who indulged in practices unexampled except in certain parts of Cornwall. In 2002, his descendants were arrested as perverts in a scandal that rocked the South Pacific.

Church, Charlotte (b.1986). Porky Welsh singer. Her teenage misdemeanours have been a godsend to tabloid editors, providing them with headlines like 'Fallen Angel Drunk in Gutter!' and 'Voice of an Angel banned from six Cardiff bars after fist fights with doormen!' The truth is, Charlotte likes a bit of rough, but the bit of rough doesn't always respond positively. When she propositioned a multi-pierced, 22-stone bar-room bouncer at the swanky Wellington Club in Knightsbridge, he suffered second-degree trauma. 'I'd rather be the sex toy of a Greek infantry battalion!' he protested. 'Who wouldn't?' replied the portly little soprano, 'but dreaming will get you nowhere.' Then she hiccoughed and poured herself another Cheeky Vimto. (FYI: this drink contains two shots of port and a bottle of blue WKD. It does not have any Vimto in it, and it is not cheeky so much as goddam rude, but there's cocktails for you.) The singer has plenty of party spirit. She can down ten double vodkas on a night out and still remember all the words to the naughty version of Ave Maria. But on her 18th birthday, Charlotte decided to forgo a night out on the razz and instead arranged a posh do for her family at a smart hotel

in Cardiff. That's not possible. There isn't a smart hotel in Cardiff. The Grand has one star but that's because it's the only hotel in Cardiff which doesn't nail the furniture to the floor to prevent the guests from stealing it.

See also CRITICISM, A STAR OFFERS; LURCH, CHARLOTTE.

Cinderella. Winsome submissive cruelly exploited by her older sisters and made to do domestic work around the house. Meanwhile, she dreamed of the day when her prince would come along and provide her with a golden charge card. After intervention from her Fairy Godpa, Max Clifford, the dotty totty was papped one night sneaking away from a nightclub wearing only one shoe (see www.celebrityoops.com for all the pics). Happily, she was followed on this occasion by her prince and thereafter enjoyed a full *OK!*-funded wedding. Unfortunately, her prince turned out to be another girl (Pat Kirkwood in drag as Principal Boy), plus, to cap it all, the prince's best friend, Dandini, was a girl too. You can imagine the tabloid headlines: CINDERS IN LESBO THREESOME.

See also MOTHER GOOSE.

Cirque

Cirque. Fashionable nightclub situated in Cranbourne Street, London WC2. Its Friday night gig is pre-eminent in clubland, so anyone looking for a suitable spot to throw some shapes on the dancefloor should take note. It boasts the best house DJs around. Joe Butler, Paul Gardener (Soul Avengerz), Maxim & Dynamix are scheduled to bless the decks so you can bank on the dancefloor filling up swiftly under the eye of host Mr Buzzard. Meanwhile, resident spinners Booker T and Bobbi and Steve will provide a fusion of funky house and US garage. Among the clubbers chilling out, expect to catch up with *Spectator* editor Boris Johnson and the lovely Tess Daly, fresh from her stint hosting the BBC's *Strictly Come Dancing* with Bruce Forsyth. Forsyth insiders have revealed that Brucie plans to release a *Strictly Come Dancing* album in time for Christmas. It will have a big-band vibe.

Clark, Alan (1927–99). Politician, popular historian and sexual profligate; the son of Lord Kenneth Clark, whose furniture he inherited, if not his intellect. Best known for his *Diaries*, published in three volumes by Weidenfeld & Nicolson between 1993 and 2002. The extended accounts in these of his various sexual escapades (including affairs with Judge James Harkness's wife and both his stepdaughters – a trio he amusingly dubbed 'the Coven') guaranteed Clark an extensive readership among subscribers to the *Daily Mail* and the *Mail on Sunday*. His wife Jane stood by him throughout his various sordid misdemeanours.

Clarkson, Jeremy (b.1958). Motor-car correspondent. In all obvious respects he's Richard LITTLEJOHN, without, perhaps, Littlejohn's wide-ranging intellectual curiosity and tolerance of opinions with which he is out of sympathy. In 2003, the BBC engaged Clarkson to front *Meet the Neighbours*, a six-part television series in which Clarkson was supposed to investigate the customs and history of our fellow members of the European Union. The self-absorbed Clarkson took this to be an opportunity for our neighbours to meet him, reducing them to embarrassed silence as he told them more about his likes and dislikes than they might have wished to hear. That said, his haircut caused them some amusement. It has recently been discovered that his name forms the anagram 'Corny male jerks'.

Cleopatra (69–30 BC). Queen of Egypt, recognized by many as the original diva. Her relationships with Julius Caesar and Mark Antony make the Jen–Brad–Angelina thing look rather suburban. It has to be granted too that her insistence on bathing in asses' milk set a standard for future diva-ish health fads. Oddly enough, horse's milk is now popular as a skin treatment, with a litre costing £7. She has been portrayed many times on stage and film, notably by Elizabeth Taylor, herself a premier-league diva.  When she stayed at the Dorchester in London in 2000, Miss Taylor demanded that her suite be repainted lilac. When she was invited to Buckingham Palace to be made a Dame of the British Empire, her bodyguards wanted to carry out a security check of the building. When the Palace politely refused, Miss Taylor said, 'Don't they know who I am?' In 1963 she played the celebrated queen of Egypt in *Cleopatra* (directed by Joseph L. Mankiewicz; screenplay by Suetonius, Plutarch, Appian and others). Having recently enticed the crooner Eddie Fisher away from his wife (the actress Debbie Reynolds), Miss Taylor quickly rid herself of him in favour of the dreadful Welsh actor Richard Burton, her co-star in *Cleopatra*. During filming, her weight ballooned to a massive 26 stone, but since the production was already a year behind

schedule (largely because Taylor and Burton rarely came out of their trailers) and £50 million over budget, the cameras continued to roll. (A further difficulty was the fact that the producer, Walter Wanger, had recently been shot in the balls by his wife and was keen to return as quickly as possible to California so that he might convalesce.) A highlight of the completed picture – perhaps its only highlight – was a scene in which a large carpet was unrolled to reveal the 16-year-old Francesca Annis (*see* LANGTRY, LILLIE) dressed in a handkerchief. The part of Cleopatra has also been taken by the actress (no one knows her name) who plays Dot Cotton in the popular soap opera *EastEnders*. The performance was judged a disappointment. It was Marlene Dietrich's habit to refer to Elizabeth Taylor as 'that British tart with the big bazookas'. It was Cleopatra's tragedy, perhaps, that she lived before it was possible for a Celebrity to check into the Betty Ford Clinic when her personal arrangements were at sixes and sevens.

Clitoris, Victoria Beckham's. Just when men had at last been educated into understanding where a woman's clitoris is likely to be found, the discovery has been made that Victoria Beckham's is located in the handbag department at Gucci in Bond Street.

Cnut the Great. *See* CANUTE, KING.

Cold sore, catchy as a. *See* BEDINGFIELD, DANIEL.

Collins, Joan (b.1933). Former Rank starlet. Is she 97? 101? 103? It's anybody's guess. Whatever her age, she looks terrible – a triumph of nature over art. That said, and when it was the other way round, the art was no great shakes, having the value, perhaps, of six graduated ducks on the wall of Simon COWELL's North London lounge. Miss Collins has written several books for Random House. Though they sell in great quantities no one has actually ever read one, so there is no way of knowing whether they are better or worse than those written by her sister, Jackie – which no one has read either.

See also CELEBRITY PUBLISHING.

Collymore, Stan (b.1971). In October 2004, Mr Collymore, formerly a soccer player and the lover of, among others, the Swedish trollop Ulrika JONSSON, was badly beaten up by eight rugby players in a Dublin nightclub. The event was celebrated by a studio discussion on an afternoon television show. It was proposed by various studio audience members that Collymore was deserving of the beating, his offence having been to give too detailed an account of former love affairs in his recently published autobiography. The following question was then put to the viewers: 'Do you not agree that the vile Collymore got his just desserts?' At the end of the programme, a relieved talk-show host was able to report that 95% of the viewing public had said 'Yes.' The next day, a Mr Arthur Grover, a serial complainer, rang the television office. Were the audience members fit to discuss the morality of kiss-and-tell memoirs, given they were in all likelihood themselves consumers of the tabloid press, asked Mr Grover. A representative of the red-top press had once asked Mr Grover whether he knew anyone who, for £5000, would say that she had had a lesbian relationship with Conservative cabinet minister David Mellor's former lover Antonia de Sancha, whether she had or hadn't. Mr Grover had been able to supply his friend Fat Michelle from South London. The newspaper was well aware of the fact that Fat Michelle and Antonia de Sancha had never met, but each was paid £5000 to talk about their imaginary affair and the story duly appeared in a Sunday rag. Mr Grover then asked the TV office what the outcome of the viewers' poll might have been if they had been asked: 'Should rugby players be encouraged to beat up people whose books are not to their liking?' A spokesman

for the programme said he failed to understand the point Mr Grover was trying to make.

See also DOGGING, CELEBRITY.

Completely natural. Bloated gay diva in dark glasses and an unbecoming wig briefly patronizing a shrieking Welsh wannabe. 'He's so totally the most famous person I've ever met but he was, like, so totally down to earth!' gasped the hyperventilating 15-year-old from Swansea.

See also LANGUAGE, BAD.

Connolly, Billy (b.1942). Gorbals loudmouth. Looks like a rag-and-bone man. If he didn't laugh so much himself (*see* CORPSING) you'd never suspect that he was trying to be funny. He used to be. That's the tragedy of Celebrity: once you've achieved it, bang goes your talent. He's married to Pamela Stephenson, a social-climbing comedienne from Takapuna.

Consolations of philosophy, the. *See* DE BOTTON, ALAIN.

Consolations of soft toys, the. *See* ELLISON, JENNIFER.

Constantine, Susannah (b.1961) and **Woodall, Trinny** (b.1965). Fading haberdashers. They should join the French Foreign Legion, which is manned entirely by former dress-designers. The Legion, which hasn't won a battle since 1910 (even when Germany is on its side), only becomes aggressive when confronted by fashion violations. If a battalion comes across a man in uncoordinated separates they shoot him dead. Trinny and Susannah would be quite at home. Laura Ashley and Charlie Adams have already enlisted and one platoon is made up entirely of redundant stitchers from Lady Victoria Hervey's liquidated boutique, Akademi. Trinny has a sister called Waggles. When the siblings did the season the rumour was that Trinny wouldn't but Waggles Woodall.

Controlling, he's like so. A pork-bellied Bermondsey girl whose father objects to her sitting around all day eating crisps and farting on the soft furnishings (*see* GOODY, JADE).

Cookery Maths, doing the. All TV schedulers are proficient at Cookery Maths. The rudiments are thus: Gordon Ramsay plus seven celebrities equals one popular TV show. Gary Rhodes plus Jean-Christophe Novelli plus fourteen nobodies equals one popular TV show. Delia to the power of seven equals one very popular TV series. Jamie times Delia (over Nigella) equals a summer blockbuster. Fanny Cradock divided by Keith Floyd equals insolvency.

Corpsing. An indulgence practised by semi-professional comedians. The straight man is so diverted by the spontaneous antics of his partner that he is reduced to uncontrollable laughter. When Peter Cook and Dudley Moore were a fashionable double act the myth grew that Cook's prevailing ambition was to make Moore 'corpse'. In fact these moments were carefully rehearsed, as would have been obvious to anyone who saw them perform more than once. Shortly before he died, Moore said: 'Peter could never have made me laugh spontaneously since I didn't find him even slightly funny. Had we rehearsed the sketches as assiduously as we rehearsed the moments when I apparently "cracked up", the show might have been more successful.' Conceited Scotsman Billy CONNOLLY is thought to be the only comedian who can make himself 'corpse' – the Scotch equivalent of spontaneous combustion.

Corrs, The (b.1995). Drippy Irish Von Trapp family. The Corrs have inexplicably enjoyed more than six weeks at number one in the UK album charts. They comprise Andrea (lead vocals, tin whistle, youngest, most winsome), Caroline (drums, bodhran,

piano, vocals, chiselled cheeks, meekest), Sharon (violin, vocals, vampiest) and Jim (keyboards, guitars, vocals, spectacles, conceited). Their music is reputedly used as a sedative in Swiss psychiatric wards. But if you like their folksy Celtic harmonies, well, that is the kind of thing you like.

See also AIR, DONNA.

Cosgrave, Fran (b.1978). Thought to be the first Celebrity famous for not being famous (a condition not to be confused with Simon Dee Syndrome – *see* DEE, SIMON). When it was announced that Fran was to be a contestant in *I'm A Celebrity, Get Me Out Of Here* in November 2004, ordinary people scratched their heads. Who is he? What is he? Is he a man? Is he a woman? Is he a cook? Is he a love rat? Is he a blonde bombshell? Is he a blonde bombshell's fella? Is he a *Corrie* cracker? Is he a totally fit STUD MUFFIN? By the end of the show, no one was any the wiser. Emerging from the jungle, fellow participant Janet Street-Porter said, 'I didn't know who he was when I went in. And I don't know now.' Happily, Janet had no such doubts about her own performance. In her Jungle Diary, published in December 2004 in the *Independent on Sunday*, she wrote: 'Day 17. I'm evicted! Everyone's gobsmacked! As I leave, many of the production staff thank me for all my hilarious contributions. Some of the women are on the edge of tears. I hadn't realized that so many people really wanted me to win. But at the end of the day, I did it my way. I left with dignity. I'm sorry we didn't discuss the plight of the pensioners or the state of the National Health Service, but this is a primetime entertainment series and I was always mindful that my role was to provide you lot at home with great television.' Mad as a dingo's bollocks.

Couples who have a claim to be recognized as the Posh and Becks of their day. *See* HELOÏSE (and Abelard); LANCELOT AND GUINEVERE; ROBINSON, MARY (and Banastre Tarleton).

Courtney Cox, Walford East's answer to. *See* SLATER, KAT.

Cowell, Simon Philip (b.1961). Music entrepreneur. He left school with no educational qualifications, but with the fixed belief that profitability is the only value. Deciding to exercise this truth as a record producer rather than as an estate agent or car dealer, he cut his teeth at EMI before being offered a position as an A & R man

at BMG in 1989. Here he produced a string of chart-toppers, mainly with a novelty vibe. Among the artists he recorded were Mr Blobby, Bob the Builder, the Teletubbies, the Bumbleweeds, Postman Pat, the Wombles, the Wurzles, the Roly Polys, three grapplers under contract to the World Wrestling Federation, Kenny the Kangaroo, the Krankies ('We're going to Spain!') and, most famously, the soap-opera actors Robson Green and Jerome Flynn. Their cover versions of 'Unchained Melody', 'I Believe' and 'The White Cliffs of Dover' dominated the charts for months on end.

By now a millionaire, Cowell then teamed up with music mogul Simon Fuller to produce *Pop Idol*, a reality show for ITV in the course of which deluded adolescents competed for a valuable recording contract. Cowell appeared as a judge, quickly securing the title 'Mr Nasty' for his ill-mannered comments on the wretched children's efforts to impress. Viewers who had heard about his 'Acid Tongue' might have been disappointed by his remarkably limited repertoire of insults. Those who were familiar with his first recorded lapse of manners may have been less surprised. At the age of four he told his mother, who was about to leave the house in a pink fuzzy hat, that she looked like a poodle. His televised 'put-downs' rarely achieve greater penetration than this, but they have considerably enriched him. He has his critics. After Cowell informed a hopeful American group that they were the 'most disillusioned he had ever seen' (he had presumably meant to say 'deluded'), Mr Graydon Carter, the editor of *Vanity Fair,* questioned whether English was Cowell's first language. Then, somewhat snobbishly, Mr Carter said that Cowell in any case 'looks like the sort of man who would say "gift", "hospitality" and "toilet"'. A rival in the music business has remarked that 'Simon is so vain that if he went to a funeral he'd want to be the corpse.' When in England he has maintained the peculiar habit of driving to Sussex at weekends to have Sunday lunch with his mother. He has never married.

Coxy, Foxy, properly **Sara Cox** (b.1974). Daughter of a farmer from Bolton, Lancashire, who breeds pedigree bulls. Lost her virginity in a sheep field. Famous as mouthy, over-familiar TV and radio presenter. Leader of the 'Ladette' movement and self-proclaimed 'Geezerbird'. Voice hoarse from shouting 'Wa-hey!' and 'Going for a wazz now!'

Cracking the American market. Desperate UK pop babe lands a walk-on part in *Lost*.

See also HALLIWELL, GERI.

Cradock, Fanny (1909–94). Like Eamonn Andrews, Fanny is of some historical interest as an early exponent of Celebrity TV. She was the first of many cooks of limited accomplishment who came to dominate the schedules. Best known for her overbearing manner (she addressed her common-law husband much as a sergeant does his footsoldiers – 'pass me the bloody bain marie, Johnnie!') and inappropriate wardrobe: she cooked in a Hartnell ball gown. Her downfall came about when she was over-critical of a viewer's home-made crème brûlée. The public turned against her and she was soon off-air. Nigella, take note (*see* LAWSON, NIGELLA).

Craven, John (b.1946). 'I never miss a programme if John Craven's in it.' You'll not hear that said.

See also WORRALL THOMPSON, ANTONY.

Crimpers to the stars. Ageing bisexuals with capped teeth. Some have the distinction of having been married to one of their clientèle; most simply flirt with them. If they ever had any brains, they have now been addled by volumizing spray and/or cocaine. Liable to cry if presented with a really skilful shingle.

See also CELEBRITY HAIRDRESSERS.

Criticism, a star offers. 'I don't like to analyse music when I'm listening to it but I will hear a song and think: you can't sing for fuckin' toffee!… You know that song, 'Jumpin' Jumpin', by Destiny's Child? Beyoncé's going nuts in it, right, and she's so out of tune that it does my head in… I can't stand Bob Dylan, he sounds like a freak… And that Chris Martin isn't any good either – he can't do any vibrato… I know that the sound of Coldplay's singing is very modern, but it's a bit wimpy and as soon as one person's done it, they're all fuckin' at it… Celine Dion does not speak at all for an entire day before she performs a concert. I admire that, but I can't see myself doing it, because I'm a loudmouthed cow' (*see* CHURCH, CHARLOTTE).

Crumpet, old lady's. *See* LLEWELYN-BOWEN, LAURENCE.

Cullum, Jamie (b.1979). Wiltshire-reared musical hobbit who croons jazz standards while playing the piano with his furry feet. *See also* MELUA, KATIE.

D

Dahl, Sophie (b.1979). Goggle-eyed supermodel with cartoon body and sucky fish lips. Suspiciously pale. It's almost as if she isn't even trying to get an Orange Nomination (*see* AWARD FOR ORANGENESS SPONSORED BY TERRY'S CHOCOLATE ORANGE). Dahl's appearance in the Yves Saint Laurent Opium advert, in which the model appeared to be pleasuring herself, provoked a large number of complaints, mainly issuing from middle-aged motorists who resented having to drive past it so quickly. Miss Dahl is the granddaughter of children's author Roald Dahl, and was the basis for Sophie, the protagonist of the story *The BFG*. She has since written a 'fairy tale for adults' herself, entitled *The Man With the Dancing Eyes*, which hinted that that the eponymous Man was Sir Mick Jagger. The book also indicated that the beautiful Miss Dahl should stick to what she clearly does best: reclining on black velvet with an expression of surprise.

Daly, Tess (b.1971). Excellent TV presenter married to Vernon Kay of the same occupation. The website www.befuddle.co.uk contained the following disobliging comment: 'Tess Daly, pictured here, may not be as drunk as she looks.' That's not very nice. The popular TV presenter may just be befuddled. Even ruder is www.dogsbomb.co.uk on which Miss Daly has been included as one of a thousand people who are more irritating than Mick Hucknall. That's just silly. A typical e-mail to www.dogsbomb.co.uk reads: 'Her voice is the most gr8ting thing ive eva herd. Shes not funny, shes not pretty, she's not talented. SM: TV LIVE is nothing wivout Ant and Dec and I think their shite. Monkeyspanker, Leeds.' And here's another. 'She shood do summit bout it bein so thin cos she and kids think its ok to be anarexic and b a knobhead at the same time. What an encouragin futur this country has. Loadofarse, Grimsby.' Miss Daly can console herself with the fact that – educationally – her detractors appear to be fractionally above the national average.

Dandies. *See* BRUMMEL, BEAU; CHRISTIAN, FLETCHER; HORSLEY, SEBASTIAN.

Danesh, Darius (b.1981). Lanky, self-regarding Scottish singer who came third to Will Young and Gareth Gates in *Pop Idol 1*. If he were to change his name to something sensible like Engelbert Humperdinck, Las Vegas might beckon in a few years time. Otherwise it will be cruise ships supporting a troupe of Chinese contortionists and a sealion act. Kilted up, he customarily wears a pubic purse between his legs.

Dangers of Absinthe, the. One shot and a stud muffin goes bananas. While filming the drama *Mile High* for Sky 1 in September 2004, pop hunk Darren DAY drank a bottle of the lethal liqueur and then trashed his suite at the Hotel Esperanza in Alcudia, a Majorca holiday resort. He threw the furniture out of the window, set fire to the curtains and targeted other guests with exploding water bombs. A Darren Day insider later revealed: 'Darren won't be touching absinthe again. When he saw the room in the morning he realized that he would have to get his priorities right.' Absinthe was banned in America in 1912 and in France in 1915.

Date rape. *See* GEORDETTES.

Da Vine, Magenta (b.1955). Odds-and-ends TV reporter who always wears dark glasses – the consequence of a morbid fear that she might be mistaken for Janet Street-Porter's prettier younger sister. When she presented *The Rough Guide Travel Show* on

BBC2, she prided herself on always dressing inappropriately. She wore rubber skirts to Swahili villages and bra tops to church in Madrid. Caught wearing a hat and twin-set at Buckingham Palace, she retired on the spot and hasn't been heard of since.

Day, Darren Christopher (b.1968). Born in Colchester, Essex, and educated at the Charles Lucas Comprehensive, where he excelled at music, drama and snooker. For a time he played on the semi-professional snooker circuit, but the lure of showbusiness proved too strong. He was soon cast as a juvenile in musical comedies, appearing in *Joseph and the Amazing Technicolour Dreamcoat* (1994), Barry Manilow's *Copacabana* (1995) and *Grease* (1999). He was also busy in the recording studio, laying down tracks of which Sir Cliff Richard wouldn't have been ashamed (indeed, of which Sir Cliff wasn't ashamed – 'Summer Holiday', 'Bachelor Boy', 'Livin' Doll' and 'The Young Ones'). Sir Cliff's musical influence is paradoxical, since the private lives of the two artists are quite dissimilar. Day has earned his Celebrity status not for his acting or singing but for his extramural activities as the Nation's No. 1 Love Rat. He has famously cheated on Anna Friel, *Corrie* babe Tracy Shaw, and Isla Fisher, who appeared in the soap opera *Home And Away*. His wedding in 2003 to a blonde dancer called Adele Vellacott was called off when he was spotted leaving Suzanne Shaw's bedroom. His relationship with Suzanne, the former Hear'Say babe, by whom he has a son, Corey, faltered when he popped out for some milk on Mother's Day 2005 (three months after Corey was born) and didn't return. After a short affair with lingerie model Cecilia Carneby, he tried to resume his relationship with *Home and Away* babe Isla Fisher. This initiative failed since Isla is perfectly happy with long-term lover, the comedian, Sacha Baron Cohen.

See also DANGERS OF ABSINTHE; PALMER-TOMKINSON, TARA.

Deayton, Angus (b.1960). Gifted TV presenter, now back on top form, happily, after his sacking from the satirical quiz show, *Have I Got News For You?*

See also HISLOP, IAN.

Debenhams, Bejewelled chavs on their way to urinate over. *See* GEORDETTES.

De Botton, Alain (b.1961). Literary novelist and wine-bar philosopher. The success of his book, *The Consolations of Philosophy* ('Philosophy undisturbed by philosophy' – Howard Jacobson), persuaded Channel 4 commissioning editors that de Botton might have a future as a Celebrity. No chance. He's too nice and too bald – not in a Celebrity bald-as-a-billiard-ball way, but like a chicken moulting in unbecoming places. Undeterred, Channel 4 televised his book *Status Anxiety* (Hamish Hamilton, 2004) – a work of nursery instruction of which Edward de Bono would have been proud.

Dee, Simon (b.1932). Former disc jockey and television presenter, one of the few to have had a disease named after him. Simon Dee Syndrome derives its name from the discovery that those who suffer from it are better remembered for having been forgotten than they would be if they were still remembered, which indeed they are, but only for having been forgotten, which they are not. Celebrity psychologist Oliver James has pointed out that, unusually, early detection of the symptoms (grandiloquent behaviour unsupported by any obvious talent) serves only to speed up the full-blown disease.

Deeley, Cat (b.1972). However did this girl from Sutton Coldfield get to advise us on our dental habits? 'Spend as much time brushing and flossing your teeth as you can,' says Cat sagely. How did she get to be the face of Braun Oral-B? It's been a rollercoaster ride. She does a bit of modelling, a bit of presenting. Then, one moment she's eating her baked beans in front of the telly, the next her mum calls up to say she's on Chris Evans. 'Mum, I'm not,' insists Cat. 'I'm sat at home, having a beer with the ladies.' Then she switches on and there's this life-size cutout of her where Des Lynam and Jarvis Cocker used to be. Now Cat's officially the whiskers. She goes on to play foil to funnymen Ant and Dec on *CD:UK* ('Oi!' she'd say. 'Stop it, you two! Now!') This larky triumvirate smashed the hegemony of Zoe Ball's *Live and Kicking*, though Cat could never be persuaded to muster up much in the way of animosity towards Zoe, despite persistent prodding from the press. Cat isn't really up to much, apart from being nice. And gargling. (NB. On one of her fan websites, in the Interesting Facts section, it says: 'Member of Storm model agency.' Gosh.)

Dell'Olio, Nancy (b.1959). The partner of Sven-Göran Eriksson, head coach of the England football team. She has been dubbed, somewhat unkindly, 'Jack Palance in thigh boots'. She once expressed a desire to be photographed naked, but no photographer has yet volunteered for the job.

Sometimes accused of exerting undue influence on Mr Eriksson, she is in fact far too busy with her own arrangements to interfere with Mr Eriksson's. She is a successful trial lawyer in her native Italy, and during Euro 2004, far from sitting on the bench with Mr Eriksson and instructing him in the proper deployment on the park of Christmas tree formations and so forth, she was fully occupied at Naples Central Criminal Court. Twenty-seven men, represented by Miss Dell'Olio, faced charges of fraud, extortion, murder, arson, assault, bombing, blackmail and slander. Her clients on this occasion were nine monks, seven schoolmasters, five doctors, three senior policemen, the Mayor and the Cardinal Bishop of Milan. All were acquitted. The chief prosecutor immediately lodged an appeal, but before this could be heard he was arrested for running a brothel.

Jack Palance's best-known screen role was as the villainous gunfighter dressed in black who stalked Alan Ladd in the cult western, *Shane* (George Stevens, 1953). Before becoming an actor, Palance was a moderately successful boxer. On one occasion he went 15 rounds with Joe Baksi – a good-natured but enormous fighter from the Bronx who famously finished the career of the popular British heavyweight champion, Bruce Woodcock. Baksi broke Woodcock's jaw in Round 1, had him on the canvas six times in Round 2 and knocked him out in Round 3. Woodcock continued to fight, but he no longer posed a threat to world-class heavyweights. He now runs a pub in his native Warrington. Mr Baksi celebrated his 85th birthday on 19 February 2005.

Democracy, the unacceptable face of. *See* REALITY TELEVISION.

Dennis, Cathy (b.1969). Think Blondie, but from Norwich. That's it. You've got her. Ms Dennis enjoyed a string of hits in the late 1980s – 'Too Many Walls' and 'Touch Me (All Night Long)'. Then she stopped singing, and turned her hand to her true talent: writing hits for other people. These include Kylie Minogue's 'Can't Get You Out of My Head', Britney Spear's 'Toxic', and Rachel Stevens's 'Sweet Dreams My LA Ex'.

See also STEVENS, RACHEL.

Dent-Brocklehurst, Henry (b.1968). Producer, playboy, dishy daddy, whatever. A prominent socialite, HD-B organizes charity cricket matches (it was at one of these that Hugh Grant first demonstrated his flipper to Jemima KHAN). In July 2000, Dent-Brocklehurst married Lili Maltese at Sudeley Castle, to which he is heir. They were paid £500,000 by *OK!* magazine – not a great deal of money bearing in mind that Liz Hurley attended in leopard-print knickers. Ms Maltese is a Hawaiian model and committed ambassador for Californian prunes. She was prune spokeswoman during National Prune Week: 'They give you a real energy boost,' she said.

Derrida, Jacques. *See* STRINGFELLOW, PETER; *VIE EN GRIS, LA.*

Descartes, René (1596–1650). French philosopher and mathematician, often dubbed the father of modern philosophy. Gilbert Ryle famously pointed out that if Cartesian dualism is true it would be possible for some Celebrities to be joined at the personality as Siamese twins are joined at the body. Whether Celebrities with one personality between the two of them could be separated like Siamese twins remains open to doubt. Professor Ryle didn't live to see the phenomenon of ANT AND DEC.

See also CELEBRITY CATCHPHRASES; CELEBRITY HAIRDRESSERS.

Desmond, Richard (b.1955). Bongo-playing newspaper proprietor. On his acquisition of Express Newspapers he was dubbed a pornographer – a label intended, and taken, as an insult in the United Kingdom, if nowhere else. Everyone likes pornography, but the British are obliged to deny this in public – a circumstance that may explain their dysfunctional attitude to a useful product. The Scandinavians put porn in their trolley as part of the weekly shop; at 8 p.m. the French settle down for an evening's viewing with their children; but the British furtively scan the magazines available on the top shelf before hiding one in their copy of the *Daily Telegraph.* Americans can watch home-grown, hardcore porn on cable TV; the British have to make do with the imported, oil-buffed bodies thrown their way by Channel 5, backed up by contributions from whichever channel Mark Thompson happens to be in charge of at the time. And while the Americans democratize visual porn with hand-held cameras, the British remain in thrall to *Carry On* innuendo and shivering 'readers' wives'. The British are no good at buying porn, and, worse, they are no good at making it – the latter rule being one to which Mr Desmond's productions were, and are, no exception. Nor, at the moment, does his touch with the *Daily Express* and the *Daily Star* seem any more secure than it was with the top-shelf material that financed their purchase. (British porn stars

should carry none of the blame for the woeful standard of the home-made product. In performers such as Miss Jo Guest, Miss Sammi Jessop, Miss Maria Sheriff and, particularly, perhaps, Miss Shanine Linton, an outstandingly attractive young woman from the Southampton area, Britain has *artistes* who are as accomplished as any in the field. They can be seen to advantage, however, only in foreign films and magazines.)

De Villeneuve, Daisy (b.1975) and **Poppy** (b.1979). Moody young ladies beloved of the *Evening Standard*'s slavering toff-rag, *ES* magazine. Daisy is a talented illustrator working in the medium of felt tip, and Poppy is a promising Polaroid artiste. They are the daughters of 1960s entrepreneur Justin de Villeneuve (properly, Nigel Davies) who discovered Twiggy and turned the stick-thin girl from Neasden into the world's most famous model. Daisy and Poppy (whose mother is Justin's second wife, American model Jan Ward) are such permanent fixtures of London society that it would take an industrial chisel to prise them loose. (Davies changed his name to de Villeneuve so that he could claim a family connection with Napoleon's most illustrious admiral.)

Dick 'n' Dom, properly **Richard McCourt and Dominic Wood** (b.1976). Grown men who, in an attempt to be popular with under tens, engage in bogie-flicking, gunk-licking and whoopee-sniffing. Compared to them, ANT AND DEC are models of sophistication. Their mind-rotting shows have prompted questions in Parliament. 'What time is Dick 'n' Dom in Da Bungalow on this week?' was one; 'Can the member for Leicester East tell me if the dunky gunk is genuine cat poo?' another.

Dickhead. The story that, when 'chatting' to Hollywood legend Ingrid Bergman, Michael Parkinson raised a glass and said, 'Here's looking at you, blue eyes,' may be apocryphal, but is significant for all that.

Dickinson, David (b.1941). Bottle-tanned buffoon. He is so weird that bookmakers William Hill are offering 7–1 on that he'll be Liza Minelli's next husband.

Dido, properly **Dido Florian Cloud de Bounevialle Armstrong** (b.1971). Name like a Medici contessa, face like a bowl of custard. Blonde, bland, blubbery North London girl with bookish parents and good connections in the music biz. Curiously difficult to recognize (*see* photograph thought to be of Dido). Makes music in the same way a polite person breaks wind – the aim is to give minimum offence, but the upshot is to put everyone else off their dinner. One of her most popular songs, 'Hunter', contained the rangy, freedom-hungry lyrics:

'I want to be Hunter again / I want to see the world again / So let me go, let me leave.'

The passion with which Dido delivered these lines was like air escaping from a slowly deflating balloon.

Dimmock, Charlie, properly **Charlotte Elouise Dimmock** (b.1966). Charlie was born in Romsey, Hampshire, the only child of Terry, a merchant seaman, and Sue, who ran a clothes shop. She spent a lot of time with her grandfather, helping him in the family vegetable garden. 'He was pleased and rather proud,' Charlie recalls, 'when I graduated from horticultural college instead of doing a forensic science course as I had originally planned.' After college, and having settled down with John Mushet, a viticulturist whom she had met when visiting New Zealand, Charlie went to work at the Romsey Garden Centre. It was there that she was spotted by TV producer John Thornicroft, who had dropped in to buy a water plant. In 1997 he needed someone to do a water feature on a gardening programme. He remembered Charlie and offered her a slot on *Ground Force*. Charlie's role alongside Alan Titchmarsh (properly Alan 'Titch' Marsh – *see* BAZALGETTE, PETER) and Tommy Walsh on the garden makeover show catapulted the bra-less Amazon into the limelight, making her a household name overnight and, to the surprise of many, the focus of the fantasies of male gardeners across the land. It also led to a series of lucrative spin-offs, including several books, a calendar and a garden gnome. Although her partner John always referred to her as 'the missus', the pair never married and split in 2001 after Charlie had a fling with *Ground Force* camera operator Andy Simmons. That relationship soon faltered and Charlie went on to form a liaison with another member of the programme's crew, sound technician Barry Smith. In spite of her soaring TV career, Charlie's aspirations remain firmly grounded. 'I'll become a dotty old dear,' she says, 'pottering around the garden.' (For another such, *see* GOLDSMITH, LADY ANNABEL.)

Diogenes (*fl.* 4th century BC). Philosopher dubbed 'the Cynic'. For a short outline of his work (and his reluctance to discuss the problem of trans-personal identity with Alexander the Great), *see* McCALL, DAVINA.

Diplomat's diplomat, The. *See* EDINBURGH, PRINCE PHILIP, DUKE OF.

Dishes, doing the. Celebrities are in unison here: doing the washing up is fabba-dabba-dabulous. It's a hobby, it's a calling. You don't believe it? Just ask Myleene KLASS – formerly of the pop group Hear'Say, now a cross-over pianist – what she's doing tonight:

> 'I'm going to take it easy at home, I actually just love relaxing and tidying up and washing the dishes.'
> *Interviewer*: 'You wash *dishes*? I thought your hands were insured for a million pounds!'
> *Myleene Klass*: 'Yeah, they are.'
> *Interviewer*: 'Do you wear rubber gloves then?'
> *Myleene Klass*: 'Oh no! I don't wear gloves, I just love doing the dishes, don't tell anybody.'

And Natalie APPLETON couldn't agree more:

> 'I love loading the dishwasher. You put them in and think, this won't get clean. And then they do. It's amazing.'

Small wonder that Natalie had a nervous breakdown on national television when, in November 2004, she participated in *I'm a Celebrity, Get Me Out Of Here.* She had expected a dishwasher to be among the luxuries provided. Something is afoot here. Perhaps only the marketing department of Fairy Liquid knows exactly what.

Dishing up the sprouts when a housemate's on the toilet. *See* APOLOGIES.

Dissertation title reported in *Hello!* magazine. *See* KHAN, JEMIMA.

Divas, pop. Forever beating their drugs and booze hells to put their singing careers back on track. Opening their hearts to the world, they say: 'I now feel whole again. I've emerged from a long, long fog. I'm clean. I'm sober. I feel reborn and I'm loving life. I came

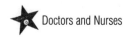

so close to throwing it all away. Now I cherish every second of the day. You sorted by any chance?'

See also ALBUM, WORKING ON MATERIAL FOR A NEW; NATURAL TALENT, A SUBLIME.

Doctors and Nurses. A nursery game of anatomical exploration popular among six-year-olds. It loses much of its charm when played out by twentysomethings on Reality TV shows; still more when indulged in by adults. In *Celebrity Big Brother 3* – in which Professor Germaine Greer made a surprise appearance – a late-night game of Spin the Bottle was suggested. When the bottle came to rest pointing towards Brigitte Nielsen, a boot-faced Danish actress in her forties, she addressed herself to Kenzie, a sweet 18-year-old pop singer from South London. 'Look at me,' said the overbearing Dane. 'Do you think I'd be good in bed?' The other housemates clapped and roared with laughter.

See also ADULT CONTENT; CHANNEL 4; GREAT TELEVISION; LYGO, KEVIN; TELEVISION WE DESERVE, THE.

Dogger Bank, rough local girls smelling like low tide on the. *See* BOURNEMOUTH.

Dogging, celebrity. Normal people admit to dogging by driving to Epping Forest and flashing their rear lights in a lay-by. Celebrities admit to dogging by informing their agents. 'Dogging is an activity which Stan has been involved in.' said Simon Kennedy, agent of troubled former footballer Stan COLLYMORE.

Dogs that are Celebrities:

- Lassie
- Son of Lassie
- Montmorency (*Three Men in a Boat*)
- Gnasher (*Dennis the Menace*)
- Scooby Doo
- Scrappy Doo (Scooby Doo's nephew)
- That doggie in the window
- Fred Basset
- London the Wonder Dog
- President Bush's Poodle (My Little Tony)
- Grommet
- Kym Marsh
- Hooch (Turner and)
- Rin Tin Tin
- Toto
- White Fang
- Whatamess the Afghan Hound (properly Prince Amir of Kinjan)
- Nana (*Peter Pan*)
- Cerberus
- Rinka (Norman Scott's Great Dane, shot dead in Jeremy Thorpe scandal)
- The Andrex Puppy
- Spot the Dog
- The Hound of the Baskervilles
- Mrs Thatcher's kennel cabinet

Dogs that belong to Celebrities. Horrible yappy little creatures of the sort that wear waistcoats in cold weather. Their number include Paul O'Grady's Buster, Paris Hilton's Tinkerbell, Geri Halliwell's Harry and Amanda Holden's Nobby and Fudge.

Doherty, Pete (b.1979). In his own words, borrowed from Morrissey, he is a 'sweet and tender hooligan' – that is to say, a sentimental drug addict. You can tell by his oversized tweed overcoat and pasty chops. Top musician and baby-faced singer with the excellent band The Libertines until his addiction to heroin and crack cocaine led to his expulsion from the band by co-founder Carl Barat. He was arrested in 2004 after breaking into Barat's flat (Barat and The Libertines were on tour in Japan) where he stole anything of value in order to fund his drug habit. He also took a mouth organ, but we told you he was sentimental. Since then, he has managed both to recognize and kiss Kate MOSS, been arrested for possession of a knife, and founded his own splinter group, Babyshambles. When he was interviewed on *Newsnight* on 21 December 2004, his mother, Jaqueline Doherty, wrote as follows to Jeremy Paxman: 'Please be gentle when you interview my son. Please be considerate with him. I feel he is very vulnerable.' Kirsty Wark did the interview instead.

See also PAXO, THE BIG BAD.

Do-Nascimento, Tania (b.1982). Shop girl from North London who participated in *Big Brother 4*. She keeps a pet koi carp and would like to be reincarnated as a bird: 'I could fly wherever and wouldn't be troubled by traffic.' After her eviction from the *Big Bruv* house, she broke up with her boyfriend, the former West Ham footballer Youssef Sofiane. He was angry that she had denied during the show that they were a couple. 'I don't understand her,' he said. 'Either we're an item or we're not.' Clearly, they're not. Happily, Dawn AIREY had been so impressed by Tania's performance that she subsequently employed her in a game show hanging upside down on a rope in her knickers.

Doukas, Sarah (b.1960). She understands the model business. As founder and chief executive of Storm, she is able, from any collection of adolescent girls, to pick out the one whose appearance is so unfortunate that even her own mother prefers not to be seen with her in public. Within three weeks, Miss Doukas has turned this peculiar-looking child into a supermodel – the face of Anna Sui cosmetics and the star of campaigns for Hermès, Moschino and Julien Macdonald. A mystery.

Dowling, Brian (b.1978). Having obligingly played the gay one in *Big Brother 2*, Brian emerged from the house victorious. Ryanair was able to announce a vacancy in its in-flight personnel arrangements, and a hysterical Davina McCall asked Brian how he intended to spend his windfall. After due consideration, he revealed that he would be upping his weekly expenditure on hair gel, possibly opting for a more expensive brand. Later, he admitted to a more sensible extravagance. He would be taking one friend to Florence, another to Barcelona. Brian, who is thought to be talented, has already done the voiceover for *The Salon,* and fronted *Brian's Boyfriends,* Trouble TV's *Celebrity Bodies* and *I'm Famous and Frightened 2.* Graham Norton is wishing he hadn't left his Professional Poof patent pending.

Drake, Sir Francis (*c.*1540–96). Although extremely short (being less than five feet in height), he was the first Englishman to circumnavigate the globe. An Elizabethan loyalist, Drake defeated the Spanish Armada, though some historians have argued that this achievement was due mainly to the weather and, to a lesser extent, to Drake's superior, the self-effacing Lord Howard of Effingham. The debate still rages in academic circles as to whether Drake was a courageous Protestant crusader or a gold-digging pirate. The evidence is contradictory. When Drake arrived in the Caribbean and changed the name of his ship from the *Pelican* to the *Golden Hind*, was it a sudden whim or an elaborate tax dodge? Did he introduce pyramid selling and blackmarket DVDs to the West Indies? Or did his devotion to the game of *boules* indicate that he was really quite bourgeois? Perhaps the talented actor Johnny Depp could be persuaded to settle the matter once and for all by giving a definitive account of the old rascal's comings and goings in a biopic.

Drink-and-drugs hell. A rite of passage through which some Celebrities must pass before achieving the peace to be found in contemplating one's priorities in a Celebrity Clinic. Whether enduring a drink-and-drugs hell (or, as Martin Heidegger put it in his masterwork *Sein und Zeit*, 1927, in relation to Nazi fatman Hermann Goering, '*Sauf-und-Drogen-Alptraum*') is a necessary or contingent condition of being a Celebrity is much debated in the philosophical schools.

Drug-shamed footie stars. 'Good evening. The time is 10.30 and I'm Fiona Bruce. Pay attention. Here are tonight's headlines.  "*Big Brother* wants Bad Boy Bosnich!" I doubt that very much. They must be on drugs too. I'm appalled. Anyway, it says here that shamed footie star Mark Bosnich is set to follow ex-lover Sophie Anderton into Reality TV. Bosses at *Celebrity Big Brother* have approached the former Chelsea goalkeeper – sacked over his £2000-a-week cocaine habit – for the next series. That's utterly disgraceful. Entirely the wrong signal to be sending out to young people. A *Big Brother* insider, speaking exclusively to the BBC's *10 O'Clock News*, said: "Mark's had a rough time of it. But Celebs who've found things hard on the outside often get a lot out of going on the show. There's time to think about things and take stock." Bosnich is reported to be keeping his options open. Very sensible. Here are tonight's other stories. Paul Gascoigne, another troubled former soccer player, intends to change his name to G8, since "Paul" has brought him nothing but bad karma. He won't be the first Geordie to change his name, of course; simply the first who isn't on a witness-protection programme. I imagine that's a joke. I hope it won't get me into trouble. They're very sensitive up north. Well, you'd be sensitive if you still kept coal in the bath. Anyway, as Huw always makes clear, we just read this stuff out. Now for the good news. Al Murray – he's hilarious, don't you think? – is to host a new ITV quiz show called *Facthunt.* You have to be jolly careful how you read that out or people think you're talking about Peter STRINGFELLOW.'

Ducks, Celebrity. *See* ORVILLE.

DUNCANFROMBLUE, properly **Duncan James** (b.1979), of the boy band Blue. Like Balloo-the-bear, Adele-from-*Hollyoaks* and William-of-Orange, DUNCANFROMBLUE is one of those celebrities who need a tripartite name. Say 'Duncan James' and people wouldn't have a clue who you're talking about. Say 'Duncanfromblue' and they immediately reply, 'What, the dishy dolt who can do Arab Springs and had a surprise baby?'

Dwarfs used as the ball in the Eton wall game. *See* JUNE CELEBRITY *FAUX PAS.*

Dyke, Greg (b.1946). Man o'the People slaphead who has the looks and manner of a small-time boxing promoter. He's forever boasting that he hasn't been to Eton or Oxbridge – unnecessarily, since it wouldn't have occurred to anyone that he had. After his resignation as director general of the BBC in January 2004, there was a brief revival in his reputation – not that he ever had much of one, except for making a great deal of money in his previous jobs, for introducing Roland Rat to the Great British Public, and for putting on some exceptionally silly programmes in his new one.

One of his first initiatives as director general had been to have a series of yellow cards printed to berate anyone who used vulgar jargon. The first one read, 'I want to make this a can-do organization the full 24/7.'

Dykons. *See* LESBIAN ICONS.

Dysfunctional families as a source of entertainment. *See* CHANNEL 4; EDINBURGH, PRINCE PHILIP, DUKE OF; GODDARD, TRISHA.

Edinburgh, Prince Philip, Duke of (b.1921). Consort. Also celebrated as the diplomat's diplomat. Born plain Philip Schleswig-Holstein-Sonderburg-Glücksburg, Prince of Greece and Denmark, he later changed his surname to Mountbatten, and on the eve of his wedding to his distant cousin Elizabeth Windsor in 1947 found himself heaped with titles: Baron Greenwich, Earl of Merioneth, Duke of Edinburgh, Phil the Greek. Prince Philip's sensitive parenting within his family has produced an assortment of well-adjusted progeny, who have themselves enjoyed a succession of happy marriages. He is worshipped as a god by the followers of so-called cargo cults in the South Seas.

Effluence. *See* ADULT CONTENT; BAZALGETTE, JOSEPH WILLIAM; BAZALGETTE, PETER; CHANNEL 4; LYGO, KEVIN; TELEVISION WE DESERVE, THE.

Elephants. Forever urinating on *Blue Peter* presenters and sitting on keepers at Howlett's, the zoo in Kent founded by the right-wing gambling-club proprietor John Aspinall. That said, elephants are rightly celebrated for their remarkable feats of memory. One famous story tells of a wildlife photographer who saved the life of a baby elephant separated from the herd on the African savannah and about to be attacked by lions. Thirty years later, the photographer, rather against his principles, agreed to take his seven-year-old son to Jimmy Chipperfield's circus. During the elephant act, one of the animals was seen to be looking very closely at the photographer, who was sitting at the ringside. After a while, it ambled slowly in his direction. Then it sat on him. It was a different elephant.

Elgar's Enigma Variations. *See* POSITIONS, CELEBRITIES' FAV-
OURITE SEXUAL.

Elliott, Grace Dalrymple (1758–1823). The wife of an Edinburgh
solicitor, Mrs Elliott was the first in a distinguished line of Celebrity
Adulteresses that includes: Margaret, Duchess of Argyll, Lady Antonia
Pinter, Edwina, Countess Mountbatten, Mandy Rice-Davies,
Amanda Holden, Camilla Parker Bowles, and, most famously,
Harriet Wilson, who, on threatening to write her memoirs, was told
by the Duke of Wellington to 'publish and be damned!'. Mrs Elliott
was consecutively, and sometimes simultaneously, the mistress of,
among many others, Lord Valentia, Lord Cholmondeley, Charles
Windham, George Selwyn (the founder of Selwyn College,
Cambridge), the Bishop of Lichfield and the Duc d'Orléans, who
changed his name after the French Revolution to Philippe Egalité.
M. Egalité was obliged to share Mrs Elliott's favours with the Prince
of Wales, later George IV.

Ellison, Jennifer (b.1982). Liverpudlian former *Brookie* babe
with the appearance of a Disney
cartoon princess. Tiny chin, tiny
waist, tiny brain, tiny feet. She
takes size four. Jennifer is now
'one hundred per cent focused'
on her singing career, which so
far includes two pop hit singles
– 'Baby I Don't Care', 'Bye Bye
Boy' – and a role in the film of
Lloyd Webber's *Phantom of the
Opera*. (However, Hollywood
moguls insisted she take elo-
cution lessons after they discovered to their surprise she

was a native English speaker. They had thought she was speaking Dutch.) Our Jen has a penchant for soft toys. When she 'went into' *Hell's Kitchen*, her fiancé Tony Richardson (27), a sunbed salesman, gave her several to take with her; in interviews in the *Daily Mail*, she repeatedly stresses that her bed is stuffed with them. This could be significant, since Jen has the soulful eyes of a Pietà, the blonde hair of a Raphael Madonna and the character of a plastic doll. When asked what she looks for in a man, she once told *FHM*, 'I like an older man, around 19 or 20. Basically, a well-heeled man. Money's nice – I don't want no scrubs!' So, now we see the real Jennifer. 'You're just a materialistic little scally!' Oh dear. We shouldn't have said that. She eyes us as if she were a fawn and we had just set fire to her tail. 'It's just that you like the finer things in life,' we say, 'like men with pots of money.' Jen starts to bawl. Quick, someone throw her a soft toy!

Elton, Ben (b.1961). Don't be wrong-footed by the 'dead common' accent. Although born in Catford, Elton comes from a long line of well-born Cambridge historians. In his early years he was a sod-'em-all aggro comedian of unquenchable verbosity. One reviewer has suggested that his logorrhoea was the result of his father, Sir Geoffrey Elton (author of, among other things, *The Tudor Revolution in Government*, Cambridge University Press, 1953), not allowing him to speak at meals until he achieved his majority. When this arrived he suffered cerebral meltdown, his brain came out of his ears and he said everything he'd wanted to say between the ages of 8 and 18. He now compiles unspeakably bad musicals. Some authorities believe his father, too, had flaws, such as over-emphasizing the role of Henry VIII's chief minister, Thomas Cromwell, in the birth of the modern bureaucratic state.

Emin, Tracey (b.1966). Crock-toothed artist who resembles a confident gypsy. Cross her palm with silver and she may give you a glimpse of her fascinating personality. Fascinating to her, anyway.

As the leader of the pack of the Once-Young British Artists, she has made a body of work about herself, whether it be *Everyone I Have Ever Slept With* – the stitched tent displayed at the Sensation exhibition that marked her arrival into mainstream consciousness and which was tragically destroyed in the Momart fire in 2005 – or her painstaking reconstruction of her own *Unmade Bed*. Her recent sortie into film is also autobiographical (with a hint of fantasy, since Margate is shown being destroyed by a bomb). Her personality is also large enough to take up the whole front row at many shows at London Fashion Week, and she has been known to attend four parties at the same time. Tracey certainly loves Tracey, and when you think about it, why shouldn't she?

Emu (1973–95). Britain's naughtiest puppet. Started out as an inanimate prop on a set in Australia. Rose to prominence under the direction of Rod Hull, a shy British vaudeville entertainer. Emu, wild-eyed, inquisitive and known for his distinctive ragged silhouette, acted as an engine of wish-fulfilment for the British public. He violently jumped the King of Chat, Michael Parkinson, and later, when introduced to the Queen Mother at the Royal Variety Show, he ate her bouquet and then head-butted the nation's favourite granny.

Endemol UK. Television production company responsible for a clutch of reality shows including *Big Brother, Changing Rooms, Ground Force, Ready Steady Cook* and *The Salon.*

See also BAZALGETTE, JOSEPH WILLIAM; BAZALGETTE, PETER; CHANNEL 4; LYGO, KEVIN.

Enfield, Edward (b.1925). Former local-government functionary who achieved a brief moment of Celebrity by publicly insulting his son, the comedian Harry Enfield. Having described his boy's TV performances as 'vulgar and embarrassing', he was informed that

10 million people customarily enjoyed them. 'That means that 40 million don't,' retorted Enfield Senior. With his reputation as a wag established, he was engaged to write a column for *The Oldie* and, accompanied by Mrs Enfield, to participate as an undeceived old timer in travel programmes for the BBC. Having arguably brought the condition of seniority into disrepute, the ageing curmudgeon has now disappeared from view.

Enjoying a pint with the lads after the game. Hospitalizing a law student.

See also ADOLESCENCE; ROASTING.

Essex Woman. *See* BOUDICCA.

Esther Rantzen melted down at Madame Tussaud's. *See* KAPLINSKY, NATASHA; RANTZEN, ESTHER.

Eurovision Song Contest, the. Warbling fat people wearing tiny clothes. Saturday night in Newcastle – all across the Continent.

See also GEORDETTES.

Evans, Chris (b.1966). Media mogul turned social casualty. Evans conceived, produced and appeared in *Don't Forget Your Toothbrush* and *TFI Friday* (whose highlights included a nose-picking contest), but in spite of these ground-breaking achievements he now sits at the bar in the Groucho Club all night, pouring back the drink and listening to the pianist playing 'Moon River' in the style of Dooley Wilson. Unsympathetic fellow members fear that the success of such innovative programmes as *Don't Forget Your Toothbrush* and *TFI Friday* (another of whose highlights was a man who ate his own vomit) may have gone to Evans's head. On one occasion he arrived at the Groucho Club and sat down heavily next to Julian Clary. 'Let's play a game,' he said. 'I ask you a question, you ask me a question. Me first. So Julian, how come your career's gone down the toilet?' Julian Clary flushed pink and held back the tears while hailing a taxi. Some might see Evans's behaviour as peculiarly offensive; others, with a better understanding of the pressures of creativity (to say nothing of life in a goldfish bowl) would be more sympathetic. As usual, Vanessa Feltz put it best. Writing in the *Daily Star* (7 February 2005), Vanessa said: 'I've lost count of the telly executives who have built entire careers on the claim that they created *Don't Forget Your Toothbrush.* They didn't. At the core of that barrier-breaking, unmissable show was one man and one man only – the maverick genius that is Chris Evans. Would he use a number-5 iron to hit fruit at the audience? He would! Would he film a senior member of his production team on the toilet? He would! For the first time on TV there was an atmosphere of authenticity. Viewers were 'aving a larf [sic] courtesy of a man they'd have been only too chuffed to bump into at their local. Suddenly television was REAL! No one has ever come close to filling Chris's shoes.' That says it all.

Eve. *See* ADAM AND EVE.

Events, overtaken by. For examples of how quickly the compilers of dictionaries can be overtaken by events – particularly when dealing with the condition of Celebrity and its fugitive nature – *see* FROST, JENNY *and* ICONIC, SO.

Extreme Celebrity Detox (Channel 4, 11 p.m.). The title of this reality show broadcast in February 2005 did not refer to the degree of Celebrity of those involved – Mina Anwar, anyone? Dominik Diamond? – but to the Detox. Fifteen Celebrities were sent off to have all the pettiness cleaned out of their lives (leaving them with what exactly?), variously trying out tai-chi, shamanic rituals, integral urine-drinking and advanced yogic disciplines by which they could introduce three-fifths of their bodyweight into their genital areas. The winner was Anwar, who turned out to have been a policewoman in the Ben Elton sitcom, *The Thin Blue Line*. In a hut in Peru she drank a local herbal brew and vomited her insides out night after night, later experiencing hallucinatory fits in the course of which she screamed repeatedly that she was dying. Afterwards she spoke of having found a new clarity.

Facthunt. *See* STRINGFELLOW, PETER.

Faithfull, Marianne (b.1949). On her latest album, *Naïve*, the croak-voiced Miss Faithfull effortlessly evokes the impression of a rootless personality worn to a smooth acceptance of life's vicissitudes. In Miss Faithfull's case, these include sleeping rough for some months in a Soho graveyard, living in Ireland and experiencing love affairs with Gene Pitney, David and Angie Bowie, Jimi Hendrix, Henrietta Moraes and three-fifths of the Rolling Stones. Mrs Moraes was married for a time to the distinguished Indian poet, the late Dom Moraes, whose first book, *A Beginning,* was published when he was just 18 by David Archer's Parton Press and later won the prestigious Hawthornden Prize for 'Best Act of Imagination'. A famous beauty, Henrietta Moraes often modelled for Francis Bacon (he characteristically made her look like something the dog's just sicked up). The story concerning Miss Faithfull and a Mars bar may be apocryphal since it was supposedly put into circulation by Mr Nigel Lilley of Scotland Yard's notoriously unreliable Drugs Squad.

Family entertainers. Bottle-tanned weirdos with their wigs worn sideways.

Famous for not being famous. *See* COSGRAVE, FRAN.

Famous for having been forgotten. *See* DEE, SIMON.

Farrell, Colin (b.1976). Incontinent Irish actor popular in Hollywood. Evidently they like dark sandpaper chins and wounded dog eyes over there. Farrell played Alexander the Great in Oliver Stone's historical epic and strained every nerve and muscle to give the most commanding performance of his lifetime. Sadly, the only thing that caught the attention of reviewers was his preposterous platinum highlights.

Fawkes, Guy (1570–1606). Catholic conspirator executed for his participation in the well-known Gunpowder Plot (1605). To this day, bonfires are lit on 5 November. City dealers in bowler hats drop thunder flashes into one another's Wellington boots. Street oiks put lighted rockets into old people's shopping baskets. Millwall supporters tack cats to Catherine wheels. Geordie rude boys hand Indian shopkeepers a fizzing fire-fountain and say, 'Hold that, Gunga Din.' In Ruislip, four-wheel-drive-men with a taste for bangs and barbecues put on novelty aprons, and, driven by evolutionary imperatives, joust with tongs in front of the ladies, get drunk and sit down suddenly in the rocket box, blowing themselves backwards over the garden shed. Are they celebrating Fawkes's execution or honouring a man who attempted to blow up the Houses of Parliament? Was he hero or buffoon? In the matter of Celebrity, the question is irrelevant. He is, after all, as famous as Jade Goody, as Dr David Starkey, as Posh Spice or Persil Automatic.

Fearnley-Whittingstall, Hugh (b.1964). Goose-stuffing lifestyle glutton who has turned a smallholding in west Dorset into a slaughterhouse. Here, unsuspecting farmyard animals end up being passed around on plates at mock medieval banquets – occasions on which, for all the world as if he were a Celebrity Historian, Fearnley-Whittingstall wears a jester's hat with a peacock feather in it. Red-faced local yokels, also comically attired in smocks and pointed boots, are instructed to 'Sit ye down!', to

February Celebrity *Faux Pas*

Gorgeous, pouting glamour model **Jodie Marsh** (32DD) confuses her KY Jelly with a tube of industrial putty and all her windows fall out. Jodie drops five rungs on Celebrity *Faux Pas* Ladder.

Celebrity Historian **Dr Simon Schama** appears on *The Parkinson Show.* The other guests are Billie Piper, Jasper Carrott and David Dickinson. Schama drops five rungs on Celebrity *Faux Pas* Ladder.

Jayne Middlemiss interviews Doris Lessing. She asks Miss Lessing whether she's ever logged on to www.celebrityoops.com.

In order to show she is a woman of the people, **Theresa May** appears in a cameo role on *Footballers' Wives*.

Tania Bryer orders tiramisu as a main course at Locanda Locatelli. The cockney waiter doubles over with laughter at this mistake, points at her, guffaws again and then calls over a colleague and repeats what she said, loudly.

'Make merry!' and to 'Imbibe deeply from the life-enhancing chalice!' To applause, a wild boar is then wheeled on with an apple up its arse. The evening ends with heavy-footed farmers and their wives folk-dancing to lute and conch.

Feeding Frenzy. *See* MEDIA INTRUSION.

Feisty. Perspiring rock chick with short legs.

See also RAUNCHY.

Feltz, Vanessa (b.1959). When Vanessa's career suddenly belly-flopped like a fat man diving into a hotel swimming-pool she managed to get herself filed under 'likely to unravel in public'. Accordingly, down-market newspaper editors and producers of Reality Television shows can now rely on her to fill the role of self-pitying exhibitionist inclined to tell us a great deal more about her private life than we want to hear. 'I was known as "Vanessa the undresser" in the lower fifth,' squeaks Vanessa. 'I can testify that the fundamentals I mastered in the stationery cupboard have stood me in better stead than anything I studied at Cambridge. I've never had to handle a slide-rule, a Bunsen burner or a lacrosse stick since I left school. But those fumbles on the back seat of the High Barnet coach have left a practical legacy to draw on with sensational effect to this very day.' That seems unlikely. In fact, rumour has it that she applies her

make-up in the morning by falling face down on her dressing-table; further that her underwear is stitched together by America's Cup sailmakers working double shifts. Neither slander has the ring of truth, but she continues to make money by vaunting an appearance and personality that most people would go to great lengths to conceal.

Fergie, properly **Sarah Margaret, Duchess of York** (b.1962). Problematic royal with the dress sense of a barrage balloon. Her gargantuan appetite for all the fleshly pleasures (shopping, stuffing, toe-licking) earned her the cruel sobriquet of 'Duchess of Pork'. However, in her new slimmed-down incarnation she travels around America as roving ambassadress for Weight Watchers. 'My name is Sarah, and I am a Bigfatgreedyguts.'

See also CHRISTMAS CELEBRITY *FAUX PAS*; RED RUM.

Ferguson Sir Alex (b.1940). What's Sir Alex doing here? He isn't a Celebrity. Notwithstanding his foul temper and unintelligible manner of address, he has a kind of animal dignity, almost a grandeur, in his simple-minded devotion to football and all its unpleasant attachments. Invite him to share a jungle hut with Tuffers, a queer ballet dancer and a weather woman in her knickers, stand well back, and you'd soon discover who was a Celebrity and who wasn't.

Ferris, Stewart. *See* CELEBRITY BODY LANGUAGE.

Fifty Ways to Look Great Naked! 'Sounds like one for us, Kevin.' It won't be long before this one appears on CHANNEL 4.

Finnigan, Judy (b.1948). The less offensive half of the sofa-bound tag-team combo which Judy forms with her husband, Richard Madely, on Channel 4's early evening chat-and-promotionzzzzzzzz show. She's certainly a proficient journalist, seldom out of step with the crassest aspects of the contemporary sensibility. Indeed, it has been claimed that, more than any other broadcaster, she reflects the hopes, fears and opinions of the ordinary person in the street. This may well be true, but why should Channel 4 suppose that the opinions of ordinary people in the street are of any interest? Her first words to Madely when they met in a Manchester television studio were, 'I'm your Mummy.' This is thought to be significant.

Fisher, Kitty (1741–67). Saucy self-promoter, royal courtesan and mistress of the notorious philanderer Augustus Hervey (1724–89). She was a favourite model for Sir Joshua Reynolds, and sat for him as Cleopatra. Arriving in London as a 19-year-old she found herself much written about in the *Public Advertiser* – publicity which was much to her taste. According to Stella Tillyard, in her essay *Paths of Glory: Fame and the Public in 18th-Century London,* 'Kitty staged a public accident in Hyde Park where crowds gathered to watch her ride, falling off her horse and exposing her pretty thighs.' Her prim 'relation' by illegitimate connection, Lady Isabella Hervey, would have strongly disapproved of such blatant attention-seeking.

See also HERVEY, LADY ISABELLA.

Fitness videos, raunchy. *See* ADAM AND EVE; GODIVA, LADY; HILTON, PARIS; TITMUSS, ABI.

Fitzherbert, Selina. *See* BRYSON, DR KIT.

Flatley, Michael (b.1961). Strict-tempo toe dancer in the Irish mode. The huge success in New York of his 87-man jig-and-fiddle bollocks, *The Lord of the Dance*, was explained by the fact that Americans couldn't believe that 87 Irishmen could remain upright for two and a half hours.

Florist, Celebrity. Pruner to the stars demonstrates on camera how to make a nosegay for Vanessa Feltz. His name is Ercole Moroni, which translates as Hercules Moron. Janet Street-Porter prefers to call him 'Perky Erky'. He fondles tuberoses suggestively, while posing in leather trousers. Millions tune in.

Fogle, Ben (b.1973). Ben is the son of a vet, Brian Fogle, and Julia Foster, an actress who has frequently worked for Michael Winner – a gene pool that seems to argue against his reputation as Posh Totty. That said, he has thin upper-class legs and the vocal pitch of a flannelled almost-gent from a long-ago Ealing comedy in black and white. You expect him to say 'Crikey!', 'By George! and 'You rotter!' in the manner of Ian Carmichael or Terry-Thomas.

After A-levels, Ben spent a gap year in Quito, Ecuador, where he helped in an orphanage and taught English. He then spent a second year off in Nicaragua where he worked alongside the American Peace Corps on a turtle-conservation project. It was when he enrolled in the Royal Navy Reserve as a midshipman, later being deployed in Spain, Norway and Gibraltar, that questions of constitutional importance began to be asked: was Ben being trained up as an honorary Royal against the possibility that all those properly in succession might meet with accidents or in various ways let the side down?

Speculation reached fever pitch when Ben spent a year on the remote island of Taransay, where he and 35 other men and women embarked on one of those outdoor self-sufficiency courses that the Duke of Edinburgh has traditionally insisted that male members of his family endure. Happily, it turned out that Ben was merely competing in *Castaway 2000*, a Reality Game Show, from which he emerged victorious. All speculation ended when Ben accepted a job on the society magazine, *Tatler*. He now co-presents *Animal Park* with Kate Humble and has appeared in *One Man and his Dog* and *Death By Pets*. A spot on *So Graham Norton* was judged to have been a mistake.

Football fans. While it would not be true to say that all football fans are boors, thugs and silly women, it is certainly the case that all boors, thugs and silly women are football fans.

Fordham, Andy (b.1952). Known as 'The Viking'. Gargantuan darts champion with roadkill on his head. On closer examination, the roadkill appears to be a hairstyle. The nation shudders when he appears on *CELEBRITY FIT CLUB*.

Foucault, Michel (1926–84). French philosopher. Born in Poitiers, Foucault was a pupil of the Marxist philosopher Louis Althusser and became professor of the history of systems of thought at the Collège de France, Paris, in 1970. He wrote a series of influential books, including *Histoire de la folie* (1961), *Les Mots and les choses* (1966), *L'Archaeologie du savoir* (1969) and *Histoire de la sexualité* (1976). Foucault argued that prevailing social attitudes are manipulated by those in power, both to define categories such as insanity, illness, sexuality and criminality, and to use these in turn to identify and suppress the 'deviants'. On his death he received a three-line obituary in the *Guardian* under the headline 'Sex historian dies'.

See also FRY, STEPHEN; PHILISTINISM, BRITISH.

Fox, Samantha (b.1969). Former glamour model, and the face of conman Peter Foster's discredited Bai Lin slimming tea. 'As far as I was concerned the tea worked,' said Sam, regretfully. She says

Foreplay

A new man's idea of. 'Excuse me for asking, but could you tell me for how much longer you're going to be "almost there"?'

A soccer player's idea of. 'These are the lads, innit. Carlton. Kevin. Jody. Keiron. Wanna be first cab off the rank, Lee?' *See also* ROASTING.

David Beckham's idea of. 'Can't talk now, Nevilly. Ring you back in five. Love you. Bye.' 'Okay babe, do anything you like to me! That's it... that's right... Hey!... mind my hair! Oh yes! Oh yes! Lower! Lower! Don't stop! That's it! But slowly. Not *that* slowly! That's better! Oh yes! Oh yes! Aaaahhhggghhhh! Pass me my mobile, will you, babe?' 'Hullo? Nevilly? You still there? Sorry about that...'

Father Christmas's idea of. Coming down people's chimneys and saying 'Ho! Ho! Ho!'

John Leslie's idea of. 'What was your name again? Doesn't matter. Tell me later. Take your clothes off and stand over there by the sink while Abi gets the camcorder out.' *See also* TITMUSS, ABI.

Sebastian Horsley offers. 'But that's enough about me. What about you? What do you think of me?' *See also* HORSLEY, SEBASTIAN.

Stephen Fry offers. 'At 10 o'clock there's a dear little film on BBC2 starring clever old me and all my darling chums at Cambridge – Ems and Kenneth and Hugh and ... where are you going, poo chops?'

she started taking it and lost weight, though she now realizes that was probably down to her seven-hours-a-day fitness regime and no-carb, no-protein diet. Ms Fox is now a lesbian and professional fist fighter, though not both at once.

Friel, Anna (b.1976). Small, suggestive actress. A puckish, faun-eyed child-woman who gives the impression that she rather enjoys life. A natural show-off and provocateur who tells journalists that 'sometimes you want to have a really good time and fuck', talks about her bowel movements while fluttering her eyelashes and, when wearing trousers, poses for photographers with her finger sticking, penis-like, out of her flies. She didn't spend long in her home town, Rochdale. At 15 she landed a role as Michael Palin's daughter in the TV drama *GBH,* and after that it was *Corrie,* and after that it was *Brookie.* As Beth Jordache in the latter, she murdered her abusive dad and hid him under the patio. Then her character snogged another girl and the nation was outraged. Complaints, angry leading articles, rocketing viewing figures – this was 1993, after all, and it was the first lesbian kiss ever seen on television. Then Anna went all upmarket. She was directed by Harold Pinter at the Almeida, starred in Patrick Marber's *Closer* on Broadway, wrote a book of *Pensées* for Orion. But then she appeared in a TV commercial sporting frog feet and the nation was relieved to discover that she hadn't lost the common touch. Last seen posing with her baby Gracie by her partner, David Thewlis, saying, 'I haven't got buckets of nannies, OK?'

Frost, Jenny (b.1980). Pop beauty Jenny has that 'just out of bed' look down to a tee. The former Atomic Kitten babe was looking quite the buffed scruff when she visited her local Tesco petrol station in North London. Even with a messy barnet and ripped T-shirt, the gorgeous 25-year-old managed to show why she's still one of the sexiest women on Planet Pop. So naturally Jenny insiders are wondering just why it's taking so long for her boyfriend, DJ Dom T, to get the saucy songbird down the aisle.

Frost, Sadie (b.1967). Flinty-faced actress and Celebrity Wife. Born Sadie Liza Vaughan, her first acting role was at the age of three in a Jelly Tots commercial. It didn't get much better thereafter on the acting front, apart from a stake going through her heart in Francis Ford Coppola's *Dracula*. She married Gary Kemp of Spandau Ballet at 19; they have one son, Finley. Next she married Jude Law, the actor, when she was 25 and he 19. They have three children, Rafferty, Iris and Rudy. Iris was admitted to hospital at the age of two in 2002 after swallowing a tablet she found on the floor at Soho House. Sadie quickly retrieved the tablet from her child's mouth since she thought it was Ecstasy. Forensic tests proved this to be the case. The child was unharmed, but the marriage of Jude and Sadie was not. They divorced in 2003, a development that Sadie imaginatively put down to their wonderful marriage. 'The love was just too strong,' she said, squirting gusts of eau denial into the air. Meanwhile, she retains her spunky, unflappable demeanour, presenting TV slots with self-effacing titles such as *What Sadie Did Next*, and *Watch Out, Sadie's About*. On the latter programme, plants in the audience ask grotesque questions about her underwear, so that she can respond with a plug for her knicker label, Floozie.

Fry, Stephen (b.1960). The stupid person's idea of a clever person.

See also JULY CELEBRITY *FAUX PAS*.

Furnish, David (b.1962). Trim, slim and manly, with a capped smile and artful highlights. Well, he has to look the part. He's the trophy wife of Elton John. Furnish was a successful Canadian advertising executive working primarily on condiment accounts (Sun-Pat Peanut Butter, Rowntree's Jelly and Gale's Honey), but his life was transformed when he was invited by a mutual friend to dinner at Elton's home in Windsor in 1993, and he became the world's most prominent gay consort since Piers GAVESTON. Allegations that Furnish is in fact bisexual have been dismissed by Elton as 'pure steaming horseshit'.

Further Celebrity Catchphrases.

'*Après moi, le déluge*' – Louis XV.
'I've started so I'll finish' – Magnus Magnusson.

G

Gallacher, Kirsty (b.1976). 'I don't like having photos taken of me in a bikini,' says Kirsty. It must be a very hard life, then, for the curvy model, because she has just finished shooting her second calendar of pretty string bikinis, modelling in her bikini for the pages of *OK!* and posing in a bikini for the cover of *Maxim*. Kirsty, the spokesperson for Slendertone, was born in Edinburgh, where she developed her sporting physique. She has also presented *RI: SE*, *Sky Sports*, and *Kirsty's Home Videos*, a programme that Prince Philip reputedly approves of. What the Queen thinks of it is unknown.

Game, the Beautiful. Twenty-two silly haircuts and three rape allegations.

See also ADOLESCENCE; ROASTING; ROLE MODEL, A GOOD.

Game-show hosts. A class of unproductive interchangeables. Useful targets for any progressive terror movement. The fixed smile develops into a rictus and the constant face-pulling eventually leads to paranoia.

See also McCALL, DAVINA.

Gascoigne, Paul (b.1968). Troubled former footballer.

See also DRUG-SHAMED FOOTIE STARS.

Gaveston, Piers (*c.*1282–1312). Foreman of the Gay, Lesbian and Bisexual Association, Dark Age division. He was the committed consort of Edward II, though the two were continually denied a civil partnership. Neither were they granted adoption rights on the two little Princes in the Tower. Generally, Gaveston was the victim of patriarchal prejudice. The royal barons were forever taking away his title, so Edward had to make him Earl of Cornwall three times over. He was finally executed while a houseguest of the Earl of Pembroke, after he was discovered in his bedroom prancing about singing 'I feel pretty' while wearing the crown jewels.

See also FURNISH, DAVID.

General public, members of the. Always 'unsuspecting'. A blessing, some clinical psychologists have argued, since no normal person would wish to be burdened with the knowledge that at any moment Davina McCall might spring out of a doorway and quiz them about their personal arrangements. Still less by the fearful expectation that, by switching over to Channel 4, they might see Vanessa Feltz testing a flatulence-free baked bean. Better to confront such emergencies when they happen. That said, broadcasters take a different view, preferring to warn customers of adult content in the offing.

See also ADULT CONTENT; CHANNEL 4; FELTZ, VANESSA; GREAT TELEVISION; LYGO, KEVIN; McCALL, DAVINA; TELEVISION WE DESERVE, THE.

Genuine, totally. Celebrities who aren't 'totally genuine' when participating in TV Reality Shows are back with the nonentities even quicker than those who 'have an agenda'. Coincidentally, and imagining, perhaps, that it was what the world was waiting to hear, the spangly-suited aggro comedian Ben ELTON once announced that he didn't 'have an agenda on Benny Hill'. What a relief!

Geordettes. What are they? 'Worra you mean, what are we? Wanna slap? I'll tell you who we are. Only the most bang up for it lasses in the entire land, like. Wanna piece of it? Do you? Do you?' And with that, the flesh-devouring, bottle-crunching womenfolk of Newcastle go braying into the town centre. Men scatter as the micro-skirted Valkyries descend on Weatherspoons. A surprising 80% of Geordie blokes reckon that, on an average night out in Newcastle, they've had their drinks spiked by man-eating babes and then been date-raped. Who knows how many victims will be claimed tonight? Bar bouncers tremble, there's panic in the barracks, footballers refuse to go out without the latest in anti-date-rape technology in their handbags, bejewelled chavs on their way to urinate over Debenhams turn through 180 degrees and run home to their mummies. The police have urged victims to come forward. Their stories will be treated in confidence and counselling will be available.

Gervais, Ricky (b.1962). In March 2004, Gervais came second in a *Radio Times* poll to discover the nation's most popular TV Personality. The order was:

1. Ant and Dec
2. Ricky Gervais
3. Chris Tarrant
4. Davina McCall.

There's no logic to it. Like a poll of 'Great Scientists' that went:

1. Patrick Moore
2. Sir Isaac Newton
3. Magnus Pyke.

Or one of 'Distinguished Thinkers', which resulted in:

1. Alain de Botton
2. Ludwig Wittgenstein
3. David Starkey.

It makes no sense. Ricky Gervais should be worried. He must be doing something wrong. But what?

See also ANT AND DEC.

Gingold, Hermione (1897–1987). One of this country's finest comediennes. We may be thankful that she didn't live to see her favourite god-daughter become the bath salts correspondent of the *Independent on Sunday*.

See also IVY, THE.

'Give him the money, Mabel!' *See* PICKLES, WILFRID.

God. His injunctions are not to be challenged – a privilege not granted to other Celebrities, for instance the Amazing Adam or Fay Presto, the sex-change close-up conjuror. The foregoing notwithstanding, God is one Celebrity you can insult with impunity. God doesn't sue. However, sources close to God sometimes sue on his behalf. In 1970, the producers of the irreligious theatrical satire, *Council of Love*, were prosecuted for blasphemy in a private case brought by Lady Birdwood of the British National Party. Since they were by this time hiding deep in foreign bank accounts, the author of the play, John Bird (of *Bremner, Bird and Fortune* and *The Long Johns*) was prosecuted in their place. He was defended by John Mortimer and found to be not guilty.

Lady Birdwood's behaviour may be accounted for by the fact that she was born under Taurus, the sign of cleanliness and decency. As Poppy Folly, the *Independent on Sunday*'s in-house astrologer, has pointed out, 'Because decent people can only take so many deviants, degenerates, drunks, peddlers, progressives, paedophiles, aerobics teachers, speculators, developers and French films, Taurus is the sign of the fascist's natural power-base. Taureans are authority-respecting, big-bodied, savings-oriented

moderate drinkers with well-brought up clean-limbed children. The Queen is Taurean and so are a large proportion of German district nurses.'

Coincidently, it doesn't follow from the fact that God doesn't sue that you can't sue him. The comic possibilities inherent in such an action have been examined on film, notably in *The Man Who Sued God* (Mark Joffe, 2001). Billy Connolly heads the cast of this disarming comedy, taking the part of a fisherman who, after insurance investigators have declared that the destruction of his boat in a storm was an act of God, issues proceedings against the Almighty. Shown on television on Christmas Day 2004, the film was judged to be 'agreeable festive fare'. In Cardiff a cow was executed as a witch on the night of 16 June 1987.

See also GOD'S MYSTERIOUS WAYS.

Goddard, Trisha (b.1957). The British Oprah, though not so fat. Trisha, whose style is tart except for when she remembers to be caring, has been through it all – homosexual husband, suicidal sister, a month as a psychiatric patient and a TV career in Australia. This qualifies her for inviting dysfunctional families on to her show and getting the audience to cheer while they implode and attack each other. One thing is clear: Trisha can communicate with disturbed people. 'I'm a vegetarian, so if I go into a steakhouse somewhere, me and the steakhouse are going to part company,' says Trisha, a trained mental-health counsellor.

Godiva, Lady (d.c.1080). The wife of Leofric, Earl of Mercia (d.1057). According to the *Flores Historiarum* of Roger of Wendover, a 13th-century chronicler, she rode naked through Coventry market place in order to persuade her husband to reduce taxes. Her legend provides provincial exhibitionists with an excuse to appear naked in public at annual pageants. She was thus the first known streaker, and a cheery influence on those who succeeded her at Twickenham (*see* ROE, ERICA), Wimbledon and – to the great displeasure of that prim old cowpat, Richie Benaud – Lord's. 'Oh dear. That's really quite unnecessary.' Were she alive today, Lady Godiva would have brought out her own raunchy fitness video.

See also TITMUSS, ABI.

God's mysterious ways. In the course of an entertainment performed in front of the Roman Emperor Diocletian (AD 245–313), Genesius, the most celebrated actor of his day, took the lead in a mocking representation of the Christian baptism. In the course of the performance he was touched by the grace of God and, when presented to the emperor, declared that he had converted to Christ. He was beheaded on the spot. God drops ten places on Celebrity *Faux Pas* Ladder.

See also GOD.

Goering, Hermann. *See* DRINK-AND-DRUGS HELL.

Goldie (b.1970). Feral DJ who had it going down, man. He was the business, his shit was mental. Back in the 90s he was the innovator, the main man for drum 'n' bass. Goldie and his merry Metalheadz were rinsing. It wasn't just his teeth that were golden (hence his soubriquet), it was everything he touched. Music, laydeez, fbjorkcredibility, man. He was friends with David Bowie, he dated Naomi Campbell, he even dumped Björk. The orphan from the Walsall care home done good. Now ageing in a mansion in Hertfordshire.

Goldsmith, Lady Annabel (b.1935). Daughter of the 8th Marquess of Londonderry. At the age of 20, Lady Annabel married Mark BIRLEY, creator of Annabel's Club in Berkeley Square. The marriage produced three children – two sons, Rupert and Robin, and a daughter, India Jane – but it came to an end following Birley's serial affairs. Lady Annabel had by then become the mistress of the groceries tycoon, Sir James Goldsmith. Their relationship began secretly, but became common knowledge in the mid-1970s, when first Jemima (who later married Imran Khan, the former Pakistani cricket captain) and then Zac were born. Although obliged to share him with two other women and their families, Lady Annabel married Goldsmith in 1978 (to legitimize their children), and in spite of the fact that Sir James had just begun another relationship in New York. Lady Annabel now lives on her own in a Queen Anne house near Richmond Park, where she spends a lot of her time in the garden. 'Solitude is a blessing,' she says. 'I rather like pruning, which is therapeutic. If you've got a worry, you can get your secateurs out and start snipping.' Lady Annabel's memoirs, *Annabel: An Unconventional Life*, were published by Weidenfeld & Nicolson in 2004.

See also KHAN, JEMIMA.

Good craic. A roomful of blethering Irishmen vomiting onto the sawdust.

Good Tyne Girls. Donna Air, *Big Bruv*'s Michelle Bass, Girls Aloud's Cheryl Tweedy, Jayne Middlemiss, *EastEnders* babe Jill Halfpenny.

Goodwin, Daisy (b.1970). Cloying TV producer-turned-presenter with eyes like runny caramels. She markets poetry books, videos and DVDs to the 'self-help generation', peddling poetry as if it were sausages. 'Well,' she sighs, reclining on a chaise longue and looking deep into the camera, 'isn't Wordsworth just the greatest comfort food?'

Goody, Jade (b.1981). Terrifying chavette role model and Chris Moyles look-alike. Came to fame as corpulent anti-star of *Big Brother 3*, and is thus regarded as the Epitome of Contemporary Celebrity. Graced the cover of *Heat* magazine's biggest-selling issue ever. *Jade's Dance Workout* video outsold even Geri Halliwell. She is under the impression that Rio de Janeiro is a footballer and that Sherlock Holmes invented the water closet. At the time of *Big Bruv*, Jade's father was serving a four-year sentence for robbery in Wandsworth Prison. We all make mistakes.

See also BRAZIER, JEFF; MOYLES, CHRIS.

Google. A 'search engine' that facilitates access to a 'web page'. This offers fanciful textual information, flashing lights and pictures of naked Celebrities alongside inappropriate sponsorship.

Gough, Darren. *See* CELEBRITY CRICKETERS.

Grammar. A system of tripwires designed to make a laughing stock of John Prescott.

Grant, Hugh (b.1961). Once perceived in America as a bumbling English prat. Then everything changed. He was caught by the LAPD being fellated on Sunset Boulevard by a back-street hooker. No longer is Grant perceived as a bumbling English prat. Now he is perceived as a bumbling English prat who likes to be fellated by back-street hookers.

Great Television. The idea of Vanessa Feltz testing a flatulence-free baked bean. 'Sounds like one for us, Kevin.' It is beyond the scope of a dictionary to analyse why, and when, the term 'Great Television' came to be used to describe only what is intrusive and ugly. A natural broadcaster, such as Michael Parkinson, Cat Deeley, Richard Madely or Judy Finnigan, would never make the mistake of describing *The Office, The Sopranos* or *Brass Tacks* as 'Great Television'. If what is 'Great' (the freakish and cruel) gradually drives out what is merely 'Good', the distinction may turn out to be significant.

See also ADULT CONTENT; AIREY, DAWN; CHANNEL 4; GENERAL PUBLIC, MEMBERS OF THE; HUMILIATING THE AFFLICTED; LYGO, KEVIN; TELEVISION WE DESERVE, THE.

Grief, recreational. Recently identified by clinical psychologists as 'the ostentatious expression of public caring at the anniversaries of Dead Celebrities'. Experts now agree that wearing coloured charity wristbands and holding silences for the deceased in high-profile catastrophes amount to 'grief substitution' and are undertaken as enjoyable pastimes, much like a day out at a safari park or waving a small Union Jack at the last night of the Proms.

See also LIVERPUDLIANS.

Grounded. Half-witted.

See also REALLY GROUNDED.

Grounded and focused. Half-witted and rude.

Growing apart. Girl band members sticking chewing-gum in each others' hair extensions, spitting in each others' cornflakes and giving one another the finger on live TV.

See also SUGABABES.

***Guardian,* the.** *See* FOUCAULT, MICHEL; PHILISTINISM, BRITISH.

Guirado, Catalina (b.1979). Model. Her physical beauty is matched only by her sweetness of nature. When she appeared on the game show, *Back to Reality,* it came as no surprise that Channel 5 viewers preferred Maureen, the toothless crone from *Driving School.*

Guinness, Jasmine (b.1975). Catwalk model and beverage heiress. Miss Guinness, a fashionable Notting Hillbilly when not at home in Ireland, has a Twenties face, Sixties legs and Thirties waist. Overall, the effect is *so* 2005. She often models accessories for her relative by marriage, Lulu Guinness (the pixie-like woman with the worldwide handbag empire). Jasmine has dated Jesse Wood, son of erstwhile Rolling Stone, Ronnie Wood, but who hasn't? Subsequently, she conceived her son Ellwood during a liaison with the photographer Gawain Rainey. (It has been suggested that this is Wayne Rooney's posh alias, though this is thought to be unlikely.) They are considering marriage, according to a Guinness insider. She is thought to have inherited her stunning beauty and unconventional approach to relationships from her grandmother, Diana Mosley.

Gwynn, Nell (1650–87). An actress whose battle honours were won in the bedroom rather than on the stage. The Koo Stark of her day.

H

Halibut, Celebrity. *See* BOURNEMOUTH.

Halliwell, Geri (b.1971). Life-style exhibitionist. Formerly a table-dancer in Turkish holiday resorts, later the fleshiest and least abashed member of the Spice Girls pop group that prospered in the late 1990s. Some commentators, driven by envy, perhaps, have compared the tubby little singer to a cockroach. Certainly, she appears to be indestructible. If the world were wiped out by a nuclear catastrophe, she'd still be there, making a nuisance of herself. Volume 2 of her ghosted autobiography, *Just For The Record,* was recently published by HarperCollins. Her guest appearance in *Sex and the City* continues to win the No. 1 spot in 'TV's Most Embarrassing Moments' compilations.

Hamilton, Neil (b.1946) and **Christine** (b.1948). Husband-and-wife slapstick tag-team celebrated for their sleazy routines. Of the two, Neil is marginally the more disquieting, if only because he has about him something of the lurker, of the upstairs-landing, stocking-footed blimper. He wears a bow tie and the flickering, insecure smile of a man about to play 'spin the bottle' in the suburbs, as if he half suspects there might be some cause for embarrassment here; Christine has no such qualms. A lachrymose battleaxe and exhibitionist, she's the only performer in Reality TV to make Jade GOODY seem dignified. Some have seen her as the reincarnation of Marged ferch IFAN, the Welsh wrestler.

Hand-holding, Celebrity. Stratagem employed, while on parade at premiéres, by girly Celebs pretending to be friends (with an added Sapphic undertow to excite the chaps). Girlpower: this is my best best besty ever mmwwwaah! As soon as they're off the red carpet and safely inside, they ditch each other in search of cocaine and John Leslie.

'HANDS OFF OUR TELLY!' 'Good evening. The time is 10 o'clock and I'm Huw Edwards. Here are tonight's headlines. "Go back to your ivory tower, so-called Dr Jonathan Miller!", storms the *Daily Star*. In a lecture, "Egg-head" Dr Miller had referred to *Big Brother 6 as* "electronic excrement which degrades the audience as much as it does its participants". Well! Naturally the *Daily Star* wheeled on one of its biggest guns, Vanessa Feltz, to shoot down the snooty prof. "What so-called Dr Miller knows about 'Great Television' could be written on a rat's arse and shoved where the sun don't shine." That said it all. Did you read about the asylum seeker, Seterah Nahwi, who is suing the government for £15,000 for the trauma of being moved to Wigan? Can't say I blame her. I'd want a lot more than £15,000 to move to Wigan, and I dare say you would too. Now for the rest of the news. 200 pensioners were drowned when...'

Handy Andy, properly **Andy Kane** (b.1966). Carpenter on TV home-improvement show *Changing Rooms*. Salt-of-the-earth foil to Laurence LLEWELYN-BOWEN's cavalier flamboyance.

Harris, Rolf (b.1933). Amiably bearded and bespectacled didgeridoo-playing Antipodean all-round early-evening entertainer. Specializes in painting, pets and vets: 'I'm afraid little Harry didn't make it through the night. His poor little heart just wasn't up to it.' Now a cult figure among students, he may have succeeded Peter Ustinov as the comic Rector of some obscure Scottish university. According to research by Ms Dymphna Lonergan of Flinders University, Australia, the word *didgeridoo*, which is unrelated to any known Aboriginal word, may be derived from the Irish *dúdaire* ('horn-blower') and *dubh* ('black') or *duth* ('native'). Is it a sign of the times that the Queen has selected Rolf to paint a new portrait for her 80th birthday? Rolf is reportedly 'thrilled to bits'. 'Can you see what it is yet?'

Heaton, Michelle (b.1981). Pert Scally, formerly of the band Liberty X. A poor man's Posh Spice, notable for her over-plucked eyebrows and the whisper of menace about her. You wouldn't want to snog her boyfriend in a hurry. But then again, you wouldn't want to snog her boyfriend period. He's Andy Scott-Lee, the goon from *Pop Idol*. His sister, in turn, is Lisa Scott-Lee, of Steps.

See also INTERCHANGEABLE POP BABES EXPLAINED IN FULL AT LAST.

Hectic lifestyle. A rubber-breasted clubber on her mobile phone. *See also* TEXT MESSAGING.

Hectic recording schedule. Posh Spice out shopping.

Hector (*c*.6th century BC). The leader of the Trojan forces in the war against Greece and the hero of Homer's *Iliad*. He killed Patroclus, the lover of Achilles, and paid for this with his life. Achilles sulked in his tent for many weeks and then suddenly emerged with a torrent of blank verse ('See, Hector, how the sun

begins to set…'). Scholars have pointed out that were Achilles and Patroclus alive today they'd be running a fish restaurant in Brighton with a largely theatrical clientèle. Alternatively, they might relocate to Sydney, Australia, the gay capital of the world. Collectors of theatrical trivia might be interested to learn that in George 'Dadie' Rylands's production of *Troilus and Cressida* for the Marlowe Society, Cambridge, in 1957, the role of Achilles was taken by Dan Massey, son of the Hollywood actor, Raymond Massey, while the part of his lover, Patroclus, was played by Bamber Gascoigne, who was later to achieve Celebrity as the questionmaster of *University Challenge.* The leading role of Troilus was taken by Julian Pettifer, who went on to have a successful career as a BBC wildlife reporter. Interestingly, at the start of the Trojan War, Achilles went AWOL, and was found hiding in the women's quarters dressed in female attire. This style tip apparently came from his mother, Thetis. Some authorities believe there is a parallel here with Victoria BECKHAM's insistence that her husband wear a sarong, beads and an Alice band, and that he speak with a lisping, high-pitched voice.

Heggessey, Lorraine (b.1963). Television executive who stunned media watchers in February 2005 by quitting her £250,000-a-year job as boss of BBC1 after five years. During that time, Lorraine, acknowledged to be a brilliant broadcaster, had delivered such challenging programmes as *Fame Academy, Celebrity Fame Academy, Strictly Come Dancing* and… er…

Hell and back, celebrities who have been to. Sophie Anderton. Frank Bruno. Cleopatra. Lady Godiva. Davina McCall. Elizabeth Siddal. Kerry Katona. Daniella Westbrook. Old King Cole.

Heloïse (1082–1150), a nun. She was loved by Peter Abelard, (1079–1142), a disputant. Recognized by most authorities as 'the Posh and Becks of their day'. Reviewing Robert Forsyth's play

Heloïse, recently revived at the Almeida Theatre in Islington, North London, Charles Spencer, the *Daily Telegraph*'s respected drama critic, wrote that their love scenes reminded him of an *aperçu* about Jane Welsh and Thomas Carlyle: that it was as well that they married each other, since this meant two unhappy people in the world rather than four; further that Mr Forsyth had 'endowed the lovers with a crushing generic banality which at once stifles any interest in what happens to them'. Whether Mr Spencer was at this point referring to Heloïse and Abelard or to Posh and Becks was not made clear. In fact, Abelard was a subtle logician, though ruled by his heart rather than his head. (Some commentators have judged that at this point the comparison with Posh and Becks loses a certain amount of purchase.) In 1078 Abelard was castrated by Heloïse's uncle, a canon of Notre Dame. There may be a lesson here.

See also BECKHAM, VICTORIA; LANCELOT AND GUINEVERE.

Henry VIII (1491–1547). Chiefly remembered now for his six marriages, Henry was in fact an accomplished administrator, and, through Thomas Cromwell, his highly able minister, laid the foundations for the modern civil service. (For a more cautious view as to Cromwell's role in this process, *see* ELTON, BEN.)

See also BOLEYN, ANNE.

Hervey, Lady Isabella (b.1980). Younger sister of Lady Victoria Hervey. The rumour that the siblings have not spoken since Lady Victoria posted it on her website that Lady Isabella's name is an anagram of 'shyly revealed labia' is entirely without foundation.

See also BEST, CALUM; HERVEY, LADY VICTORIA FREDERICA.

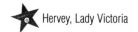
Hervey, Lady Victoria Frederica (b.1976). Beaky posh tart and *soi-disant* It Girl. Older sister of Lady Isabella HERVEY and half sister of the 7th Marquess of Bristol (1955–99). The 7th Marquess was a homosexual heroin addict who ordered up rent boys in the middle of the night as if they were pizzas. Their father was the 6th Marquess, known as 'Victor Hervey, Mayfair's Playboy No. 1'. On one occasion he drove his car into a taxi rank to see whether the vehicles would buckle like a concertina. They did. After boarding school, Lady Victoria went to work for Michael Winner, thus gaining valuable experience of how common people behave. She was already demonstrating an ability to get her priorities right. A dinner date with Prince Andrew finished after the first course when she left for an engagement at a lap-dancing club. Various sorties into the boutique business have ended in disappointment, but she has made her mark on the public imagination by clubbing without her clothes and snogging Paris HILTON. Tara Palmer-Tomkinson once called Lady Victoria 'cringey and tragic', but would probably snog her anyway. In a 1996 interview, Lady Victoria told a reporter: 'I used to think my title would count against me in life, but I now realize it will be a great help.'

Hewitt, Major James (b.1959). Royal love rat. The rumour has it that during the 1991 Gulf War his men followed him 'out of a vague sense of curiosity'. Diana, Princess of Wales, slept with him, but she'd sleep with anyone, and anywhere: in service lifts, in doorways, up chimneys. Even Auberon Waugh packed a condom in his pocket when he lunched with her at Kensington Palace. Hewitt was nicknamed Timeshare by his friends as he simul-taneously swore his love for Diana, proposed to his girlfriend Emma Stewardson and had a fling with a Bosnian refugee, Aida Basic. 'He used to tear my clothes off,' reported Miss Basic, 'carry me into the bathroom and take me against the plumbing.' Among his present celebrity initiatives, Major Hewitt now wrestles for ITV in the early evening under the cognomen 'Upper-class Clarence'.

At least one love-rat insider has pointed out that while Hewitt has been accused of many things, being upper-class isn't one of them. His father was in trade; his grandparents in service.

See also MAJOR JAMES HEWITT OFFERS FOREPLAY.

Hilton, Paris (b.1981). Looks like a shivering whippet dipped in bleach. But in all other respects, the Diana Cooper of her day. She is the great-granddaughter of hotel magnate Conrad Hilton, granddaughter of Barron Hilton and grand-niece of Nicholas Conrad Hilton (Elizabeth Taylor's first husband.) In November 2003 a private video of Miss Hilton locked into a variety of strangely unimaginative sexual positions with her boyfriend, Rick Solomon, was circulated on the internet. Her father was highly embarrassed, as was natural. His daughter had filmed the video in the top suite at the Marriott Hotel. Happily, family harmony has

been restored. To make amends, Paris filmed a livelier video, this time at one of her father's hotels. She subsequently appeared in the Reality TV show *The Simple Life* in which she and her best friend, Nicole Richie (the daughter of the ballad singer, Lionel Richie), tried to live like farm hands, attempting to muck out horses and, hilariously, to eat carbohydrates. Paris's first book – *Confessions of an Heiress: A Tongue in Chic Peek Behind the Pose!* – was published in America by Fireside in 2004. HarperCollins are believed to have stepped in with a seven-figure offer for the British rights. The 'book' contains such sensible pieces of advice as: 'Never, ever wake up before ten. Never go to bed before three. Normal hours are for normal people.' Ms Hilton, clearly an abnormal person, charges $200,000 for appearing for 20 minutes at parties. 'If it's in Japan, I get more,' she claims. Paris is engaged to Greek shipping heir, Paris Lastis. It has been said of her that she has the merit at least of making Tara Palmer-Tomkinson seem like a useful member of society.

Hislop, Ian (b.1961). Those who had previously admired the editor of *Private Eye* for his speed with the smart riposte were disappointed by his failure to support his friend and colleague, Angus DEAYTON, when the latter was dismissed from *Have I Got News For You?* Deayton's offence had been to enjoy himself in a Manchester hotel room. Why was Hislop so disloyal? Could it be that he was irritated not just by Deayton's attractive appearance but, more importantly, by the fact that, unlike Hislop himself, he had mastered the most important of a comedian's many skills: the art of comic

timing.

See also NEW YEAR RESOLUTIONS.

Holbrough, Charlotte (b.1979). A WPC in the South Wales Police who scooped £1 million as the first winner of *Survivor UK*. Dubbed 'Charlotte the Harlot' for no better reason than that she apparently had oral sex up a tree with a fellow contestant, she certainly had the last laugh. A young woman of heartbreaking beauty, she refuted the theory that the viewing public will only vote for those of limited intelligence and unprepossessing appearance (*see* ADAMS, HELEN; GOODY, JADE; KATONA, KERRY; PASQUALE, JOE). After her triumph, she returned to her husband, also a policeman, and hasn't been heard of since. She hasn't even written a book for HarperCollins or announced an ambition to star as Roxy in *Chicago*. A mystery.

Hoppen, Kelly (b.1960). You want a distressed ceramic fondue dish? You want to turn your window box into a Japanese sand garden? You get Kelly. Or rather, you get Kelly's book, since Kelly is running a worldwide furnishings empire as well as bonking a premier league footballer (Sol Campbell) so she won't have time to install it herself. Kelly, who looks like a soigné Charlie Dimmock, or a cut-price Nicole Kidman, depending on how close you get, specializes in restrained, tasteful, neutral décor with lots and lots of taupe.

Horsley, Sebastian (b.1962). Formerly employed by L'Homme, an escort agency accommodating rich, randy women of a certain age, and a composer of slaughterhouse prose for the now defunct *Erotic Review*. Horsley currently poses as a performance artist and self-advertising dandy. He walks round Soho in a pink suit and is rumoured to be writing a book for HarperCollins. In September 2004 he surprised Radio 4 listeners by announcing that he visited a different prostitute every afternoon. In spite of the provocation his appearance must be to other Soho residents, he is beaten up on a regular basis only by tiny knob-headed Scotsmen on visits south and by tarts when he attempts to smuggle his crack pipe into their apartments.

Howard, Michael (b.1940). Slippery immigrant with an id wee of prinincing wids.

See also BONKING BORIS.

Humiliating the afflicted. In September 2004, Mr Arthur Grover, the serial complainer, took issue with the producers of *The X-Factor,* a talent show featuring, as Celebrity Judges, Simon Cowell ('Mr Nasty'), Louis Walsh, a pop impresario, and Mrs Sharon Osbourne, the wife of Mr 'Ozzy' Osbourne, properly John Michael Osbourne, the rock-and-roll singer dubbed 'The Prince of Darkness'. Mr Grover had been offended by the fact that the more deluded of the contestants had clearly been drummed up simply to be mocked. He suggested that even better peak-time family viewing would be provided by a show, provisionally entitled *Take a Pot Shot at a Paraplegic*, in which the severely disabled were lined up like coconuts at a funfair, thereafter being targeted at a distance. The winner of the contest would be the Celebrity who could knock the largest number of crippled old folk out of their wheelchairs. To his surprise the producers of *The X-Factor* did not get back to him, but Mr Grover has since sold the idea to another

production company. The programme is scheduled for Christmas 2005. Sharon Osbourne is the daughter of Don Arden, a thuggish promoter in the popular music field once described as the 'Al Capone of pop'. Mrs Osbourne, herself an agent, is, by contrast, a flirty woman with a squeaky voice. Her husband 'Ozzy', who once tried to strangle her, is among the acts she represents.

See also CHANNEL 4; COWELL, SIMON; GREAT TELEVISION; OS-BOURNE, JOHN MICHAEL 'OZZY'.

Humpty Dumpty (*fl.c.*1820). Generally considered to be the first Celebrity Victim of the ATKINS diet. The story of his falling off a wall is untrue and was probably invented to save his dietician's reputation. Grossly overweight, Humpty Dumpty was engaged in his daily circuit training when he suddenly went spplattttt like a wet shopping bag.

Hunniford, Gloria (b.1940). That rare phenomenon, a Celebrity who has never forgotten who she really is. She's always been like this, unfortunately.

See also WINTON, DALE.

Hunter, Rachel (b.1970). Suburban clotheshorse who has done as well as anyone could with the looks of a Takapuna shop girl. Formerly married to Rod Stewart, she responded to the news that he was marrying again with all the grace and charm we have come to expect from Antipodeans. She looked her successor up and down and said 'Is it a man or is it a woman? Have you felt its crotch?' Rachel recently hosted a press event to announce that she had become a patron of Born Free, a charity that helps lions and gorillas. The press corps, unmoved by pictures of lion cubs, shouted 'WHAZ ROBBIE LIKE IN BED, RACH?' – a reference, it is thought, to Rachel's short fling with Robbie Williams. Hunter, a burly blond, recently presented the show *Make Me a Supermodel*, otherwise known as Give Me An Eating Disorder.

Hurley, Elizabeth (b.1966). Actress and model. Many point to the night she wore 'that dress' as the moment when she achieved 'A-list' status in Tinsel Town. Not so. It was after Hugh Grant revealed that at her point of crisis she made a noise like a live crayfish being dropped into a pan of boiling water.

'Hutch', properly **Leslie T. Hutchinson** (1892–1963). Cocktail-bar baritone whose style was thought to have influenced Chester Harriott, the father of the family entertainer, Ainsley Harriott (*see* AINSLEY!). Throughout the 1930s, 40s and 50s, 'Hutch' entertained the aristocracy at fashionable London nightclubs such as Quaglino's and the Allegro. His rendition of 'I Could Have Danced All Night' from Lerner and Loewe's musical *My Fair Lady* was a particular favourite among postwar débutantes. Quaglino's has since become one of the less agreeable restaurants in Sir Terence Conran's ever-expanding chain. According to Celebrity Chef, Gordon Ramsay, it dispenses school meals in a room resembling the eating area of an ocean-going liner *c.*1930.

I

Icarus. Arguably the first Celebrity. Hit the headlines in major burn-out. Rumoured to be alive and well and living above a bar in Mykonos. He is a frequent visitor to Diana's tea-towel boutique.

Iconic, so. A term that Celebrity Pundits fall back on when they wish to indicate that something or someone is important even though they are not sure why. Scarlett Johansson was the 'iconic' face of 2004. The Libertines are an 'iconic' band. Bridget Jones's oversize knickers are 'iconic'. What will become iconic next? Don't bet against the Andrex PUPPY.

If all else fails, diversify. What every canny Celebrity knows. This maxim is responsible for the Cliff Richard 'Miss You Nights' perfume range, the Mark Birley deodorant, the Kilroy-Silk pantyhose collection, Twiggy cosmetics, and the Victor Sebriakoff yoga mat. And who can blame them, frankly? It's better than taking in paying Antipodeans. Send all cheques, plus postage and packaging, to: PO Box Strapped For Cash, Hasbeenville, La-la-land.

Ifan, Marged ferch (1696–1793). Welsh harpist and wrestler. Oral tradition describes her as a large and exceptionally strong woman who could wrestle any man to the ground. Young men in the district treated her with respect even when she was 70. Her husband, the harpist Richard Morris (d.1786), was no match for her, which suggests that it was she who courted him. She is said to have given Morris two severe beatings: after the first, he married her; after the second, he joined the Methodists. She is thought to have been a role model for Christine HAMILTON.

Il Divo. Four smirking lads bringing pop opera to the masses. Dubbed 'the Phwoar Tenors', the group, whose repertoire includes 'My Way' sung in Italian, was assembled by Simon COWELL after a two-year search. Mr Cowell has described the group as his finest achievement. Others have argued that this accolade should go to the Robson and Jerome Tribute Night that Cowell presented at the Civic Hospitality Rooms, Purley, Surrey, in September 2004.

Ill-judged attempts to become Celebrities by supposedly serious people. Will Self participating awkwardly in Vic 'n' Bob's *Shooting Stars.* Leader of the Conservative Party expressing support for tear-jerking Scousers before Champions League final. Erstwhile Conservative MPs wearing fishnet stockings in a touring production of *The Rocky Horror Picture Show*, later showing off on *QI,* Stephen Fry's bum-sucking quiz show. Germaine Greer talking about her bits on *Celebrity Big Brother.* What's to come? Cherie Blair displaying 10

Downing Street on *Through the Keyhole*? Norman Foster and Quinlan Terry on *Changing Rooms*? Professor Susan Greenfield, Doris Lessing and AS Byatt in a special one-off edition of *The Golden Girls*? Baroness Mary Warnock on *Grumpy Old Women*? Roger Scruton on *Animal Hospital*? Osama bin Laden on *What's My Line?*

Ingram, Major Charles (b.1959). Fishy ex-army officer in regiment once commanded by Field Marshal Sir Claude Auchinleck. Cashiered after attempting to swindle £1 million from producers of *Who Wants To Be A Millionaire?* by complicated system of coughs supplied by educated friend in audience. Having failed in this ambition, he has prospered in Reality Television. Last seen in Channel 4's *The Games,* succumbing to an unpleasant up-and-under applied by Mr Gay UK in semi-finals of wrestling event. Mr Gay UK (real name, Jarrod Batchelor) lost in the final when he was locked in a head scissors by Charlie Dimmock, the burly gardener. Mr Gay UK was unconscious for six days, but survived. Gorgeous pouting glamour model Jodie Marsh (32DD) blamed her poor showing in the high hurdles on her mishap with the KY Jelly and industrial putty (*see* FEBRUARY CELEBRITY *FAUX PAS*). The Auk must be turning in his grave.

Ingredients, the best. Flown in daily from the south of France, lovingly prepared by Gordon Ramsay, served to a party of bankers, digested, evacuated and thereafter flushed by a system of drains and ducts (*see* BAZALGETTE, PETER) into the North Sea along with the rest of Endemol's effluence – *Big Brother, The Salon, Changing Rooms, Fame Academy, Ground Force.*

Insiders, celebrity. Forever writing calumnous dictionaries or fawning memoirs:

- ✎ *I Danced for Mussolini* – Sethma Caspers
- ✎ *I was Monty's Double* – Meyrick Clifton-James
- ✎ *I knew 3,000 Lunatics* – Victor R. Small, MD
- ✎ *I was Elvis's Secret Woman* – Gwen Jones
- ✎ *Chef to Queen Victoria: the Recipes* – Charles Elmé Francatelli
- ✎ *I was Saddam's Son* – Latif Yahia
- ✎ *I was Quisling's Secretary* – Franklin Knudsen
- ✎ *I was Hitler's Maid* – Pauline Kohler
- ✎ *I was Jacqueline Kennedy's Dressmaker* – Mini Rhea
- ✎ *I was Keith Richards's Drug Dealer* – Tony Sanchez
- ✎ *I was Ena Sharples' Father* – Tony Warren
- ✎ *Woody and Mia: the Nanny's Tale* – Kristi Groteke
- ✎ *I was Bono's Doppelgänger* – Neil McCormick
- ✎ *I was Roosevelt's Shadow* – Michael F. Reilly
- ✎ *I was Stalin's Bodyguard* – Achmed Amba
- ✎ *Major Major: Memories of an Older Brother* – Terry Major-Ball.

Intensely human. A neurotic mess.

Interchangeable pop babes explained in full at last.

- ⇔ Claire Richards (blonde Leo from Steps)
- ⇔ Faye Tozer (bright blonde Scorpio from Steps)
- ⇔ Kimberly Walsh (dirty-looking Scorpio from Girls Aloud)
- ⇔ Nadine Coyle (blonde Scorpio from Girls Aloud)
- ⇔ Sarah Harding (dark Scorpio from Girls Aloud)
- ⇔ Nicola Roberts (redhead Libra from Girls Aloud)
- ⇔ Jessica Taylor (choker-wearing Cancer from Liberty X)
- ⇔ Kelli Young (black, serious Gemini from Liberty X).

Interchangeable Pre-Raphaelite babes explained in full at last.

⇔ Maria Cassavetti (Greek muse to Burne-Jones)
⇔ Annie Miller (barmaid and muse to Holman Hunt)
⇔ Fanny Cornforth (Cockney redhead and mistress of Rossetti)
⇔ Dorothy Dene (auburn-haired muse to Lord Leighton)
⇔ Alexa Wilding (dressmaker and muse to Rossetti).

Interchangeable soap babes explained in full at last.

⇔ Nikki Sanderson (dimpled *Corrie* star)
⇔ Jenny James (toothy *Corrie* star)
⇔ Suranne Jones (worried-looking *Corrie* star)
⇔ Tina O'Brien (tiny *Corrie* star)
⇔ Michelle Ryan (chinny *Enders* star)
⇔ Jill Halfpenny (pronounced Ha'penny – pouty *Enders* star)
⇔ Kim Medcalf (pert *Enders* star)
⇔ Lucy Benjamin (frazzled *Enders* star)
⇔ Charlie Brooks (*Enders* star with Neanderthal forehead)
⇔ Amy Nuttall (bewildered *Emmerdale* star)
⇔ Sheree Murphy (sensible *Emmerdale* star).

Ivy, The. Celebrity restaurant. Once the preferred meeting place for theatrical grandees. Misattributed anecdotes abound. On one occasion, the great comedienne, Hermione GINGOLD, was mortified to discover that she was wearing the same hat as Dame Sybil Thorndike, sitting at the next table. Leaning across, she tapped Dame Sybil on the arm, pointed to her hat and roared with laughter. Dame Sybil responded with a frosty smile, and continued with her lunch. Surprised by this reaction, Gingold spent the rest of lunch pointing to Dame Sybil's hat and laughing. Dame Sybil's manner remained icy. It was not until she got home that Gingold discovered that she herself was not wearing a hat that day.

It was at the Ivy that Coral Browne was asked by Noel, or possibly Ivor, whether a distinguished actress had survived an operation. 'Indeed,' replied Coral at the top of her voice. 'They opened her up but all they found was Olive Harding's gardening glove.' Miss Harding, a formidable woman, was Miss Browne's agent.

On one occasion, Sir John Gielgud was surprised to find that Sir Alec Guinness had joined his table. 'Oh my God,' said Sir John. 'For a terrible moment I mistook you for that frightful bore Alec Guinness.' 'I am Alec Guinness,' said Sir Alec. 'I meant a different Alec Guinness, of course,' said Sir John. These days you are likely to find Michael Parkinson sitting on one side of you and Denise Van Outen on the other.

Jagger, Bianca (b.1950). Born Bianca Perez Morena de Macias, in Nicaragua. Party queen turned humanitarian campaigner. Met Mick Jagger in Paris, where she was a student, and he a tax exile. Once tried to impress a UN delegation in Geneva by riding into their conference on a white horse, wearing a zoot suit.

Jagger, Jade Jezebel (b.1972). Daughter of Sir Mick and his first wife, Bianca. Resident of Notting Hill and Ibiza. Fortunate person. Looks like a Hawaiian hoola girl. Said to design jewellery, most recently for Garrards. Hobbies include boyfriends (Josh Astor, Piers Jackson, Ben Elliott, Dan MacMillan, Pharrell Williams) and babies (Assissi, Amber). Two years ago she was said to be setting up a chain of eco-friendly hotels in beauty spots around the world. The project has not been heard of since.

Jagger, Lizzie (b.1984). Daughter of Sir Mick and Texan female impersonator Jerry Hall. Best friend of Leah Wood, Ms Jagger once dated John Lennon's son Sean. 'It is clear,' say researchers from Brokeback University, Memphis, 'that Ms Jagger is suffering from the rare but debilitating condition, nepophilia, characterized by an obsession with famous people's children. In her case, the condition is magnified by auto-nepophilia. This disease has one inevitable but tragic outcome: marriage to Lisa-Marie Presley.' In the meantime, Ms Jagger models for the cosmetics house Lancôme, quite a coup for such an unfortunate-looking young lady.

Jagger, Sir Mick (b.1943). Shrunken head with a knighthood. In 1970 he said, 'I'd rather be dead than singing "Satisfaction" when I'm 45.' Today, he's 63 and still singing it. In a bid to restore his leathery complexion, he lives on a diet of milky-skinned virginal girls.

See also DAHL, SOPHIE.

Jet. Celebrities 'jet'; ordinary people 'fly'. As was noted by Salter, De Santos and Horrocks-Taylor (*The Celebrity Syndrome: Notes Towards a Diagnosis*, Sussex University Press, 2004), 'Celebrities jet into Heathrow looking tanned and relaxed.' Ordinary people fly into Luton after a two-week break in Benidorm with sunstroke, dysentery and the remains of their transported breakfast products and toilet rolls.

Jobs. Ordinary people have jobs. Celebrities have schedules.

John, Elton, properly **Reginald Kenneth Dwight** (b.1947). Ena Sharples look-alike but without her dress sense. If he didn't exist, Barry Humphries would have had to invent him. Seen here arriving with partner David Furnish at Taiwan airport in September 2004, the excitable gay plonker screamed 'You're all ugly fucking pigs!' at fans waiting to take his photograph.

Johnson, Boris. *See* BONKING BORIS.

Jones, Bridget (b.1995). Maritally obsessed dimwit. Her belief that a woman's destiny is to be saved by a Knight in shining Armani may have set feminism back a hundred years. *See also* ICONIC, SO.

June Celebrity *Faux Pas*

Topless model **Jakki Degg** loses out to fellow tabloid scorcher **Leilani Dowding** in the final of *Page 3 The Weakest Link Special.* Stumped by killer question, 'What is the capital of Spain? Madrid? Or Madras?' **Anne Robinson** attempts caustic comment but is rendered silent by recent botox treatment, which has left face as immobile as a supermarket chicken straight from the freezer. Robinson drops 10 rungs on Celebrity *Faux Pas* Ladder to general applause.

During a photocall at a charity polo match, a gust of wind blows **Nell McAndrew's** skirt up, revealing a grey supersize pair of pants with a control top.

Natasha Kaplinsky hears her name called out at the Art Achievement Awards Ceremony. She rises to her feet, kisses her boyfriend, leaps onto the podium – and is told to please sit down. The award is in fact a posthumous lifetime achievement tribute to Wassily Kandinsky.

Charlotte Church decides to become a mime artiste. She tells her life story through this medium in a show directed by Steven Berkoff. It is not a critical success.

Jeffrey Archer attends 4 June celebrations at Eton College. Claiming to have been a 'wet bob' (1953–8), he enters the old boys' coxless pairs with his son William. He and William are steered to victory by a dwarf hidden in the boat's stern. Later, he is disqualified and escorted off the premises. By royal charter granted by Henry VI, the dwarf is then used as the ball in commemoration Wall Game watched by the Queen.

Jayne Middlemiss interviews the Dalai Lama. She asks him whether he's ever considered a carb-free diet.

Jones, Norah (b.1980). Prettyish daughter of Ravi Shankar. Filed under jazz, she enjoys a certain amount of cred. An alternative view is that her easy-listening vibe is the missing link between Carole King and Tony Bennett. Her sound casts a warm glow round your living room, but then so does a lampshade – and you wouldn't pay £30 to sit in the Clyde Auditorium, Glasgow, and listen to a lampshade for two hours.

Jones, Steve (b.1978). STUD MUFFIN reporter much to Celebrities' taste. When the Welsh T4 presenter interviewed Pamela Anderson in 2003 he retired with her to her suite at the Savoy Hotel and didn't come out for a week. The ambitious cub reporter also swapped numbers after an interview with Angelina Jolie, and has been lusted after by US pop babe Ashlee Simpson. Granted, he is an unambiguously handsome young man, rather in the mould of the late film actor, Errol Flynn. Flynn was born in Australia and what was thought to have been twins turned out to be the infant actor and his penis. This may or may not be significant.

Jones, Vinnie (b.1966). Soccer player and film actor. A hard man by his own account, Jones was a footballer of negligible talent. His conduct as a player was a disgrace. The short journey from making a fool of himself on the football field to doing the same in films such *Lock, Stock and Two Smoking Barrels* (Guy Ritchie, 1998) has not proved difficult. Judged to have 'screen presence', Jones now divides his time between London and Los Angeles, appearing on *Ready Steady Cook* and examining his priorities.

Jonsson, Ulrika (b.1967). Swedish trollop and weather woman, celebrated for fucking footballers and Gladiators, some called Rhinoceros, others not. Now happily married to Mr Wright.

July Celebrity *Faux Pas*

Vanessa Feltz takes part in her children's sports day. In the obstacle race, she gets stuck in a drain and has to be rescued by the fire brigade.

Jeffrey Archer, wearing last year's rented Moss Bros topper with the price-tag sticking out, gatecrashes the Royal Enclosure at Ascot. Repossession men collar him in the Pimm's tent and take away his hat.

Jayne Middlemiss interviews Noam Chomsky. She asks him whether he watches *The Osbournes*.

Invited to a dinner party, **Clive Anderson** gets his secretary to ring his hostess to check out the other guests. Even Tina Brown never did that, and she's the daughter of a film producer.

Martine McCutcheon, trying to crack the American market, is overheard telling a waiter: 'I'm the Madonna of the UK.'

Stephen Fry attends a Buckingham Palace garden party. He buttonholes the Queen, questions her, quotes Kafka, quotes 'Plum' Wodehouse. 'Surely it was the immortal Jeeves who said…' He deploys ten words that he has memorized that morning from the dictionary. He shows her his personal organizer. He shows her a hole in his trousers. He asks her which of Peter Cook's surreal flights of fancy is her favourite. 'Mine was the occasion when he told little Dudley that the worst job he'd ever had was removing lobsters from Jayne Mansfield's arse. Sheer genius.' He turns to the Duke of Edinburgh. 'And whose Widmerpool are you?' He eventually leaves with a pocketful of sandwiches. Fry drops ten places on the Celebrity *Faux Pas* Ladder.

Jordan, properly **Katie Price** (b.1978). Unfortunate-looking glamour model. A deformed torso on sparrow legs. Prior to her appearance on *I'm a Celebrity, Get Me Out Of Here* (*see* ANDRE, PETER), doctors warned the busty slapper that if jungle leeches attached themselves to her satirically enhanced bosoms they might explode (Sky News, 22 January 2004). The story that her silicone implants have now been classified as potential WMDs by UN weapons inspectors may be apocryphal.

In August 2005, it was announced that Random House had signed up the pneumatic sexpot in a two-novel deal. Jordan's prose has frequently been compared to Nabokov's. 'Who's he?' queried the hotly tipped authoress, 'He sounds like a nob.'

See also SLANGING MATCHES, THE MOTHER OF ALL.

Jubin, Shell (b.1983). While participating in *Big Brother 5* – from which she emerged in fourth place – Shell discovered that she had been awarded a 1st-class degree from Aberdeen University in the History of Art. She sweetly celebrated this achievement by taking off all her clothes and running around the compound. 'Thank goodness it wasn't Michelle Bass who had been awarded a degree,' commented Davina McCall, for once echoing the nation's feelings.

Just like you and me. Terrifying column in *OK!* magazine which, week by week, sets out to prove that you are just like Amy Nuttall, say, or Claire SWEENEY. Claire spends seven hours in make-up every day, just like you! Claire has hysterics when she doesn't get nominated for a TV Quick Award, just like you! Claire flosses with hairs from the Devil's head, just like you!

Kaplinsky, Natasha (b.1972). Equine TV presenter, alleged by the *Daily Mail* to subsist on a diet of steel filings, sequins and other women's fiancés. In order to get a more accurate picture of her daily diet, it might be sensible to examine her CV. The daughter of Polish-South African Professor Raphael Kaplinsky, she grew up in Kenya. When she moved to the UK aged six, she saw a television for the first time. 'When I saw this magic box,' she recalls, 'I was absolutely transfixed, and I just knew I had to work in television – it could be anything, so long as I could be on that screen.'

After an unhappy career at Oxford University (she was studying under Tom PAULIN) she progressed quickly to presenting the main evening news for Meridian TV, aided by her mentor Lloyd Bracey. (Some choose to put 'mentor' in inverted commas.) She powered on to ITV London, Sky News and BBC Breakfast. Then she was invited to take part in *Strictly Come Dancing*. 'I fought tooth and nail to avoid participating,' she says. 'I did everything in the world, including trying to break my legs.' She must think we're stupid. In the end she foxtrotted so beautifully that she won the show. During the filming, her dancing partner Brendan Cole left his fiancée Camilla Dallerup, who had performed with David Dickinson. Everyone thought the worst. And ratings rocketed. The following year she was on our screens ushering in the New Year of 2005, the most prestigious slot in TV. At Madame Tussaud's they are currently melting down Esther Rantzen and pouring her into a Kaplinsky-shaped mould.

Katona, Kerry (b.1981). 'Good evening. The time is 10.30 and I'm Huw Edwards. Here are tonight's headlines: "He's Frantastic Says Queen of the Jungle!" Troubled pop babe Kerry Katona is flying off for a sunshine break with TV jungle hunk Fran Cosgrave – leaving the kids in the temporary care of estranged husband Brian McFadden. Brian will be thinking, "Good riddance!" He's just swapped Kerry for gorgeous Aussie songbird, Delta Goodrem, formerly the girlfriend of Australian tennis hunk Mark Philippoussis. Extraordinary. Would you dump Mark for a boy band wuss? No? Nor would I. Anyway, Kerry's sorted (excuse the vernacular; the Director General wants us to be "more street"). Last night, a Kerry Katona insider claimed that Cosgrave is falling for the blonde cracker. Curvy Kerry, 24, has been boosted by daily visits from Fran while recovering at the Priory Clinic from the breakdown of her marriage. Fran, 26, has a baby with Kerry's former Atomic Kitten bandmate Natasha Hamilton. Are you following this? I can't make head nor tail of it. Never mind. The hunk – that will be Fran – has been sending Kerry flowers at the clinic and keeping her spirits up with texts and phone calls. Now Kerry has agreed to fly off to Spain for a holiday with her Jungle Hunk, leaving love-cheat Brian to look after Molly, three, and 20-month-old Lilly Sue. That's what she thinks. You and I know he'll be with Delta.'

Kensit, Patsy (b.1968). Patsy's godfather was Reggie Kray, the legendary East End gangster. Mythology has it that when he leaned over her cradle, he said, 'She's a cracker and all.' And so Patsy proved to be: pouty, unflinching, with a consistently sceptical expression. Her first role on television was in a Bird's Eye Peas commercial, in which she raised one eyebrow to great effect despite being only four years old. She then appeared as Mia Farrow's daughter in *The Great Gatsby*. Over thirty more film roles followed, including the meaty part of Crepe Suzette in the adaptation of Colin MacInnes's novel *Absolute Beginners*.

Patsy, who fronted the rock band Eighth Wonder to some success in Japan, is drawn to rock star men, three of whom she married: Dan Donovan of Big Audio Dynamite, Jim Kerr of Simple Minds, and Liam Gallagher of Oasis. She found Gallagher when she was looking for a man 'with a bit of a brain'. She got exactly that with half-wit Liam. Since their divorce, Patsy has been subject to a good deal of stress. In order to keep her career, she had to keep her figure, and in order to keep her figure, she had to risk losing her nose by sticking to her favourite method of weight control. But the loss of her nose would have brought about the loss of her career. Happily, *Emmerdale* came to the rescue with a role for Patsy as rich bitch Sadie King.

See also BABIES' NAMES, SHOCKING CELEBRITY.

Kettners. According to royal insiders, Camilla Parker Bowles's first words when she met Prince Charles were 'My great grandmother did it with your great grandfather. How about it?' She was referring to Edward VII and the woman who was probably the favourite of his many mistresses – Mrs Keppel, properly Alice Frederika Edmonstone, the wife of the Hon. George Keppel, an officer in the Gordon Highlanders. It was the king's habit to dine Mrs Keppel in a private room at Kettners in Romilly Street, Soho, now the flagship restaurant in the popular Pizza Express chain. From tea time onwards, and in deference, perhaps, to its former eminence, a pianist plays dance tunes in the strict tempo style. The restaurant's relaxed atmosphere has made it a favourite meeting place for cutting-edge lexicographers working in collaborative tandem for the Orion Publishing Group. On most days, Abi Titmuss and Keith Waterhouse, Tania Do-Nascimento and Dennis Norden, Katie Price and Peregrine Worsthorne, Kenzie and Professor Germaine Greer, *Big Bruv*'s Nush Novak and Lord Deedes, Johann Hari and Marcelle D'Argy-Smith are to be seen at adjoining tables, heads bowed over work in progress.

Khan, Jemima (b.1974). Born Jemima Marcelle Goldsmith, daughter of Sir James Goldsmith, the late asset stripper celebrated for his fear of rubber bands. Jemima is a statuesque beauty labouring under the weight of too much hair and a compulsion to be a Good Person. This was characterized in childhood by a concern for the welfare of ponies, and later by concern for the women of Afghanistan. At 21 she abandoned her attempts to gain a degree in English literature at Bristol University and instead married the celebrated Pakistani cricketing all-rounder, Imran Khan, of whom her father Sir James said: 'He'll make an excellent first husband.'

Jemima converted to Islam, changed her name to Jamila, and moved to a cramped flat adjoining Imran's father's house in Lahore. She won cheers on the campaign trail in 2002 when she spoke in Urdu to entreat women to vote for her husband's Tehrik-e-Insaaf party, and was further honoured by having a range of condiments named after her, including Jemima's Tangy Ketchup. She also launched Jemima Khan Designs, a fashion range described by the *Scotsman* newspaper as 'a wonder to behold', but one which was shortly discontinued. A son, Sulaiman, was born, followed by another, Kasim. Then, seven years after leaving Bristol University, she suddenly returned to become the only under-graduate in history whose dissertation title was reported in the pages of *Hello!* magazine.

To quash speculation in her husband's country she took out a full-page advertisement in several Pakistani newspapers, declaring: 'It is not true to say that Imran and I are having difficulties in our marriage. This is a temporary arrangement and, inshallah [God willing], I will be coming back to Pakistan once my studies are completed. Besides, without in any way wishing to disparage the culture of the Western world, into which I was born, I am more than willing to forego the transient pleasures derived from alcohol and nightclubs.' By 2004, however, she was back on the razz, hiccupping out of Annabel's on her 30th birthday in a gold strapless frock in the company of the floppy-haired British film star, Hugh GRANT. In photographs the pair look as if they both know something no one else does. Perhaps they had hidden a kipper under Imran's bed – which might explain the man's persistent expression of distaste. Their divorce was announced shortly thereafter.

See also GOLDSMITH, LADY ANNABEL.

Kidd, Jodie (b.1978). Gaunt toff who's simply mad about polo. Model turned divot-stomper. From stick-insect centrefold to galloping centrefield. Dotty totty with a mission to bring polo to the lives of 'everyday people' – even the really poor ones who have to muck out their own ponies. Host of many lavish polo galas, open to mere Members of the General Public. But would you pay £200 for a ticket? Would you pay for a smack in the mouth? It is predicted that, in scenes reminiscent of the storming of the Bastille, the seething mob will one day invade her polo gala and hang her upside down from a flagpole in the Laurent-Perrier tent. Alternatively, she may one day star in a TV adaptation of a Jilly Cooper novel. No prizes for guessing which one.

King of seam to dancing queen, from. *See* GOUGH, DARREN.

Kisses, Celebrity.

- Red carpet fraudulent ones.
- Back-stage pussycat ones.
- Imaginary ones (when stars blow them at a make-believe fan situated just to the left and behind the press corps).
- Judas ones. Entirely motivated by aggression, e.g. when Sadie FROST bumps into Sienna MILLER at Glastonbury.
- Film-set ones that are far more passionate than required and go on long after the director has called 'Cut!' – the beginnings of adultery.

- Chat-show gay ones. Stephen FRY plants a great wet one on Russell Crowe. Everyone's embarrassed except Crowe.
- Ones with lips pulled back over teeth like rubber fenders (*see* ASH, LESLIE).
- French, tongue-diving bonding ones used in Mafia, Royal Marine, Masonic and Benchers' initiation ceremonies.
- Teeth-clacking ones (as when Esther RANTZEN meets Janet STREET-PORTER).
- Ones between footballers (especially back in the hotel).
- The financial adviser (between the toes).

Klass, Myleene (b.1978). Tart who tinkles. Alternatively, and depending on your point of view, a glamorous pianist working in the cross-over field. But would Myleene rather be sitting at the piano or writhing on top of it in a torn vest? You may have to visit her steamy personal website and download her videography to find out. The classically trained musician has a strong pedigree: her grandfather was head of the Vienna Opera; her musician mother hails from the Philippines.

When she appeared on the game show *Pop Stars* in 2003, her former teachers were disappointed that she had swapped semi-breves for semi-nudity. Hear'Say followed, and the fastest-selling album of all time, but Myleene hated it. Particularly, she hated fellow popstrel Kym MARSH, whom, to this day, she accuses of looking like Shrek. Touring was misery. She used to call room service just so she'd have someone to talk to. You can see why the weight piled on. 'The more people commented on the weight I was putting on, the more I ate. Just to show them I was not going to conform.'

But now she's solo, things are better, says her official biography: 'Her fast food hell and eating and piling on the pounds because she was miserable days are over. She's vivid, happy and flawless.' The

ex-boyfriend trying to blackmail her is over too, which has to help. But what helped most of all was crying on the Frank Skinner show, which made her famous.

What's up now for this bundle of neuroses, talent and bad taste? With her soft-classical solo album *Moving On* nominated for a Brit and going gold, she appears to be in business. It includes everything from Bach to Braveheart, because, as Myleene wisely says, we all know more about classical music than we think: 'Everyone remembers the ET theme, but they don't realize it's classical music.' Myleene, according to her website, is 'full of molten emotions. It is a banquet of them. Better than that, it doesn't have a label. It is unexpected and epic.'

L

Lagerfeld, Karl (b.1940). Scary fashion designer who never takes his dark glasses off and hates all women. A very good friend of Janet Street-Porter, who has amusingly dubbed him 'Lagerlout'. Recently hunted down by crippled women semi-paralysed by his latest couture item, the STILETTO PANTS. They chopped off his ponytail and sewed his elbow to his arse.

Lamour, Gwendoline (b.1979). London's premier fan dancer. A burlesque star whose ivory skin, hourglass figure and on-line merchandise shop make her the UK's answer to Dita Von Teese. Ms Von Teese has in fact sent her a perfumed notelet asking her to desist from her 'tribute act'. Ms Lamour is thought to be plotting a revenge assassination attempt involving a chandelier and one silk stocking.

Lancaster, Penny (b.1978). Lingerie model who married well. (Don't say 'Well, what?', it's rude.) Caught public attention when she performed triumphant 'I got 'im' dance at an Awards ceremony, widely taken as a Big Bird tribute in honour of her husband, Little Bird (a.k.a. Rod Stewart). Rod's ex, Rachel Hunter, watches, her chin wobbling. Both Rachel and Penny model lingerie and are fundamentally interchangeable. L'Ultimo, the lingerie chain, catches onto this, and, in a winning publicity coup, fires Penny and in her place hires... Rachel Hunter! Justice is done, virtue rewarded. Thongs of praise. Penny down ten places on Celebrity *Faux Pas* Ladder.

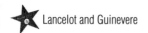

Lancelot and Guinevere. Who are these legendary lovers? Julie Andrews and Robert Goulet? Vanessa Redgrave and Franco Nero? Keira Knightley and Ioan Gruffud? Cherie Lunghi and Nicholas Clay? Who knows? One thing is for sure: it is impossible to spell her name. Guenevere? Guieneverre? Papua New Guieneve? In this, she has something in common with Keira Knightley, whose name was misspelled on the cover of *Vogue*, July 2004. A sub-editor was reportedly sacked for this offence. Here's the point, however. If Lancelot and Guinevere existed, they preceded Heloïse and Abelard as the Posh and Becks of their day.

See also HELOÏSE AND ABELARD; LEGEND, THE ARTHURIAN.

Langtry, Lillie (1853–1929). Savvy lady, official royal mistress and entrepreneur. Born Emilie Le Breton, only daughter of the Dean of Jersey. She had five brothers, which meant she was not denied a classical education like many of her sex. Married at 19 to Edward Langtry (owner of the yacht *Red Gauntlet* and burgher of South-ampton) she arrived in London convalescing from typhoid and in mourning for her younger brother Reggie. Yet she still managed to sparkle when invited to Viscount Ralegh's house in Lowndes Square. Postcard portraitist Frank Miles whipped out his notepad and made a line drawing of his first impression of her (the sketch does not exist, and this story may be apocryphal, but all Celebs are embellished by hindsight). She soon sat for John Everett Millais (*see* SIDDAL, ELIZABETH) and his portrait of her in her simple black dress, entitled *A Jersey Lily*, earned her that soubriquet.

In 1877 she became the mistress of Albert Edward, Prince of Wales and Queen Victoria's son. They were widely-known to be lovers, and their romance resembled the modern Celebrity Pairing – they were seen out dining together and driving together; photographed arriving at Heathrow looking tanned and relaxed, papped leaving Boujis together... They even shared a love nest in, um, glamorous BOURNEMOUTH.

Mrs Langtry had style and daring: when presented to Queen Victoria, she wore three ostrich feathers in her hair, the symbol of the Prince of Wales. At the height of her fame she was a consumer icon, as the charming ditty by a Miss Dorothea Mapelson (thought to be the pseudonym of a fat male hack) indicates:

There's the Langtry this and the Langtry that,
The Langtry bonnet and the Langtry hat,
The Langtry slipper and the Langtry shoe,
Langtry purple and a Langtry blue,
The Langtry carriage and the Langtry cot,
And every woman's hair in the Langtry knot.

But the affair with the Prince of Wales came to an abrupt halt when she arrived at a fancy-dress ball dressed in the same outfit as him. When he had a tantrum (understandably, since one royal dressed as a Nazi at a fancy-dress party is a scandal but two is a crisis) she responded by tipping ice down his back. Instead of calling her a pretty little pickle, he threw her out on her arse.

Undaunted, however, she became a star of the stage and conquered America (Langtry, Texas, was a town named after her by the infatuated judge Roy Beane). It is, perhaps, this indefatigability that made her beloved of the gay community (Oscar Wilde said 'I would rather have discovered Lillie Langtry than America'). She brought out Langtry-branded wine, owned several racehorses and was paid a seven-figure sum by HarperCollins to write her memoirs. She was about to launch a range of underwear (projected title, Love Lillie X) when she died in Monaco, aged 76.

In 1975, Francesca Annis took the part of Lillie in a television series, *Edward the King.* Although widely admired for her work on stage and in films (in 1971 she had played Lady Macbeth in Roman Polankski's *Macbeth*) Miss Annis – in keeping with the times – only achieved red carpet Celebrity when, in 1996, she became the lover of the British film star Ralph Fiennes. Mr Fiennes

was 20 years her junior (they had met, appropriately, when she had played Gertrude on stage to his Hamlet) and, in order to accommodate her in his arrangements, he was obliged to rid himself of his current partner, the actress Alex Kingston. Miss Kingston had recently made an impact on the British public by appearing in the TV series *Moll Flanders* without her underwear. Miss Annis, for her part, was obliged to leave her partner since 1976, the American photographer, Patrick Wiseman, by whom she had three children.

See also CLEOPATRA.

Language, bad. Channel 4 commissioning editors expressing themselves in Camden adenoidal – 'Like it will be totally brilliant, right, Tuffers with maggots in his pants, okay, postmodern, kinda ironic, yeah, at the end of the day, like literally, know what I mean?' – *That*'s bad language, not 'Bollocks to you, you twat'.

Laverne, Lauren (b.1978). TV-friendly tough cookie. Born Lauren Gofton in Sunderland, she became a member of teen girl band Kenickie Fried Chicken, who had a number-24 hit with the song 'In Your Car' in 1997. But despite all this, Lauren has gone on to have a successful career as Xfm DJ, TV presenter (*The Big Breakfast, RI:SE, Pop, Buffy Returns...* at one time, she was presenting four programmes a day) and all-round music maven. Perhaps this is due to her cool, calm manner, dextrous way with swear words and rather lovely appearance (think Lauren Bacall meets Mackenzie Crook).

Lawler, Kate (b.1982). It will not have escaped the notice of wannabes that, by appearing in various magazines in her underwear, *Big Bruv 2* winner Kate Lawler earns more in a week than Darcey Bussell does in a year. Kate is currently the girlfriend of the soccer player Jonathan Woodgate, who was recently transferred from

Newcastle United to Real Madrid. In 2002, Woodgate took part in an assault on an Asian law student and was sentenced at Leeds Crown Court to 100 hours of community service.

See also ROLE MODEL, A GOOD.

Lawrence, T.E. *See* POSITIONS, CELEBRITIES' FAVOURITE SEXUAL.

Lawson, Nigella (b.1960). To make this tasty TV chef, follow these simple steps. Take one prominent Conservative MP and one Jewish heiress, and breed. Give the child a funny name, and watch it simmer with resentment. Do not be alarmed when it goes lumpy and left wing while a young Oxford undergraduate. Give it a few more years and it will become curvaceous and wildly interested in cupcakes. Dress in tight-fitting womanly twinsets, add a little tongue-flicking sauce, a hint of self-parody, and serve once a week on the television. Healthy audience appetites guaranteed. WARNING: over-consumption of Nigella can lead to envy and self-doubt. As an antidote, remind yourself that she has lost her sister, her mother and her husband to cancer, and that she has cut the size labels out of most of her clothes.

Legend, the Arthurian. If there is a historical basis to the character of King Arthur (*c.*500 AD) he would have been famous as a warrior fighting the German invaders in the late 5th and early 6th centuries. Since there is no conclusive evidence for or against Arthur's historicity the debate will continue. Inseparable from the Arthurian legend are its geographical structures. Many of the myth's key sites – Tintagel Castle, St Michael's Mount and Dozmary Pool (the lake on Bodmin Moor into which Sir Bedevere cast Arthur's magical sword, Excalibur) – have been claimed by the

Cornish. On the other hand, it has been calculated that 47% of Cornishmen are their own grandfathers, and that it is a mistake, therefore, to rely on anything they say. What cannot be denied is Arthur's influence on literature, art, music and society from the Middle Ages to the present day. In Malory's *Le Morte d'Arthur*, Arthur marries Guinevere, whose father gave him the celebrated Round Table as a wedding present. Central to the myth is the downfall of Arthur's kingdom. In the chronicle tradition, the kingdom is undermined by the treachery of his nephew Mordred, whom Arthur had left in charge while he conducted some business abroad. In the romance tradition, that treachery is made possible by the adulterous love of Guinevere and Lancelot, the most illustrious of Arthur's knights. If LANCELOT AND GUINEVERE existed they have some claims to have preceded HELOÏSE AND ABELARD as the Posh and Becks of their day. More recently, Lerner and Loewe's musical *Camelot*, based on T.H. White's *The Once and Future King*, made money for those involved in spite of employing, in its stage and screen versions, Richard Burton and Richard Harris. However, the show contained one song, 'If I Should Ever Leave You', which may have been a consolation to those undergoing personal unhappiness at the time – the symptoms involving shopping in Safeway in their pyjamas and ordering unsystematically in restaurants. 'I'll have fishcakes *à la bonne cuisine* as a starter, please. And then I'll have fishcakes *à la bonne cuisine*. Oh dear, here comes the cabaret, Fay Presto, the gender-swap magician'.

Legris, Jean-Luc. *See* BRYSON, DR KIT.

Lesbian icons (a.k.a. **Dykons**).

- Sappho
- Pam St Clement
- Alex Parks
- Virginia Woolf
- Eddie Izzard
- Valerie Singleton
- Jackie Clunes
- Julie Burchill, for a few weeks several years ago
- Rhona Cameron
- Celia Imre
- Dale Winton
- Most of the Baader-Meinhof Gang
- Kitten from *Big Brother 5*
- Sarah Waters
- Jodie Foster
- Sue Perkins
- Sandi Toksvig
- Amanda Barrie
- Sam Fox
- Tufty
- Xena, Warrior Princess
- Greg Dyke
- Peter Dyke
- Offa's Dyke
- Dick van Dyke
- Brendan Behan's younger brother, Les
- Vita Sackville-West
- The boy who put his finger in the Dutch dyke
- The cast of *Prisoner Cell Block H*
- Saffron Burrows, in the afternoons

London, salt-of-the-earth folk born in the East End of.

Barbara Windsor

Dirty Den

Ron an Reggie K

Linda Robson

Mike Read

Al Capone

Eliza Doolittle

Dick Van Dyke

Madonna

Pauline Quirke

The Boston Strangler

Lucky Luciano

'Dutch' Schultz

Patsy Palmer

Liberty X. Pushy delinquents showing off. Runners up on ITV's *Popstars: The Rivals*. Soon showed themselves not to be losers with a number-one hit in 2002.

Like. Following the American critic, Maggie Balistreri, British linguists studying the deployment of the word 'like' in contemporary Celebrity Usage have uncovered nine different categories. These include the vague 'like' ('This was back in, like, October' – Kate Lawler, *Big Brother 2*); the self-effacing 'like', where the speaker does not want to sound priggish ('I, like, care about the environment and stuff' – underwear model Caprice, *Celebrity Big Brother 3*); or the betrayer 'like', a signpost to insincerity ('Oh this is, like, so not an imposition!' – Lisa l'Anson, *Celebrity Big Brother 3*). There is the undercutting 'like', used to introduce some uncommon piece of knowledge, without making the speaker sound too pretentious ('That's, like, the capital of Italy. Or something' – Jade Goody, *The House*); the apology 'like', where the word acts as an admission of complete inarticulateness ('I was, like, wow!' – Tara Palmer-Tomkinson, *I'm a Celebrity, Get Me Out Of Here 2*); or the staller 'like', the verbal equivalent of a thought bubble ('You're from Belize. That's like... south!' – Ainsley Harriott, *Ready Steady Cook*). Language experts see these, and similar, evasions as evidence of the infantilization of society, in which linguistic habits are passed up from adolescents to parents, rather than the other way round. As Miss Balistreri points out in her study, 'This is corrupt. To value the way an adolescent speaks is a lie in itself.'

See also ADOLESCENCE; WORDS, CELEBRITIES' FAVOURITE.

Little Britain. Cutting-edge comedy show. Three catchphrases. Two fat wallies. It is particularly popular with Judy Finnigan's children. There may be a lesson here.

Littlejohn, Richard (b.1951). A London cabbie from hell who has managed to find employment as an aggro columnist on the *Sun*.

Liverpudlians. Work-shy grief junkies.

See also BONKING BORIS; GRIEF, RECREATIONAL.

Llewelyn-Bowen, Laurence (b.1965). Swag merchant, prince of flock and sultan of the stencilled pineapple. TV decorator with his own wallpaper shop and a flair for bombast. Gilderoy Lockhart made flesh, and with a way with papier-mâché. The unthinking old lady's crumpet, Laurence has starred in innumerable episodes of *Changing Rooms*, the BBC1 interiors programme that also introduced the nation to Linda Barker and Handy Andy. Laurence looks like the sort of man who'd sign his name with florid curlicues descending half way down the page. In fact, that's exactly what he does. No cheque or Christmas circular goes without at least six self-aggrandizing swirls. Larry Llelly Bolly, as intimates call him, looks like a King Charles spaniel on heat, or a porn star trying his hand at Restoration drama. One of the vainest men in England, he takes to the streets with two burly bodyguards, there to protect him from the hordes of Llelly-crazed women hurling themselves in his direction. No such assaults have ever been seen. Notwithstanding all the pomp and campery, LLB is happily married and a talented designer, responsible for the Criterion restaurant in London's Piccadilly and the Royal Opera House's refurbishment. He is also intelligent enough to present himself, for the benefit of early evening viewers, as less intelligent than he actually is.

Lloyd-Webber, Lord Andrew (b.1946). Musical comedy composer who looks as if he's wearing his face inside out. In May 2002, 100 people were asked whether they'd rather see *Phantom of the Opera* or remove their own appendix with an oyster fork. A remarkable 82% said they'd rather see *Phantom of the Opera*.

When he asked an acquaintance why people took an instant dislike to him, the acquaintance replied, 'Because you're a cunt'.

Logan, Gabby (b.1972). Cheerful, well-built front person and soccer pundit. Her breezy, scrubbed-up style may be an inheritance from her father, Terry Yorath, a willing midfield water-carrier with Don Revie's Leeds United team, which made its mark in the 1970s. Her marriage to Kenny Logan, the muscular Scottish wing three-quarter, has honed down some of the rougher edges, but you'd still expect to find her in the saloon bar of a public house sharing a pint with the lads. Before meeting Gabby, Kenny had a long affair with Kirsty Young, who is customarily to be seen perched on a desk in her little boots and hairstyle, reading the News for Channel 5.

London cabbies from hell. Richard Littlejohn. Jeremy Clarkson. Helen Chamberlain. Dawn Neesom. Janet Street-Porter. Paul Dacre. Kelvin McKenzie. Michael Winner. Wayne Rooney's Auntie Effie. Rebekah Wade.

London's sewage system. *See* BAZALGETTE, JOSEPH WILLIAM; BAZALGETTE, PETER; CHANNEL 4; ENDEMOL UK.

Loos, Rebecca (b.1969). Having been bombarded for months, it is alleged, with squalid text messages from the English soccer player David Beckham, the hauntingly beautiful Miss Loos claims to have taken pity on the randy little ball-bender and consented to a brief affair. For this putative act of mercy Miss Loos was called 'a sleazy senorita' in the *Daily Mirror*, 'a foreign scrubber' by Richard Littlejohn in the *Sun*, and, surprisingly, 'a Dutch bunk-up' by Terence Blacker in the *Independent*. Most remarkable, perhaps, was Mr Dominik Diamond's contribution in the *Daily Star*. 'David Beckham bint Rebecca Loos is buying a luxury half-a-million quid flat for cash. I hope it has a lovely bathroom. I certainly wouldn't want to touch her unless she had had a damn good wash.' There is a photograph of Mr Diamond above his column. It is not immediately obvious how he imagines that he might find himself in the company of Miss Loos. Latterly, enjoying a successful celebrity career in the wake of her Beckham allegations, Miss Loos proved herself ever compassionate when she obligingly masturbated a pig on TV's *The Farm*. And the cheeky 'parp, parp!' which she let off at the dinner table on *Celebrity Love Island* (2005) was, surely, a winning indiscretion.

Love-split pop babes. Forever trying to pick up the pieces after their three-year marriages to boy-band hunks collapse, as a rule failing in this respect and checking into a Celebrity Clinic, generally the Priory in Roehampton, London.

See also KATONA, KERRY.

Lulu, properly **Marie McDonald McLaughlin Lawrie** (b.1948). Compact singer and hardy survivor. A pop chameleon, Lulu had a hit before she was 15, had a fling with David Bowie, married Maurice Gibb, and then the hairdresser John Frieda. In the 90s she became a mascot for Take That, joining them on the single 'Relight My Fire'. Born in Glasgow, Lulu was the daughter of an offal dresser. The act of 'dressing' offal is not ornamental. Its first recorded usage, according to the OED, is in Defoe's *Journal of the Plague Year* (1722), in which he refers to a man who is 'the dresser of the Offale sharpening his Knyfe'. It is part of the processing of the carcass that occurs after bleeding and before packaging, and is perhaps best described, in layman's terms, as evisceration. An offal dresser operating independently might also be described as a speciality butcher.

Lurch, Charlotte. 'Good evening. The time is 10 o'clock and I'm  Huw Edwards. Here are tonight's headlines: "Arse-Up In the Gutter!" Oh dear! Sozzled singer Charlotte Church lands on her backside after another night on the toot. Only two months ago she vowed to give up her bad-girl antics for good. Right. And pigs might fly. Last night, the badly behaved little singer got well barrelled, though her new boyfriend Gavin Henson, the conceited Welsh rugby centre three-quarter, drank only mineral water. All right – they were celebrating Wales winning the Grand Slam for the first time in 37 years, and I'm as patriotic as the next Welshman. But since when did a Welsh centre three-quarter wear a fake tan, spiked hair and silver boots? Did the legendary Bleddyn Williams take the field in full make-up? I don't think so. You may argue that a lot of men wear make-up these days – David Beckham, Boy George, Dr Renée Richards – but Welsh rugby players? I think not. Talking about rugger, I've been reading an excellent book, *The Celebrity Syndrome – Towards a Diagnosis* by Salter, de Santos and Horrocks-Taylor. Interestingly, Dr Horrocks-Taylor is the son of Phil Horrocks-Taylor, the celebrated outside-half who distinguished himself for Cambridge University, the Harlequins and England in the 1950s. Horrocks-Taylor's side-step off either foot was so razor-sharp that he was obliged to change his boots at half-time, since his starting pair had, like the tyres on a Formula One racing car, been worn to a shred. On one occasion, he was said to have dummied the entire opposition XV into the West Stand at Twickenham, where, to their annoyance, they were obliged to pay £15 each for their seats, but the story may be apocryphal. Horrocks-Taylor led the famous Cambridge University XV of 1957 which fielded twelve current internationals, including – and apart from Horrocks-Taylor himself – Andy Mulligan at scrum-half, David Marques at lock forward and at wing three-quarter 'the Flying Scotsman', Arthur Smith. "Give it to Arthur!", the Cambridge supporters used to cry as soon as the ball emerged from the scrum. This incomparable XV took the field against Oxford and were stuffed 0–9. Henson, by the way, is no relation of Leslie Henson, the great English musical comedy star, and a favourite of my father's. My father never missed a show if Leslie Henson was in it – least of all if it also starred Fred Emney, another favourite of his. Emney was very fat, you may remember. He used to come on dressed as a boy scout – short trousers, top hat, monocle – smoking a cigar. "Has anyone seen a boy scout wearing a top hat, a monocle and smoking a cigar?" he used to ask the audience. "Yes!" the audience would scream. "Thank God," said Emney. "I thought I was lost." Made my father roar with laughter, God bless him. More about that later. Now for some even better news. Last night a bus-load of comedians plunged over a cliff. All saved! Except Mark Lamarr! So that was a result. The rest of the news now follows...'

Lygo, Kevin (b.1961). Previously director of programmes at Channel 5, Lygo succeeded Mark Thompson as chief executive at Channel 4 when Thompson was appointed director general of the BBC in 2003. He is thought to know what makes 'GREAT TELEVISION', but the jury is still out on whether his grip on the concept is as secure as predecessor's, or as Dawn AIREY's when she was at Five. That said, programmes such as *The Day My Tits Went Bust!*, *Going Down in the Valley: A Look at California's Sex Industry*, *Big Brother*, *Celebrity Big Brother*, *Porn: A Family Business* and *The Sex Inspectors* suggest that the rolling freak show put in place by Mark Thompson is in safe hands.

See also TELEVISION WE DESERVE, THE.

M

McCall, Davina (b.1967). Hyperactive TV front-person and recovering drug addict. Davina, to the disappointment of the general public, is, by her own admission, no longer 'a party animal on the club scene'. When working on the door at the Double Bass, a fetish club in London's Soho, Davina, whose job it was to attract the customers, stood outside in her suspenders (*see also* STRING-FELLOW, PETER). Those were times of which Davina prefers not to be reminded. 'From my late teens until my mid-twenties,' she has revealed, 'I went out clubbing every night and took a lot of things to keep going. I was a drug addict, a complete mess. You name it, I took it. Cocaine, ecstasy, even heroin. I was a completely different person then' – an accomplishment, it has to be said, that philosophers have always judged to be impossible since it breaks the first of the three laws of logic: 'Everything is itself and nothing else.'

The authoritative *Dictionary of Philosophy* (Peter Owen, 1973) makes no mention of Miss McCall, but the entry for Diogenes is relevant. '**Diogenes** (4th century BC). Philosopher, known as the Cynic. He lived in a barrel and when his compatriots were preparing for war against Macedon he rolled in his barrel up and down the street in order, he said, that he might seem to be busy too. When Alexander the Great asked whether there was anything he could do for him, he replied, 'Yes, you can get out of my way.' Alexander countered by saying that had he not been Alexander, he would have liked to have been Diogenes – a reply which, while graceful in the circumstances, raised intractable problems in the philosophy of trans-personal identity that the old Cynic chose not to discuss on this occasion.' Miss McCall has, in like manner, always resisted attempts to draw her into a discussion of the problem. Whether this reluctance is part of her 'recovery' is not known.

McAndrew, Nell (b.1975). Disobliging glamour model. When in November 2003 she entertained the British Army in Iraq she had a hissy fit when told that she would have to use a chemical toilet. Where are the old standards? As the comedian Paul Merton pointed out (*Have I Got News For You?* October 2003), 'When entertaining the troops in World War II, Dame Vera Lynn would shit anywhere. A true professional.'

McCartney, Heather Mills (b.1971). 'Good evening. The time's 10 o'clock and I'm Huw Edwards. Here are tonight's headlines. "Guess What Lady McCartney Has Said Now?" Appearing on the *Larry King Show* in America recently, she told Mr King of a meeting she'd had in Moscow with the ex-Soviet leader, Mikhail Gorbachev. "You remind me of Raisa," she reported Gorbachev as having said. "You both have this unquenchable love of mankind." If you say so, Heather. Now for the latest on Posh and Becks. The front page of today's *Daily Star* describes Posh as "A perfect Fairy Tale Princess!" That's nice. However, on page 7, it says of her acting ambitions, "We advise her to audition for the part of an Ugly Sister in the Hackney Empire's panto this year!" Confusing or what? Here at the BBC we say: "Get your act together, *Daily Star*!" Last night, the wife and I saw *Four Weddings and a Funeral*. Not the film. Les Dennis's diary for 2006. The rest of the news now follows...'

McCartney, Sir Paul (b.1941). Singer and composer, formerly with The Beatles. In October 2001, Sir Paul McCartney announced that he had proposed marriage to ex-model, Heather Mills, after receiving instructions from an owl. Sir Paul understood that the bird was passing on a message from his first wife, Linda, who was giving the couple her blessing from 'the Other Side'. Sir Paul was

once a pupil of Maharishi Mahesh Yogi and would have known that in India three hoots from an owl mean that a woman is to be married into the family. Nearer home, Edd Prynn, arch druid of Cornwall, has said, 'The owl is a strong messenger.' Sir Paul has frequently taken mind-expanding substances.

McCartney, Stella (b.1971). Bib-designing daughter of Sir Paul McCartney and his first wife Linda, *née* Eastman. Mini-Macca on heels, who customarily wears an unimpressed, pouty expression on her face, probably a consequence of having eaten so much bean curd. Ms McCartney, or Mrs Alasdhair Willis, as she now is, has never eaten meat or used leather in her creations, nor will she sit on a leather chair (unless she's really, really tired and her heels are killing her). 'Stelly', as she is known to her pal 'Melly' (Madonna), wanted to make a bit of a splash when she put on her final graduation show at Central St Martins School of Fashion in 1995. So she got Naomi Campbell and Kate Moss to model her knitwear, while her Daddy sang 'Yesterday' and did the hand jive in the front row. You can imagine how popular she was with the other students. She was soon appointed chief designer of the Parisian fashion house Chloe, where she reinvented the all-in-one spangly jump suit for the 1990s. But she can be forgiven for this, because she has also been involved in much-relished arguments: publicly falling out with her former co-designer Phoebe Philo, refusing to sit on the chairs at her father's wedding...

McCoist, Ally (b.1968). Cackling Scotch soccer twit.

McCray, Raymond (b.1940). Bank robber. In January 1983 members of the Robbery Squad interrupted a performance of *Snow White and the Seven Dwarfs* at the Shaftesbury Theatre, London. They ran on stage and arrested Raymond McCray, a professional wrestler, in connection with a £45,000 hold-up at a bank in Ilford. McCray, a 3-foot dwarf, had been able to avoid surveillance cameras because his head had remained below the counter throughout the raid.

McCririck, John (b.1942). Offensively right-wing tic-tac man married to Booby. Affects a deerstalker and cape while presenting the racing on Channel 4. One TV critic has claimed he has 'all the charm of an armpit', but this may be harsh on armpits. In January 2005, and in the company of, among others, Professor Germaine Greer, the underwear model Caprice, Sylvester Stallone's mother and Bez, an apparently retarded maraca player with Happy Mondays, he participated in *Celebrity Big Brother.* Over dinner one night he announced that when flying to America

it was his custom to travel Executive Class and to put the Booby in the Cattle Truck. His fellow housemates seemed a little shocked, but Professor Greer walked out of the show because she thought the fat tipster was being bullied. That it would have been better, had that been the case, to stay in place to defend the frightful McCririck didn't seem to have occurred to the scatterbrained old polemicist. He is now considering offers to write for the *Daily Mail.*

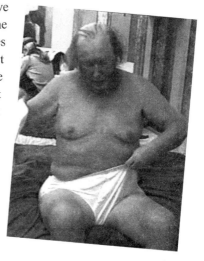

McCririck Syndrome. By strange coincidence, a condition named after its discoverer (the American psychiatrist, Dale McCririck, 1901–77) which afflicts attention-seeking children. Feeling that they are unappreciated, they draw attention to themselves with actions which they know will shock and disgust their peers.

Mackenzie, Aggie (b.1959) and **Woodburn, Kim** (b.1941). Comical charladies who have caught the public's imagination with their TV programme, *How Clean Is Your House?* Kim, who has a barmaid's bosom and a *Carry On* hair-do, occupies the ground once covered

March Celebrity *Faux Pas*

Dawn French, as part of her continuing campaign against body fascism, revives Nell Dunn's *Steaming* in the West End with a cast of fat people. Dawn takes the lead, supported by Pauline Quirke, Lisa Riley, Amy Lame, Miriam Margoyles and Lisa Tarbuck. Christopher Biggins makes a guest appearance as Vanessa Redgrave.

One of the **3am Girls** uses the word 'ontological' in her column. The editor of the *Mirror* sacks her on the spot.

The Royal Family Celebrates **Prince Philip's** birthday by playing the 'Which Celebrity Would You Rather?' Game.

Richard and Judy or Des and Mel?
Joan Collins or Hugh Hefner?
Barbara Windsor or Dirty Den?
Rebekah Wade or Richard Littlejohn?
Carlos Acosta or Stephen Gately?

'No, no, *no* Edward. You *still* haven't understood the game.' Harry tries to divert attention away from Edward by passing on a joke currently popular at Pangaea. 'Here's one! Daddy recently ran over one of Gran's corgis, do you see? Squashed it flat!' Cries of horror. Old Lady Fermoy (103) faints dead away. 'Daddy, damned upset of course, carried the little corpse down to the great lake for a ceremonial burial service. A genie emerged from the lake. "I am the genie of the lake," he said to Daddy. "I can grant you one wish." "Marvellous," said Daddy. "Please could you bring Mummy's corgi back to life?" The genie shook his head. "I'm really sorry. I'm only a genie. I'm not God. I can't create life. Do you have another wish?" "Well," said Daddy. "I'm recently married, do you see? Could you transform my bride into the most beautiful woman in the world?" The genie scratched his head. "Now… about the corgis …"' **Camilla Parker Bowles** runs weeping from the room, followed by Charles ('Actually I thought it was jolly funny, don't you know?'). Prince Philip barks with laughter. 'That's my boy!'

by the drag comedian Dick Emery, aiming a volley of flirtatious *doubles entendres* at terrified scruffs and slatterns. Aggie is small and Scottish and does the science bits. Some clinical psychologists have pointed out that most of Aggie and Kim's customers need psychiatric help, not the attentions of two cleaning ladies. This is obviously true but Channel 4 are to be congratulated for recognizing that mental deficiency as entertainment has always appealed to the British sensibility.

McKenzie, Kelvin (b.1946). Flabby-faced bully.

See also LONDON CABBIES FROM HELL.

McFadden, Brian (b.1980). Former member of Westlife, a boy band which did well for a collection of tone-deaf, spud-faced chancers. Once Brian looked like a pretty little builder; now he has been remodelled as a haunted hippie. Joining Westlife at the age of 18 caused him to spend his formative years perched on a stool, wearing a white suit; alternatively, sitting on a chair the wrong way round doing cover versions of Barry Manilow songs.

In spite of this promising start, McFadden has had a rocky ride. For one thing, he has had to have his personal stationery altered on a number of occasions. At the age of 19 he changed his Christian name from Brian to Bryan in order to make it easier to sign autographs (Colonel Gaddafi would do well to take note). Since leaving Westlife in March 2004, Bryan has reverted to his original Brian. He had resigned from the band, he said, because he wanted to spend more time with his wife, former Atomic Kitten and Jungle Queen, Kerry McFadden (*née* KATONA) and their two daughters, Molly and Lilly Sue. That was a mistake. The Jungle Queen shortly discovered that Brian had 'engaged in a sex act' with a pole dancer on the night before their wedding. A Jungle Queen insider exclusively revealed to the *Daily Star* that in retaliation for this offence Kerry intended to take Brian for £10 million. And this was

the couple who were once so close that insiders affectionately called them 'Fish and Chips'. A further consequence of the divorce was that Brian lost the title 'Celebrity Dad of the Year', which he had won in 2003, despite composing a song entitled 'Sorry, Love Daddy'. 'I'm so confused about everything,' he says. We'd have taken his word for it, even if he hadn't already been snapped with songbird Delta Goodrem.

McKeith, Dr Gillian (b.1959). Droopy-eyed Scot who claims she is 'The World's Top Nutritionist'. That seems unlikely. Despite having her own series, Channel 4's *You Are What You Eat*, plus a best-selling book accompanying the show and a whole range of food products with her name all over them, Dr Gillian McKeith is in fact no more a qualified nutritionist than Emma Bunton is. Granted, she has two degrees: one is in language and linguistics, the other in international relations. Her only scientific qualification is a correspondence course from a non-accredited college formerly known as The American College of Holistic Nutrition. This institution charged her approximately $3000 for her PhD. McKeith's advice on how to energize the liver and oxygenate the blood is demonstrably mumbo jumbo, and she was awarded a Bad Science Award by the *Guardian* in 2004. She even lists 'unconditional love and light' as the nutritional contents of her Love Bar, priced £3.99. Yet the point of Dr Gillian McKeith is not to be a nutritionist, but a Celebrity Nutritionist. Her unattractive appearance has convinced the public that she must be an expert in something, otherwise she would not be on the television. Moreover, she has the ability to prod an obese mother from Romford until she cries. A second series of *You Are What You Eat* is in production.

McLoughlin, Colleen (a.k.a. **Queen Colleen of Mersey**) (b.1986). Heir apparent to Posh Spice. A blonde bruiser who manages to make any expensive designer item she wears look like it came from a rip-off stall in Torremolinos, Colleen is currently the partner of soccer player, Wayne ROONEY. The two have been sweethearts since they were 13. But how does it feel to be Queen Colleen? One moment you're a schoolgirl performing in a production of *Bugsy Malone* at St John Bosco School, Liverpool. The next thing you know your boyfriend is a superstar, you've had a cameo appearance in *Hollyoaks* and you're

hobnobbing with Posh Spice. Then trouble looms. Not only does a prostitute claim to have slept with your fiancé, but she also says that she spent their night of passion thinking about which Pot Noodle flavour she was going to have after her shift (chicken or beef and mushroom?). This does not look good. Who wants a man who inspires thoughts like that? Slap him, Colleen. And then max out his cards on a spending spree in New York with two friends. 'It was brilliant,' said one. 'We spent, spent, spent.' The racks at Bloomingdale's are still empty, and the sales assistants still in therapy. ('Like, these three wild hoodlums ran in, calling to each other in a strange language... I thought we were all gonna die.') All was going well until British customs officials were alerted when a card linked to Rooney was used to make a cash withdrawal so large

(an estimated £40,000) it triggered a security alert. Back on British turf, Colleen was hauled over by customs, who ransacked her bag expecting to find Hermès leather, silk scarves, Tiffany's diamonds… Officials, however, couldn't find anything. 'Just a lot of cheap tat from Torremolinos,' said one, perplexedly.

Madely, Richard (b.1956). Blundering presenter of early-evening family television, married to Judy FINNIGAN. Once, when interviewing the former president of the United States, Bill Clinton, Madely, in a delirium of inappropriate self-importance, compared an early misfortune of his own (he was once falsely accused of shoplifting) with Clinton's involvement in the Monica Lewinsky fiasco, even managing to suggest that while he, Madely, had been innocent, Clinton could claim no such mitigating circumstance. 'Hey, believe me, I understand where you're coming from,' said the Channel 4 buffoon. 'But it must have been worse for you. After all, I knew I would be vindicated.' The former president was rendered speechless. In other respects, and despite a hairstyle unsuitable for a man of his age, Madely resembles a stalwart of the PTA and Tenants' Association, interfering in the lives of his social superiors and issuing directives in Water Board English. 'Would tenants kindly refrain from leaving main doors unsupervised when the caretaker is off-site…' 'Bicycles left in the common parts will be removed…' At the age of 50, he attaches himself to what he thinks are the latest street constructions like other people pick up dog shit. 'I *so* don't want to go to that particular place at the moment…' 'What am I *like*!…' 'Word up…!' 'Sorted…' 'Total respect, my man…' 'Pukka!' 'Judy and I were chilling out the other night when…' 'Just how surreal was it when you discovered that your toddler had lost both legs in a bomb outrage… ?' Small wonder that Channel 4 have locked him in place with a £2 million golden-handcuff arrangement.

Madonna, properly **Madonna Louise Veronica Ciccone** (b.1959). Now a naturalized Briton who speaks exclusively in cockney rhyming slang. In middle age she has developed the thigh strength of a Bulgarian weightlifter. With it, she is able to pick up her husband, English film director Guy Ritchie, and pack him in like a car-crusher in a wrecker's yard. In spite of his acquired tough-guy image and his friendship with former soccer hooligan Vinnie Jones, Mr Ritchie, a former public schoolboy, is rumoured to enjoy the experience. Today his wife's songs are enjoyed by 8-year-olds at jelly and ice-cream discos.

See also BABIES' NAMES, SHOCKING CELEBRITY.

Magee, Debbie (b.1960). She wanted to be the Margot Fonteyn of her generation, her Odette-Odile causing swooning balletomanes to shower the stage with diamonds and floral tributes. She'd have settled for understudying Noreen Sopwith at the Ballet Rambert. She ended up married to a conjuror and fisting a pig in a reality show for Channel 5.

Major James Hewitt offers foreplay. Into the Montpeliano with Caroline, a senior tottie. Calls her by her surname to show he's seriously interested. Talks about his hangover. Scans room for friends. Relieved by arrival of Paddy from the Blues and Royals. Persuades Paddy to join them. Swaps experiences, endorsements, accidents, bun fights, Vanessa's capacity. 'I hear she goes like a rocket!' Shows reluctance to leave Paddy. Has frequent nightcaps. 'The night is yet young!' Helped into driving seat. Questioned by policeman. Attempts to charm him: 'Do you mind? I'm trying to sleep?' Gets a beating. At home, assumes favourite position (head down the lavatory). Passes out *in vaginam.* Later, reads note from Caroline. 'You spastic! See you at the Drinkwaters!'

See also HEWITT, MAJOR JAMES.

Manners Makyth Man. *See* WINCHESTER BY-PASS, THE.

March Celebrity paranoia. Celebrities can't go out because they think they look like Billie PIPER. It's worse. They look like Kerry KATONA.

Marino, Dan (b.1969). Legendary quarterback with the Miami Dolphins.

See also WORLD CUP 2006, ENGLAND'S PROSPECTS IN.

Marsh, Jodie (b.1980). Gorgeous, pouting glamour model (32DD), distinguishable from the others by her nose, which is shaped like a ski jump, after the manner of the late Bob Hope's. Tattooed across Jodie's back are the inter-  twined names of murdered friend Kim, and her deceased chihuahua Pixie. When she heard the news of Pixie's death, Marsh says she collapsed on the floor, shouting 'Please God, no!'. The taciturn comedian, Jack Dee, has remarked that what he admires most about Jodie is 'her refusal to be pigeon-holed, at least on a first date'.

See also SLANGING-MATCHES, THE MOTHER OF ALL.

Marsh, Kym (b.1976). Mannish ex-Hear'Say pop star who, by her own admission, inclines to flatulence and corpulence. Born in Wigan, she was already making music for a local record company at 13. How long is too long, Kym?

Martin, Chris (b.1977). Devon-born goody-goody. When not emoting as front man of Coldplay (the band Alan McGee, former head of Creation records, described as making 'music for bedwetters'), Martin is forever dousing himself in cream to make a point about free trade and holding forth about the benefits of hemp seeds. He and his wife Gwyneth Paltrow (and baby Apple) are happiest when holed up at home in St John's Wood feeding each other live bioorganic yoghurt and watching nature documentaries.

See also BABIES' NAMES, SHOCKING CELEBRITY; CRITICISM, A STAR OFFERS.

Masquerading as a Celebrity. In the summer of 2003, Michael Hammond was a young man working in a branch of the Abbey National in Brighton. Suddenly dissatisfied with his lifestyle, he moved to London and started to hang around in nightclubs where Celebrities gather. His stories of having had affairs with, among others, Lisa Snowdon and Dannii Minogue didn't seem particularly unlikely and in no time he was described in gossip columns as a 'film consultant', a 'theatre producer' and 'a pop music mogul'. Setting his sights higher, he began to attend polo matches and was rewarded when Sky Television engaged him to present a programme about polo shot in Windsor Great Park. He was no longer masquerading as a Celebrity: he had become one. If he had confined his activities to the Met Bar and similar Celebrity rendezvous, he might in time have had a real affair with Lisa Snowdon or Dannii Minogue; been invited to produce a film; become rich and famous and a polo-playing friend of Harry Windsor. Unfortunately, he began to impersonate first a doctor and then a police officer, and shortly found himself in court. Commenting on the case in the *Independent*, Philip Hensher remarked: 'Mr Hammond wasted a lot of people's time, and made himself look more important than he really was. If there's a better definition of a real Met Bar "Celebrity" I can't think what it is.'

Material, working on new. Washed up (*see* BECKHAM, VICTORIA; HALLIWELL, GERI, et al).

Matthews, Meg (b.1967). Pushy trollop, and that's just what her friends think. Once a blonde bombshell; now more of a blonde bombsite. Born on Guernsey and brought up in South Africa, Meg sold wigs in Kensington Market and organized music PR. Then her flatmate Rebecca de Ruvo started going out with Oasis frontman Noel Gallagher. Not for long. As Mrs Gallagher, Meg inspired the song 'Wonderwall', and had a column in the *Sunday Times* Style Section entitled 'Yeah!'. This was written for her, but unfortunately by people who didn't seem to like Meg particularly. They had her saying things like 'In preparation for my exotic holiday, I've dyed my hair platinum blonde ... I like my hair to match my credit card.' Consequently, she was not popular with the public. Still, she shifted copies of *Elle* magazine when she was its 'candid' nude cover star, though readers of a bilious disposition regretted turning to the page where her pierced reconstituted nipple was on display.

See also BABIES' NAMES, SHOCKING CELEBRITY.

Maze at Longleat, Celebrities thought to be lost in the.

- ⬀ Selina Scott.
- ⬅ Shergar.
- ⬇ Vic Reeves.
- ⬋ Gareth Gates.
- ⬀ Chris Evans.
- ⬍ Boy George.

Media intrusion. A public relations own-goal.

'Meeting, I'm sorry, he's in a'. On a podium at a Celebrity Clinic having his personality ignorantly analysed by others in the group. 'It's not my fault. It's a disease.' Smart agents now by-pass the Ivy, Soho House and the Groucho Club and, with the contracts in their briefcase, head straight for the Priory Clinic in Roehampton or

Broadway Lodge in Weston-super-Mare. 'Sign here, Sir Tony. One day at a time. Group hug, everyone?' The story that Ed Victor was on one occasion mistaken for a patient and thereafter spent three days cleaning the latrines with a toothbrush is apocryphal but no less significant for all that.

Melua, Katie (b.1984), pronounced MELL–oo–wah. Sweet, sensible girl-child who warbles. Waif going on 40. If the Prince of Soft Jazz is Jamie Cullum, then Katie Melua is his equally squidgy right royal sister. Born in the former Soviet republic of Georgia, then resident in Northern Ireland from the age of 9, Ms Melua looks like she stepped out of a Freeman Hardy Willis Catalogue: curly bonce, pointy chin, tame eyes. Her singing has the bite of a marshmallow sandwich. Terry Wogan is a big fan as is the Queen. Katie hangs out with a lot of middle-aged saddos, like her mentor Mike Batt and the other frumpy bandmates she tours the world with, checking into Travel Inns with them and living it up occasionally at Happy Eaters. Just look at the newsletter on her website: 'Having turned 20, soon I'll be all responsible, with slippers and a cuppa every night watching *Emmerdale*. Hold on, I already do that!' Poor Katie. Expect teenage rebellion – stickers on her bedroom walls, ripped jeans even – at the age of 32.

See also CULLUM, JAMIE.

Members of the general public. Always lost for words. 'I can't put it into words, Chris.' 'It probably hasn't sunk in yet.' 'That's right, Chris. It hasn't really sunk in yet.'

Men whose hearts sing at the thought of Petsy getting a thoroughly rococo seeing-to even if it's not something they'd have time to do themselves. *See* BONKING BORIS; WYATT, PETRONELLA.

Messenger, Melinda (b.1971). Swindon-born glamour girl with baby-doll eyes, simian jaw and pumped-up knockers. Basically, a Donald McGill cartoon made flesh. Formerly a hostess with Britannia Airways, Melinda came to prominence in 1996 by posing in a bikini in a double-glazing advertisement, accompanied by the slogan 'Class Behind Glass'. This provoked many complaints, mainly from elderly gentlemen who were trying to acquire the posters but found they had already been nicked from the local bus shelters. The story was taken up by the *Daily Star* and the *Sun*; Melinda's TV career then kicked off with *Eurotrash* and culminated in *Melinda's Big Night In*. Melinda's main appeal has always been her ability to look as if she's really enjoying herself. It was ironic, therefore, that when she retired to spend time with her husband Wayne and children Flynn, Evie and Morgan, she suffered severe postnatal depression and even contemplated suicide. In the archives of British pin-ups, Melinda Messenger is filed under 'Heart of Gold' – after Barbara Windsor and before Nell McAndrew.

Middle England. *See* REAL WORLD, THE.

Miller, Sienna A skinny little girl nicknamed 'Squit' emerges from public school (Heathfield, since you ask), keen to show off acting abilities honed over years of school plays ('I was the lead in *Charley's Aunt* and everything, yah?'). She takes a bit of a gap year in New York, doing drama at Lee Strasberg Theatre and Film Institute. Then she meets Jude Law on the set of the film *Alfie*. And – whoosh!!! She becomes a pin-up star, a style guru, a full time Celebrity Girlfriend: pictures of her are everywhere; it's Page One news when she wears a new hairband. As Vanessa Thorpe put it in the *Observer*, she was 'traded on the celebrity market like pork belly'. She's even up there on cover of *Vanity Fair*, wearing a Donovan cap and cocking her leg like a labrador in Hyde Park, but never mind that, she's British and we're proud. (Unless we happen to be Sadie FROST, Jude's ex-wife, of course.) Then Sienna, happily ensconsed in Primrose Hill with Jude and child-substitute dogs Porgy and Bess, suddenly loses her astrological advantage. Overnight she goes from the House of Soho rising to the chute of tabloid despair. Jude's children's nanny (pretty, like a charity shop version of Sienna and appointed by Sadie Frost, but that's another story) tells the tabloids that Jude is having it off with her. Ouch. And this comes just as Sienna is finally proving herself as an actress on the West End stage, appearing as Celia in David Lan's production of *As You Like It*. The critics were not kind, however. Wrote the *Independent*'s Paul Taylor: 'I once saw a 13-year-old girl give a subtler and more captivating performance as Celia in a school play... Miller approaches emotion with all the finesse of somebody beating a carpet.' Oh dear.

Minnelli, Liza (b.1945). Barmy singer.

Moorish, Lisa (b.1972). Average singer and talented celebrity baby-mother. Ms Moorish, who sings with her band Kill City, has a daughter, Molly, by Liam Gallagher (conceived a week after he married Patsy Kensit) and a daughter Estile by Pete Doherty. While some might think that Ms Moorish's arrangements betoken a free spirit, the *Sun* thinks no such thing. Its two-line editorial of 8 August 2005 read: 'Lisa Moorish is worried that her two little girls will end up like their fathers. She ought to be more concerned that they turn out to be a slapper like her.'

More Celebrity Catchphrases.
'E = mc^2' – Albert Einstein.
'Give him the money, Mabel!' – Wilfred Pickles.

More examples of Dawn's rethink. Programmes of a thoughtful nature currently being formulated by Dawn AIREY at Sky TV include one in which participants are told that they've won the

lottery. A pensioner is presented with a cheque for £5 million by Page 3 Scorcher, Leilani Dowding. Cue riot in the studio, fizz and whizzbangs. Then they say it was all a joke! Tears. Despair. Heart attacks. Nervous breakdowns on camera. Audience rocks with laughter. Cue titles. An even better idea is currently being conceptualized by Ms Airey – working title *Superstar UK*. Dawn boasts that it will 'shatter the dreams of all pop wannabes' by making them inadvertently compete to discover who is the least talented among them. Gifted teenagers will be turned away sobbing, and caterwauling fat girls given bonus points. After a 15-week series, the triumphant winner will be told that he or she was in fact the worst in the show and can now count him- or herself a national joke. Next week we beat kittens with a mallet. Artaud has nothing on this. Dawn understands television.

More is More. *See* VERSACE, DONATELLA.

Morris, Jane (1839–1914). Pre-Raphaelite 'Stunner' – in the words of Dante Gabriel Rossetti. W. Graham Robertson preferred to call her 'the Delphic Sybil'. Henry James found her to be a figure of 'fearful intensity'. Born in Oxford, the daughter of a groom, she was spotted by Rossetti and William Morris at the theatre. Morris married her in 1859 and taught her to weave, while Rossetti painted over a hundred pictures of her. Rossetti and 'Janey' Morris are thought to have begun a romantic involvement in the late 1860s. In 1871 Morris and Rossetti took a joint tenancy of Kelmscott Manor, Oxfordshire, where – during Morris's annual visits to Iceland – Janey fulfilled her role as Rossetti's model, muse and idealized lover. In 2004 their love triangle was dramatized in a play by Peter Whelan entitled *The Earthly Paradise*. The contemporary beauty, Miss Saffron Burrows, took the part of Jane Morris, and was judged by the critics to have given a 'luminous' performance. Miss Burrows, a socialist and native of Hackney, is a close friend of the Old Labour curmudgeon, Tony Benn.

Moss, 'Cocaine' Kate (b.1973). Cockney sparra supermodel now considering her options. As a phenomenon of late capitalism, she used to be able to flog any luxury merchandise going. You simply sat her down, mussed her hair up a bit, put an expensive handbag in her lap, took a photo and – boom! Everyone wanted to buy the handbag. Extraordinary.

Born and bred in Croydon, she was 'spotted' at 14, on holiday at JFK airport. In the 1990s, she pioneered the fashionable 'heroin chic' look by looking bandy-legged and resentful. These days she's a mother, model and party animal. Being all of these at once brings the moral majority out in a rash, of course. It's simply not fair. What about baby Lila-Grace? What about the child's poor abandoned father Jefferson Hack? Mothers shouldn't spend time in rehab and should definitely not celebrate their 30th with a party at Claridge's during which some of the guests engage in 'a polymorphous gang bang' (Peter Conrad's construction for her 'Beautiful and the Damned'-themed party). Moreoever, they shouldn't date grubby young rockers like Pete DOHERTY, who wooed her with the ditty 'What Katy Did'. (Perhaps it was the way his crack-addled eyes rolled back into his skull that particularly attracted her.) And as for her looks, well, says Conrad, 'the beauty she sells when modelling is leaking away like the ice sculpture Mark Quinn did of her. Her nocturnal antics... must inevitably accelerate this loss.' Tut tut tut. We say, Kate – go for it. And what does Kate say? Not much, since she hasn't given an interview since 1994. But the supermodel did drop one pearl of wisdom as she swigged vodka from her hip flask. 'Fuck all the mixers,' she said.

Mother Goose. She isn't a mother, and she isn't even a goose. She's a broad comedian, usually from the north of England, wearing striped stockings and an apron.

See also CINDERELLA.

Mothers, Celebrity. The loss of a child in tragic circumstances greatly enhances their own profiles and guarantees them a place on Richard and Judy's sofa.

Moyles, Chris (b.1974). Gobby, obese disc jockey. The only person in the entertainment industry to make Chris EVANS seem likable.

Music, pop. An accurate expression of the debased culture that supports it. As the style and *objets* writer, Stephen Bayley, has observed, 'When you have the sort of slaphead bruiser in a black AMG Mercedes and all his retinue of cutpurses, cony catchers, priggers, palliards, fraters, Abraham-men, bawdy-baskets and rufflers who comprise the music industry … only then do you understand the full-on meretricious horror of joining everyone for 'Breakfast with Johnny Vaughan' at Capital FM.'

See also VAUGHAN, JOHNNY.

Musos. The most essential Celebrity Accessory since babies (potty training was a bit too real). And soccer players have had their day. (Anyone for a ROASTING? Where's the camcorder?) Jordan, Natalie, Emma B, Cameron, Nicole, Gwyneth, Drew – none of them would be seen dead clutching anything other than a muso this season. This, presumably, is because they are so authentic. Sort of troubled-looking, most of them, with great cheekbones. Plus, they understand the mechanics of fame and never get the chance to snog a co-star on set. The downside? Imagine having to go to all those noisy gigs. And no girlie Celeb will ever be able to watch herself on TV because her muso will have chucked the set into the swimming pool. And sleeping with groupies is part of a muso's job. Commitment isn't. If you find yourself shacked up with a university drop-out who claims he's 'in a band' but who hasn't touched his Strat since GCSE, seek help. There's a helpline for everything these days.

My Side of the Story. Ghosted bollocks (*see* AUTOBIOGRAPHIES, CELEBRITY WARTS 'N' ALL).

Mystery blondes. Forever comforting love-split telly stars in nightclub toilets.

Mystery stud muffins. Forever snogging Gail PORTER after her marriage has gone tits up.

Nabokov, Vladimir. *See* JORDAN.

Name recognition. Whipple and Golan, clinical psychologists at Warwick University, have devised a test by which it can be discovered how long it takes a Celebrity, when flicking through a 48-page newspaper, to pick out his or her own name from thousands of words of closely printed text. Preliminary results are as follows:

Simon Cowell	0.000000 secs *
Chris Evans	0.000001 secs
Geri Halliwell	0.000019 secs
Michael Winner	0.000211 secs
Johnny Vaughan	0.001377 secs
Richard Park	0.097688 secs
Richard Madely	1.000760 secs
Pierce Brosnan	1.127670 secs

* (the time taken was too short to be measured)

Narcissistic personality disorder. *See* COWELL, SIMON; PUT-DOWNS, ACID-TONGUED; STREET-PORTER, JANET.

Natural talent, a sublime. Heading for drug-related oblivion and a stay in the funny farm.

Never-never-lunch. A lunch date that is cancelled and deferred every few days for an indefinite period of time. It has evolved as a mutual agreement between Celebrities who don't like each other very much but want to keep their options open. With the advent of super-intelligent electronic personal organizers it has become possible for these negotiations to continue for years without either party knowing about it.

Newcastle, flesh-devouring womenfolk of. *See* GEORDETTES.

New Year Resolutions, Celebrity:

Jeremy Paxman: 'To work on my self-esteem. To look in the mirror each morning and say, "I like me."'

Chris Evans: 'Must be kinder to all the people whose only fault is that they want to be me.'

David Beckham: 'To get in touch with my masculine side.'

Victoria Beckham: 'Must smile (showing teeth) at least once a week.'

Anna Raeburn: 'To give myself less abundantly to others. To find time for me.'

Vanessa Feltz: 'To rely less on my sex appeal and more on my intellect.'

Su Pollard: Must keep regularly updating Su's Snippets on my website. Think of the fans, Su. They can't be left in the dark about my comings and goings!

Richard Madely: 'To listen to all those people who think I'm a natural to be the next James Bond.'

Emma Bunton: 'To stop hanging out with Mel C. She's dragging me down. She's not even D-list now.'

Natasha Kaplinsky: 'Must show my caring side. Say "How are you?" to at least five people every day. Try to listen to the answer.'

Calum Best: 'Watch less television. Must get out more.'

Ian Hislop: 'To learn the tango (harmony, speed, aplomb). To make a real effort to finish a P.G. Wodehouse novel. To get in touch with my feminine side. To cancel my subscriptions to *Nuts* and *OK!* To log on less often to The Iconophile's Tanya Roberts Reliquary (www.homunculus.com). To master the art of comic

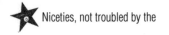

timing'.

Niceties, not troubled by the. Common and conceited *(see* STREET-PORTER, JANET).

Nightmare, a normal person's worst. In their paper referred to above under ADAM AND EVE, the team of clinical psychologists at Sussex University argued that the website www.celebdaq.co.uk 'usefully demonstrates the fact that a Celebrity's primary function is to act out in public a normal person's worst nightmare. The normal person thus experiences a kind of catharsis – as if he or she had attended a parodic performance of a Greek tragedy, the only difference being that, far from being a flawed hero, the Celebrity at the centre of this particular drama is already held in contempt by the audience. The latter condition is essential to the process. No normal person would rejoice to see things go wrong for an authentic hero, for a person who has won our respect *(see* REDGRAVE, SIR STEVEN). But the calamities that are visited on – to name a random sample – Neil and Christine Hamilton, Vanessa Feltz, David and Victoria Beckham, Chris Evans, Naomi Campbell and Geri Halliwell are comic rather than tragic and our pity is all too easily withheld' (Salter, Horrocks-Taylor and De Santos, *The Celebrity Syndrome: Notes Towards a Diagnosis*, Sussex University Press, 2004, page 17).

See also CELEBDAQ.CO.UK.

Noble, Emma (b.1971). Grubby glamour model born in Sidcup. She was briefly married (2000–3) to James Major, son of the former Conservative prime minister John Major. The Conservative Party is still in considerable disarray.

No-frills, what-you-see-is-what-you-get Yorkshire folk. Michael Parkinson. Geoff Boycott. Pete Waterman. Keith Waterhouse. Wilfred Pickles. Ray Illingworth. Brian Close. Lord Hawke. Boy George. Gianni Versace. Julian Clary. Harvey Proctor. Quentin Crisp. Rock Hudson. A.L. Rowse. Sergei Diaghilev. John Inman. Peter Tatchell. Charles Hawtrey. Liberace. Jean-Paul Gaultier. Danny La Rue. Dale Winton. Mrs Shufflewick. Elton John. Noël Coward. Matthew Parris. Stephen Fry. Kenneth Williams. Ivor Novello. Will Young. Larry Grayson. Paul O'Grady. Wayne Sleep. Judge James Pickles QC. Sir Bernard Ingham.

Nolan, Anna (b.1968). Lesbian nun who performed adequately in *Big Brother 1*. Happily, she didn't belong to an order whose members refuse to undress when taking a bath, arguing that it would be immodest to allow God to see them in the nude. In *Sceptical Essays* (1959), Bertrand Russell pointed out that this tactic was in vain since, if God could see through bathroom walls, it would follow that he could, if he so wished, see through a nun's habit too. Malcolm Muggeridge dismissed Russell's point as being 'the logic of the bucket-shop'. Miss Nolan tried to engage fellow-contestant, Scouse builder Craig PHILLIPS, in a discussion as to the merits of Russell and Muggeridge's arguments, but failed to catch his interest.

No longer at loggerheads. Leggy models Rachel HUNTER and Penny LANCASTER have at last called a truce in their war of words over Rod Stewart. Penny says: 'We're not exactly best friends, but I won't in future be quite so rude about the floppy-bosomed old trollop.'

Norton, Graham (b.1964). Comedian. 'Ignorant and spiteful... a consistently dehumanized view of humanity... everyone is degraded on Norton's show, especially women... the product of a stupifyingly degenerate and repugnant mind...', Matthew Norman, the *Independent*, September 2004. 'Sounds like one for us, Kevin.' 'Too late, I'm afraid. Mark Thompson has already clamped him in a £4 million golden handcuff deal.'

See also ADULT CONTENT; CHANNEL 4; LYGO, KEVIN.

Nose. In humans and other primates, the prominent structure between the eyes. The name of a short story by Gogol. Once, it was a footballer's legs that were the first to go; now it's his wife's nose.

Now working in the music business. Formerly a Celebrity Criminal with convictions for GBH, extortion and drug smuggling.

Nowak, Nush (b.1979) Appeared on *Big Brother 4*, where she became famous for her blond good looks and for snogging her fellow-contestant Scott Turner. A year later, she made a bid to continue her celebrity by giving an interview to *OK!* magazine. 'I'm into giant earrings at the moment, and I'm a toe-ring and flip-flop kind of person too.' Oh dear. Revelations like that will get you nowhere, Nush. Only sex with a famous person can save you now.

Nutritionists, Celebrity. *See* ATKINS, DR ROBERT; HUMPTY DUMPTY; McKEITH, DR GILLIAN.

Obituaries, Celebrity. *See* BUÑUEL, LOUIS; FOUCAULT, MICHEL; PHILISTINISM, BRITISH.

Oddie, Bill (b.1941). Bumptious twitcher.

Offers, considering the. Desperate UK pop tottie trying to crack the American market. 'I'm looking for something which will really stretch me' (*see* HALLIWELL, GERI).

Old King Cole. Arguably the first Celebrity Crack Fiend. Little is known of him except that 'He called for his pipe in the middle of the night.'

See also HORSLEY, SEBASTIAN.

Oliver, Jamie (b.1975). Essex busybody. According to his New York agents, 'he is part of a culinary revolution which aims to take the fear factor out of cooking'. He is determined to bring the vernacular into haute cuisine, and to that end calls tomatoes 'matie', the blender 'a happy chappy', the tablecloth 'geezer' and the clientèle 'peeps'. He runs a charity restaurant in London's Hoxton, called 15, which is staffed by urchins recruited in a spirit of philanthropy. Philanthropy, is, after all, a dish best served cold. His charity is called Cheeky Chappies. No one in the history of Celebrity is more determined not to be pompous than Jamie Oliver – a laudable ambition, but one that,

October Celebrity *Faux Pas*

Celebrity historian **Dr David Starkey** appears naked in a TV commercial advertising L'Occitane's new Almond Shower Oil. In a voiceover he recommends it as being very soft on the skin. 'It lathers up nicely,' he says, 'and the smell is full-on gardenia.' Down five rungs on the Celebrity Ladder. He later boasts that 'among Celebrity historians mine is now the most valuable brand'. Falls off ladder and goes head first into ornamental fishpond.

The Queen and Prince Philip invite King Gyanendra of Nepal and his good lady to stay at Windsor Castle for the weekend. They ask them to bring a joint of meat and half a dozen bottles of claret. They turn off the central heating in their bedroom and show them where the pay phone is for outgoing calls. They send them out on Saturday morning with £5 and a shopping list (dry goods, fuse wire, light bulbs, hoover bags, Savlon, toothpaste, dog food, creosote). On Sunday, they make them go to church, make them go for a raw walk after Sunday lunch, make them watch a demonstration of a little mole being despatched by revolving spikes flying into its brain ('Completely painless!') and pack them off to London before drinks. The Queen makes a profit of £37.93 on the weekend. She drops seven rungs on the Celebrity *Faux Pas* Ladder.

ironically, carries its own pomposity. The self-important little cook has now guaranteed himself several appearances on the *Parkinson Show* and in all probability an effing knighthood by appointing himself 'School Meals Supremo'. He seems to believe that today's children will be the first to die before their parents. So what? Oliver is married to his childhood sweetheart Juliette ('Jools') Norton and has two 'kids' of his own. No surprises there, then.

See also BABIES' NAMES, SHOCKING CELEBRITY.

Omai, the Noble Savage (*c.*1753–76). A native of the island of Huahine, near Tahiti. He was befriended by Captain Cook, with whom he travelled to Britain in 1774. He was the first South Sea Islander to be seen in Britain and became the darling of society and the ultimate dinner guest. No soirée, banquet or public execution was complete without him. He was painted by Joshua Reynolds in 'the habit of his country'. A play based on his life, *Omai; or a Trip Around the World*, was performed at the Theatre Royal, Covent Garden, in 1785. He went to the races, shot game on the Yorkshire Moors, watched teeth being pulled in surgeons' demonstrations and similar entertainments. Then Omai was presented to George III and Queen Charlotte, whom he apparently greeted with 'How do, King Tosh!' His ascendancy was complete. Every Celebrity needs a catchphrase, and this was his. The king paid for his lodgings in London, and his vaccination against smallpox even made the public prints. But the pressures of life in the spotlight proved too much, and he returned to Huahine in 1777. Captain Cook's men built him a house on the shore, and their parting was, by all accounts, 'a most Affecting Scene'.

On the mend after suffering depression. Pug-nosed Queen of the Jungle sues errant husband for £10 million. Later she is named 'Celebrity Mum of the Year, 2005'.

See also KATONA, KERRY.

Optical illusions. Cut-price Celebs who have nothing to declare except their symmetry. Like so many two-for-one offers, you get them home only to discover you never wanted one, let alone two. Here they are, the Glade Air Fresheners of Celebrity life. The Olsen Twins, Mary Kate and Ashley. Luke and Matt Goss. The Cheeky Girls. The Aitken girls. Tweedledum and Tweedledee. Ant and Dec. Jennifer Ellison and Kerry Katona.

Orgies within spitting distance of Buckingham Palace. *See* BODYGUARDS, THE QUEEN'S.

Orville (b.1984). Duck gone bad. Once cute, creaky and wished only to fly, he has now manipulated his minder Keith Harris into performing with him in a stage show advertised as containing 'adult content': *Duck Off* – 'not for the easily offended'.

See also ADULT CONTENT.

Osbourne, John Michael ('Ozzy') (b.1948). Musician celebrated for biting the heads off bats. His most famous band was Black Sabbath, established in 1969. A feature of the band's act was to be verbally abusive to the audience. This made them popular, particularly in America. By 1974 Ozzy was enjoying an enviable lifestyle. 'We bought dope and fucked anything that moved,' he has recalled. 'I can't do anything in moderation. If it's booze I drink the place dry. If it's drugs I do the lot and then scrape

the carpet for crumbs. I was spending $1000 a week on drugs. I overdosed about a dozen times.' There was a downside, however. He shortly met, and later married, Sharon, the daughter of his former agent, Don Arden. A flirty, irritating little woman, she has recently made her mark on television. They have three children, two unattractive and one invisible. *See* OSBOURNE, KELLY.

Osbourne, Kelly (b.1984). Princess of Darkness. Hip munchkin. Vicky Pollard meets Jo March. The spirited daughter of Sharon and 'Ozzy' Osbourne, Kelly became the archetypal Little Miss Stroppy after her family became the subject of a Reality TV Show, *The Osbournes* (2002–). She launched a singing career on the back of this with a moderately successful album, *Shut Up*, and a disappointing cover duet with her father called 'Changes'. It is believed that her retiring sister, Aimee (who didn't appear in *The Osbournes*, but who has been taking music lessons for years) is the 'real' singer in the family. Kelly is unimpressed. 'Aimee's a bitch, to tell the truth.' She is equally candid about herself. 'I know nothing about anything,' she says. She was as abruptly self-critical when asked to wear a skimpy midriff top for a teen-magazine shoot. 'I was, like: "I think you've neglected to notice that I'm fat. I'm not wearing that."' She carries her puppy-flub proudly. 'Christina Aguilera and Britney Spears can both kiss my fat arse.' Kelly has been more vulnerable in her relationships with boys. She was quickly ditched by her first love, Bert McCracken of the rock band The Used, and then with equal speed by Rob Aston of The Transplants. Get out of the dumpster, Kelly.

See also OSBOURNE, JOHN MICHAEL ('OZZY').

Palmer, Patsy (b.1972). Cheerful redhead known primarily for her portrayal of Bianca in *Eastenders*. Subsequently she has undertaken more highfalutin thespian work, such as Imogen Stubbs's play *We Happy Few*. Though her performance was well-received, the play was not. She launched her own brand of Brown Sugar Body Lotion in 2002.

See also IF ALL ELSE FAILS, DIVERSIFY.

Palmer-Tomkinson, Tara (b.1972). Self-styled 'Posh Tart'. When, in 2002, Tara was joined in *I'm A Celebrity, Get Me Out Of Here* by the soap actor Darren DAY, insiders hoped that the serial love rat might at last have met his match: the feisty Tara is known to take hard-core revenge on anyone who two-times her. An initial jungle flirtation took place, but Day rejected Tara as soon as the show was over. By way of retaliation, Tara plastered Mayfair telephone kiosks with cards advertising Day as a sex-slave in a suspender-belt. No one rang Day's number to take advantage of the services offered, so the joke rather misfired. Mark Thompson hopes to produce *I'm a Celebrity, Get Me Out Of Darren Day's Bedroom* as his first big ratings winner since joining the BBC. It has been discovered that Tara's full name is an anagram of 'I am a plonker. Not smart.'

Pantomime catcalls, unwelcome. 'Your career's behind you!'

Parents, Catherine Zeta Jones's. *See* STAR-STUDDED SALON OPENING.

Parker Bowles, Camilla (b.1947). Jolly old bat turned blushing bride of Prince Charles. When they married at Windsor in 2005, it was a little known fact that within her bouquet was concealed: 40 Rothmans, a lighter, another lighter for back-up, one hip flask containing Famous Grouse, two labradors, several tins of Winalot, a thermal waistcoat and a pork pie. Camilla is called 'the Rottweiler' by Diana fans (who once made an attempt upon her life using a barrage of bread rolls); Prince Charles calls her Gladys. When the pair were first officially photographed leaving the Ritz in 1999, so many flashbulbs went off that the film footage could not be used on the television as it was considered a danger to epileptics.

See also KETTNERS.

Parkinson, Michael (b.1935). It has been noted by Salter, Horrocks-Taylor and De Santos (*The Celebrity Syndrome: Notes Towards a Diagnosis,* Sussex University Press, 2004) that not all Celebrities are exhibitionists; some are natural voyeurs and have the capacity to take on the protective colouring and mannerisms of their Celebrity environment. Chat-show legend Michael Parkinson, for instance, can moderate his appearance, voice and manner according to his interviewee: vacuously mid-Atlantic for an American, grittily provincial for his mates from Barnsley. When

interviewing the late David Rappaport, an actor of restricted growth, he shrank to the size of a dwarf.

Party monster. *See* RUSHDIE, SALMAN.

Pasquale, Joe (b.1960). Squeaky-voiced low comedian whose frequently repeated catchphrase, 'Me crackers are killing me!', ensured that he prevailed against strong opposition (including Janet Street-Porter) in *I'm a Celebrity, Get Me Out Of Here 2004.* It is not clear what he meant by this, but he was immediately offered a contract to appear in television advertisements for Jacob's Cream Crackers.

Paulin, Tom (b.1949). Choleric poet and Oxford don who wears too much blusher when appearing on *Newsnight Review* (formerly *The Late Review*). Paulin's Belfast accent and affected manner are easily impersonated. Just say, 'This book's utter banality disgusts me,' and twitch a little. The attendant comic possibilities have brought about his cult Celebrity status. An indie band has been named after him, and he is amusingly mimicked on television sometimes by Alistair McGowan, sometimes by a plastic puppet called Tom Tortoise.

Paxo, Big Bad, properly **Jeremy Paxman** (b.1950). Smirking interviewer with a brain like a cat o'nine tails. Presents *Newsnight* on BBC2 like a wolf wearing a tie, giddy on his own daring and looking conspiratorially at the viewers, who, he thinks, know he is a wolf in a tie, and admire him for it. While not making animal-rights protestors, international human-rights lawyers or child-protection bureau chiefs crumble like over-ripe Stilton in his fingers, he also likes to sautée anyone foolish enough to think they have a chance on *University Challenge.* Even Paxo's hobbies are gladiatorial: 'There is nothing I like better than sitting on the bank of a river trying to deceive some stupid fish,' Paxo says, of fishing.

Pelling, Rowan (b.1978). Founder and former editrice of the *Erotic Review*, with a smile like a sun lamp. All the queers, dears and hacks of London want to bask in it. Couples sitting three tables away at the Groucho Club have been known to wake up the next morning with a tan. La Pelling, eldest of five siblings born to a Kent doctor and his wife (who, she constantly reminds us, was a publican, despite her plummy accent), wants very much to be filthy: she edits a dirty mag, she poses in her undies on her Christmas card, she goes on TV talking about dildos, under Hobbies in *Who's Who* she puts 'buying vintage underwear'. But the harder she tries, the more obvious it becomes that she's actually a rather jolly, upright woman.

Persaud, Dr Raj (b.1956). Prating psychiatrist who suffers from a compulsion to sound off in the media at any available opportunity. Faced with himself as a case study, he would certainly find something despairing to say about it in the pages of one of the more high-minded national newspapers. Put him in Persaud's Corner, somebody.

Personality, not a natural beauty but with a terrific. Fat and noisy. 'My friends all say I'm totally mad!' An essential character defect for wannabes who want to become holiday reps on a Greek island. Once in place, they signal their availability by lying arse-up over dry-stone walls, losing out to visiting Italian girls with long legs and twinkling feet.

Philistinism, British. When the distinguished French philosopher Michel Foucault died in 1986, the *Guardian* entitled its three-line obituary 'Sex Historian Dies'. When Gilbert Ryle died in 1976 he was given a 17-line obituary in *Le Monde*, not, incidentally, under the amusing headline, '*Le Spectre en Dehors de la Machine*'.

See also FRY, STEPHEN.

Phillips, Craig (b.1978). The first winner of *Big Brother*. He won on the man-of-the-people ticket, elected by a public who were disillusioned with slippery arriviste Nasty Nick (*see* BATEMAN, 'NASTY' NICK) and ready to embrace scally handyman Craig's speak-as-I-find manner and lost-puppy eyes. Craig melted the nation's hearts further by handing over his £70,000 winnings to a toddler who needed an operation. Happily, Craig immediately recouped the money, and made a great deal more, from newspaper stories and public appearances. His attempts to become a pop star ended in disappointment, but he has carved out a niche for himself on daytime do-it-yourself television programmes, such as *Big Strong Boys* and *Boyz in the Wood*. He has made enough money from these to buy himself a house in Shropshire.

Phillips, Zara (b.1982). Daughter of Princess Anne and Captain Mark Phillips, from whom she has inherited expertise in three-day eventing. Generally referred to by the tabloids as 'sassy' and 'raunchy', Zara is famous for wearing evening dresses split to the waist. Rearrangements in her personal life have involved the replacement of former boyfriend, jump jockey Richard Johnson, with Mike Tindall, Bath and England's beefy centre three-quarter, of whom it has been said that he tackles like the crack of doom. In December 2004 the *Sun* newspaper was able to announce, under the headline 'Oh Scrummy!', that Tindall and Zara would be celebrating Christmas together; further, that Tindall would be meeting Zara's grandmother, the Queen. Speaking exclusively to the *Sun,* Zara said: 'I think Christmas will be a chilled-out affair this year – I don't do stressed. I just get on with it and have a laugh.' With a mischievous glint in her eye, the raunchy royal, who is 11th in line to the throne, added: 'It makes me smile sometimes when people think that, because I'm royal, our Christmas Day is dull. Far from it – believe me!' Royal insiders have told the *Sun* that when the love-birds are together 'they can't take their hands off one another!'

Philosophers. *See* CELEBRITY HAIRDRESSERS; DESCARTES, RENÉ; DRINK-AND-DRUGS HELL (for Martin Heidegger); FOUCAULT, MICHEL; GOD; McCALL, DAVINA (for Diogenes).

Philosophers, wine-bar. *See* DE BOTTON, ALAIN.

Pickles, Wilfrid (1904–78). Amateur actor who made his first broadcast for the BBC's North Regional service in 1927. Pickles began announcing in 1938 and was an occasional newsreader (the first with a regional accent) from 1941. His sign-off line, 'And to all in the North, good neet', caused indignation among traditionalists, but by the end of the war he was a Celebrity. He then had his greatest success as the host of *Have a Go!* (1946–67), radio's first popular audience-participation show, in which ordinary folk did party pieces and answered simple quiz questions. Pickles's catchphrases, 'How are yer?', 'Are you courting?' and 'Give him the money, Mabel' (a reference to his assistant, Mabel Myerscough), were much quoted, and the show's title remains an epitaph to the stupidity of ordinary people. Pickles also presented another sentimental show, *Where Are They Now?*, which united long-separated friends, and which stands as the most obvious influence on performers such as Cilla Black and Matthew Kelly. At his height he was an accomplished presenter. It was only later that his style, like that of Hughie Green, came to be regarded as condescending.

Pietersen, Kevin (b.1980). Celebrity cricketer. Following England's September 2005 Ashes victory, the mongoose-maned South African turncoat (25) was reputedly offered 'the best part of £200,000' by Random House for his autobiography. 'Auto-biographies used to be written at the end of a great career,' commented Peter Oborne in the *Evening Standard*. 'Pietersen should be working on his deeply flawed technique, not looking back from an imaginary pinnacle at a handful of meagre accomplishments. He is a victim of a modern conceptual error: the equation of promise with achievement.'

See also CELEBRITY CRICKETERS.

Piper, Billie (b.1982). 'One of Swindon's brightest stars', our Billie is doing rather well. She of the chipmunk chops and buxom appearance first sprung onto television in an advert blowing on bubblegum and shouting 'Pop!' A few singles ('Girlfriend' and 'Honey to the B') later and she was Britain's favourite underage attention-seeker. After a happy, brief marriage to Chris EVANS (the two took time out to wear each others' clothes and drink Stella) Billie left him, scrawling 'Be A Happy Chappie' on his wall while the couple's possessions were sold at auction. Evans now looks wearied, as if he doesn't want to be Chris Evans any more but simply can't help it. But Billie is still wearing her ponytail on the side of her head and leaping around coltishly. Her stint as Doctor Who Christopher Ecclestone's assistant Rose Tyler is thought to presage a fulfilling acting career.

Pleasuring oneself on a billboard to the endangerment of passing motorists. *See* DAHL, SOPHIE.

Politically incorrect. Vulgar and offensive (*see* CLARK, ALAN; CLARKSON, JEREMY; LITTLEJOHN, RICHARD).

Political volte-face, Geri Haliwell's. Ginger Spice endorsed John Major in a 1997 interview in which she expressed opposition to the Euro. 'You can't make pounds and francs and liras and pesetas equal,' she astutely pointed out. In 2001, she defected to New Labour.

Pollard, Su (b.1949). Demented actress made famous in the 1980s by appearing on television in *Hi-de-Hi*! She now posts 'Su's Snippets' on the Su Pollard website. It is not clear who she

imagines might be reading them. 'Yes, it's me! I must apologize for the short delay between this and my previous "snippet"! I luv that word. More snippets soon, promise. I've just got time at the moment to keep you all updated with a few bits and pieces... then I've got to go to Pinewood to record my *Weakest Link*. Plus I'm trying to learn my *Vagina Monologue* for the opening night in Dartford. I am sorry to disappoint anyone who was planning to come and see me (performing in *Annie*) in Cork... Sad to say my lovely pussy Michael passed away a couple of weeks ago of kidney failure. No donations or flowers please. Luv, Su.xxx'.

Pop babes. Forever being rocked by family tragedies just when they've got a Christmas single to promote. In November 2004 Leanne (19) found herself mourning the death of a third relative in as many months. The Irish beauty was devastated when a second cousin twice removed died from a heart attack at the age of 96. She immediately took time out from her hectic schedule to give herself space to grieve. A Leanne insider revealed: 'She's in a really bad way, as you can imagine. To have lost three family members in such a short time is tragic. She was rocked by a double bereavement in July when her grandad's 84-year-old step-sister and her Uncle Reg by marriage passed away within just ten days of each other. Leanne cancelled a photo shoot on Friday and flew back to Cork to be with her family.' The other girls in her band were reported to have been extremely supportive. Leanne's loss came just as the band were busy promoting their Christmas single, 'Love Ya Baby', and their new album, *Ain't Nothin' Goin' On*.

Porn: A Family Business. 'Sounds like one for us, Kevin'.

See also ADULT CONTENT; CHANNEL 4; LYGO, KEVIN.

Pornography, on the usefulness of. *See* DESMOND, RICHARD.

Prince Harry's Birthday *Faux Pas*

The royal family has assembled at Windsor Castle. After dinner they play the 'Which Celebrity Would You Rather?' game.

'Nicholas Witchell or Jennie Bond?'

'John McCririck or Clarissa Dickson-Wright?'

'Jeremy Clarkson or Fiona Bruce?'

'Michelle Marsh or Lucy Pinder?'

'You what?'

'I said Michelle Marsh or Lucy Pinder, grandma.'

'And who might they be?'

'Page 3 stunners, grandma.'

'Well, we don't want any of that, thank you very much, Harry. Have you forgotten how to play the game too?'

'Oh be quiet woman. It's the boy's birthday. And at least he isn't a frightful little pansy. My turn! Rebecca Loos or Kirsty Gallacher?'

'Philip… !'

'Go on, Harry!'

'Thanks, grandpa. Kate Lawler or Tess Daly?'

'That's my boy! My turn again. Jodie Marsh or Catalina Guirado?'

'Philip! I've heard enough! I forbid you to continue!'

Things turn nasty. They criticize each others' spending habits, deride each others' workload. They exchange insults. 'Stuffy old bag!' 'Greek parasite!' 'Kilted prude!' 'Attic philistine!' 'Nazi!' 'Mini-skirted rugger groupie!' 'Absentee landlord!' 'Delinquent parent!' 'Poof!' 'Vegetarian drip!' 'Adulterous soak!' 'Arthritic xenophobe!' 'Heavy-featured Hanoverian!' 'That's it! I'm off to bed!'

They stump off in separate directions down draughty corridors. Old Lady Fermoy (103) discovers that Harry has balanced a bucket of water over her door and made her an apple-pie bed. Prince Philip and Prince Harry drop ten rungs on Celebrity *Faux Pas* Ladder.

Porter, Cole (1891–1964). American song-writer. At the age of 46 both his legs were smashed in a riding accident. For the rest of his life he was crippled and in great pain. We learn from Philip Larkin that 'from then on a kind of patrician stoicism, coupled with consummate professionalism, assumed command. "My things," Porter would say, and his manservant would bring him a container of sharpened pencils, dictionaries, thesauruses and other books, a box of cough drops and a Cutty Sark and soda. He would sit at the piano in agony and work uncomplainingly on his matchless output of beautiful songs. When callers asked him how he was, his invariable reply was "Very well, thank you. Now, what's your news?"' (*The Supreme Sophisticate*, from *Required Writing*, Philip Larkin, Faber and Faber, 1982). Some commentators have put Porter's courage down to simple good manners. More perceptive critics, such as Vanessa Feltz, have pointed out that Porter, because of his patrician inheritance, never had to endure the terrible pressures to which today's maverick geniuses – Elton John, the Gallaghers, Chris Evans, Robbie Williams – are subjected. 'Geniuses such as Evans', Feltz has pronounced, 'are entitled to rewrite the rule-book.'

Porter, Gail (b.1971). TV presenter and nude nymphet who enjoyed a brief burst of popularity at the end of the millennium. Born in Edinburgh, she hoped for a career in television. So she sent out a demo tape of herself 'going slightly mad running round the garden!' wearing Wellington boots and a bikini. Soon enough, she was presenting children's TV shows, always managing to be cheerful, pert and smiley. Then she was 'talked into' doing some nude shots for *GQ*, which she immediately regretted, then a few more for *Esquire*, then again for *FHM*, then again for *Maxim,* then again for *Loaded,* then again for... Throughout, she was able to retain an air of Scottish wholesomeness, as if she always had her Quaker Oats for breakfast before doing a girlie shoot. Imagine her surprise when she woke up one morning to find that *FHM* had projected her nude form onto the Houses of Parliament. 'There I was all over the 6.30 a.m. news, thank you very much!' She went on to present *Top of the Pops*, where she met her future husband Dan Hipgrave, a guitarist from the band Toploader. Hipgrave insiders report that he was surprised, when he moved in with the little presenter, to discover that her fridge contained nothing but vodka and face cream. Gail insiders subsequently revealed that she had struggled with anorexia for nine years. After the birth of her baby, Honey, she suffered postnatal depression. The Hipgraves' marriage was over, and so was Gail's presenting career. She made a suicide attempt in March 2005. A week later, she attended the *Valiant* premiere in London, after which she was papped snogging a mystery stud muffin.

Posh to go Demi-naked! 'Good evening. The time is 10 o'clock and I'm Huw Edwards. Here are tonight's headlines. "Posh to go Demi-naked!" Good grief! That can't be a good idea. The former Spice Girl, who is expecting her third child in March 2005, is rumoured to be in discussions with *Vanity Fair* magazine about posing naked before she gives birth. Here in the BBC's Newsroom our advice is, "Keep your kit on, Victoria!" Unfortunately, she's determined to follow in the footsteps of Tinsel Town legend Demi Moore and do a shoot showing off her bump. Extraordinary. A source close to Posh told the BBC's *10 O'Clock News*: "Posh's soccer star hubby, David Beckham (29) is happy for her to pose naked as long as it's done in perfect taste." So that's a blow. Never mind. Here's another conjuring story. Mr Lenny Chipowe, a magician from Chingford, assured a small crowd that if everyone gave him one pound they could bury him alive for two and a half hours. A Mr Bassett, also from Chingford, gave him the money and helped to bury him. Having waited for the time to elapse, the crowd dug him up. He was dead. His wife said, "Something must have gone wrong." Well, there you are. Meanwhile, here is the rest of the news. Lord Archer's attempt to break the cross-Channel swimming record has

failed. It was discovered that he was wearing a small outboard motor attached to his trunks beneath the waterline. Now for the rest of the news…'

Positions, Celebrities' Favourite Sexual.

- ☙ **The Brooklyn Bridge**
- ☙ **The Arab blackmail** (over a barrel, as favoured by T.E. Lawrence)
- ☙ **Elgar's Enigma Variations** (pretentious)
- ☙ **The Nobu** (expensive)
- ☙ **The Comic Relief** (silly. They can't be that hungry in Africa)
- ☙ **The Tom Cruz** (bisexual)
- ☙ **The Bonking Boris** (*see* The Nobu *above*)
- ☙ **The Winchester By-pass** (polite. Manners Makyth Man)
- ☙ **The Hammersmith Flyover** (dangerous)
- ☙ **The Make Carol Smillie** (naff)
- ☙ **The Tess daily** (routine yet satisfying)
- ☙ **The Charlie Dimmock** (very dangerous)
- ☙ **The Sadie Frost** (al fresco in winter while being thrashed with a rolled-up copy of *Heat* magazine and being forced to listen to Björk's Greatest Hits)

Post-modern, terribly. Them. Taking photos. Of us. Under siege from a blitzkrieg of photo-firing paparazzi from across the red carpet, the savvy modern Celeb, well versed in Baudrillard, retaliates by whipping out her tiny digi-camera and snapping back.

Potter, Harry (first published 1997). Worldwide cash cow and saviour of the publishers Bloomsbury. The character Harry Potter is a plucky orphan with a lightning zigzag mark on his forehead, a bit like Gorbachev's. He also has a good sense of school spirit, a bit like Tom Brown. His age, however, is contentious: in the first book of the existing tetralogy, *Harry Potter and the Philosopher's Stone*, Harry's birthday, 31 July (the same as the author J.K. Rowling's) falls upon a Tuesday. This would make his date of birth 1979. But in the subsequent instalment, *Harry Potter and the Chamber of Secrets*, it is indicated that he is only 12, making his year of birth 1980. Can you believe that people care enough to have worked all this out? How sad are they? And are you almost as sad for having read this entry? Quick, quick, turn to another.

Prunes, a committed ambassador for Californian. *See* DENT-BROCKLEHURST, HENRY.

Punk rockers. Spike-haired careerists who end up presenting nature programmes, many involving dolphins. Sid Vicious is an exception to this rule. 'Popper?' 'Not while I'm working on a lexicon, thank you.'

Puppy, the Andrex (b.1987). Another Celeb who achieved fame too soon, too easily. A camera-natural from an early age, it was at only 13 months that he was found to be dispensable by the industry that had made him a star. In a cruel twist of fate, his TV replacement was none other than his own younger brother. Suffering from Celebrity burnout and a three-grand-a-week crack habit, he was admitted to the care of Betty Ford. When his TV royalties dried up, his agent, Ed Victor, put him a state-run care home in Battersea, where he is often to be seen wandering the corridors at night repeating 'Soft, strong and long...'

See also ICONIC, SO.

Put-downs, acid-tongued. Playground insults without the sophisticated edge. Often associated with 'narcissistic personality disorder', a phenomenon recently discovered by American psychiatrists. The syndrome is defined as 'a pervasive pattern of grandiosity, need for admiration and lack of empathy'. It rarely calls for hospitalization but certainly leads to antisocial behaviour

See also COWELL, SIMON; STREET-PORTER, JANET.

Ramsay, Gordon (b.1958). Viking who cooks. Born on a Glasgow council estate, he spent his youth footballing in a semi-professional capacity. When not perspiring on TV's *Faking It, Ready Steady Cook* and *Hell's Kitchen,* he runs the restaurant at Claridges, as well as Gordon Ramsay at 68 Royal Hospital Road. Amaryllis in Glasgow has gone bust. Hooray. His trademarks are an angry perfectionism and a florid face. He can rustle up a cep omelette while issuing filthy put-downs and running olive-oil-smeared fingers through his blond hair. You can see why women find him so attractive.

Rantzen, Esther (b.1938). She'd sit in Dictionary Corner with Richard Stilgoe rather than never be seen on television again.

Raunchy. Sweaty rock chick stinking like a sea lion.

See also FEISTY.

Reality Television. The unacceptable face of democracy, the revenge of the socially excluded and ungifted – the hideous upshot causing fury among the traditionally privileged.

Really grounded. Common and stupid (*see* ELLISON, JENNIFER).

Real People. Anyone who isn't a Celebrity. When Real People appear on television their status changes. They become Celebrities. Confusion arises when their careers falter. Do they become Real People again, and eligible, therefore, for a second bite of the cherry? The debate continues. Clinical psychologists Salter, Horrocks-Taylor and De Santos have argued that 'If Celebrities have no shame, Real People have no dignity' (*The Celebrity Syndrome: Notes Towards a Diagnosis*, Sussex University Press, 2004). The team offers no view, however, on whether an ex-Celebrity can, after an appropriate interval, make a comeback as a Real Person. The management of 'Back to Reality' – a 'Look-Alike Agency' for Celebrities whose careers have collapsed but who now hope to make an impact as Real People – take the transition to be possible. Emma BUNTON would do well to join, and other Celebrities on the point of signing with 'Back To Reality' include:

Jonathan Ross *(comical bus conductor)*
Phill Jupitus *(bludgeoning saloon-bar funnyman)*
Robbie Williams *(lippy youth who's come to bleed the radiators)*
Michael Parkinson *(South Coast dancehall habitué in rented DJ and remedial pumps)*
Geri Halliwell *(editor-at-large,* The Independent on Sunday*)*
Peter Andre *(Cypriot spiv operating in the Turkish sector)*
Simon Cowell *(camp co-pilot on cut-price airline)*.

Real World, the. The *Daily Mail*'s ontology. Esher residents barricading themselves behind the privet hedge against asylum seekers camping in the shrubbery.

See also ALPHA *MAIL*.

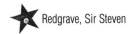

Redgrave, Sir Steven (b.1966). Five-times Olympic champion. As a Celebrity Psychologist has pointed out, 'The line between a normal person and a Celebrity sometimes becomes blurred. It is not the case that inside Dame Mary Warnock, Ruby Wax is signalling wildly to be released or that inside Professor John Fuller, Dr David Starkey is struggling to get out; however, a famous person of hitherto unchallenged dignity is sometimes prevailed upon to take the stage as a Celebrity: a part for which he or she is totally unsuited. Celebrities are born, not made. A Celebrity must have a protective carapace of innocence; be quite unaware of the effect he or she is having on normal people, that their function is to be held in contempt by the generality. After Sir Steven Redgrave won his fifth Olympic gold medal an attempt was made by outside agencies to turn him into a Celebrity. He created the "Five Gold" leisure/sportswear range (can you see what he did with the title there?) and appeared in utterly degrading Admiral Car Insurance adverts. But no matter how much he was manipulated, all these enterprises were doomed to failure. Sir Steven lacked the "Celebrity gene". What do you think of my new hairstyle? I'm rather pleased with it. By the way – I've just brought out a new range of bath unguents and skin care...'

See also NIGHTMARE, A NORMAL PERSON'S WORST; STREET-PORTER, JANET.

Red Rum. Celebrity Horse. He's even mentioned in *A Hundred Things You Didn' t Know About The Royal Lovebirds* (Pan Books, 1986) by Talbot Church, 'The Man The Royals Trust'. Mr Church writes: 'When she was at school at Hurst Lodge in Surrey, the future Duchess of York was asked in Divinity class who was born in a stable and had thousands of followers. "Red Rum", replied flame-haired Fergie.'

For other Celebrity Horses, *see* BUCEPHALUS; SHERGAR.

Rees, Maureen (b.1942). Les Dawson lookalike who achieved National Celebrity in 1998 by failing her driving test 17 times. She is no longer in great demand but is thought to earn more than she did as a cleaning lady.

Retired hookers.

- ♀ Janie Jones
- ♀ Mandy Rice-Davies
- ♀ Lindi St Clair
- ♀ June Upstairs
- ♀ Pretty Marie
- 'Y' Brian Moore ('Mooro')
- 'Y' Sean Fitzpatrick

Reverse swing. A saucy technique developed in the Punjab and refined in the back streets of Swansea. 'Sounds like one for us, Kevin.'

See also CELEBRITY CRICKETERS; LYGO, KEVIN.

Reynolds, Sir Joshua (1723–92). Mario Testino in a frock coat.

Rhodes, Gary (b.1960) Spiky-haired Gillingham barrow boy with some culinary expertise. Gary knows his onions, doesn't mince his words, can tell you which side your bread is buttered on, and is happy to reheat any other kitchen cliché you can think of during his frequent TV appearances. Yet something about Rhodes makes the heart sink. Faced with the prospect of eating a TV dinner and making mindless chatter while watching Gary Rhodes cooking a TV dinner and making mindless chatter, suicide suddenly seems a tempting option.

Ricardo (b.1970). Cross-dressing barber prone to hissy fits. That said, you wouldn't climb over him to get at Jade GOODY. Excellent legs.

Richard, Cliff (b.1940). 'I can't talk now. I'm off to buy the latest Cliff Richard single.' You won't hear that said. A mystery.

Right on, depressingly. Observing the conventional courtesies.

See also POLITICALLY INCORRECT.

Right to know, the public's. The BBC's right to lead the *10 O'Clock News* with wet-lipped details of the latest toddler strangulation.

Roasting. *See* FOREPLAY, A SOCCER PLAYER'S IDEA OF.

Roberts, Tanya, properly **Victoria Blum** (b.1954). Admirers of Miss Roberts are advised to boot up at the first appropriate opportunity and visit The Iconophile's Tanya Roberts Reliquary, www.homunculus.com, where they will find a comprehensive list of this delightful artist's films. It is generally acknowledged that her best work can be seen in *Sheena, The Jungle Queen* (1984). Those who argue that Miss Roberts isn't really a British Celebrity are overlooking the fact that the ongoing soft-core cinematic porn rivalry between her and Miss Shannon Tweed formed the backbone of Dawn AIREY's imaginative late-night scheduling when she was in charge at Channel 5.

Robinson, Mary, *née* Darby (1758–1807), also known as Perdita. One of the most admired, reviled, painted and written-about women of the 18th century, Mary Robinson arrived in London from Bristol at the age of 16. When scarcely out of her teens, she married the dissolute Thomas Robinson. She had ambitions to go on the stage and was hired by David Garrick to play Perdita in *The Winter's Tale* at Drury Lane. Here she was spotted by the Prince of Wales, known as Prinny. He dubbed himself her Florizel, and pursued her hysterically. But after a short, intense liaison, he grew tired of her.

Her next lover/protector was Prinny's best friend, Viscount Malden. Then she took up with Banastre ('Butcher') Tarleton, a popular hero of the American War of Independence. By now she was regarded by the public as little more than a courtesan, and her union with Tarleton was commemorated in a Gillray cartoon, which featured Mary with her legs in the air. The relationship lasted for 15 years, though Tarleton's family was horrified by his association with such a notorious woman.

As was noted by the perceptive critic Suzi Feay when reviewing *Perdita: Royal Mistress, Writer, Romantic* by Sarah Gristwood (Bantam, 2005), 'The phrase "actress, model, whatever" is a modern one, but Perdita was the ultimate "whatever". She couldn't go shopping without a press of people materializing around her. Her exploits were written up in the gutter press. Her clothes were scrutinized and copied. Sarah Gristwood can't quite resist the urge to call Mary and her lover Banastre Tarleton "the Posh and Becks of their day", and, much as visiting football fans sang pornographic chants about Mrs Beckham, Mary became the focus of scurrilous prints, fantasies and bawdy verse.'

When Tarleton was summoned by his parents to France, Mary, following him post-haste to Dover, suffered a terrible and mysterious injury. She was paralysed from the waist down (with what is now thought to be rheumatoid arthritis) and never walked again. At this point she published a series of long autobiographical poems, much admired by Wordsworth and Coleridge. Thus in the end, the shop-soiled glamour model influenced the Romantic movement. More than one commentator has pointed out that it's a bit like discovering that Hedy Lamarr invented radio-controlled nuclear missiles. Which in fact she did.

See also IF ALL ELSE FAILS, DIVERSIFY.

Roe, Erica (b.1961). Streaker.

See also GODIVA, LADY.

Rogue, a loveable. An elderly drunk trailing disappointed tradesmen and bewildered wives.

Role model, a good. A soccer player not currently on a charge. A soccer player not currently in rehab. A soccer player who hasn't recently beaten up his wife.

Romark, properly **Albert 'Bert' Leywood** (1923–91). The most celebrated television conjuror of his day. In 1971 he announced that he was going to give a public display of his psychic powers. 'I'm going to drive blindfold through Ilford,' he said. On 12 October he placed two coins, a slice of dough and a thick band across his eyes. Then he climbed into a yellow Renault and set off down Cranbrook Road. After twenty yards he drove into the back of a parked police car. A large crowd formed round Romark, who said, 'The car was parked in a place where logic told me it wouldn't be.' He shortly retired, his slot on TV being filled first by Ali Bongo, later by Paul Daniels.

Rooney, Wayne (b.1987). In December 2004, local residents in posh Wilmslow, Cheshire, were disturbed by the news that soccer ace Wayne Rooney planned to rent a £3000-a-month mock-Tudor house in the area. Celebrities already living there included Sir Alex Ferguson, *Corrie* veteran William Roache and radio sports pundit Stuart Hall. Particularly concerned were a forty-caravan-strong group of Roma Gypsies who had recently bought a plot of land from millionaire farmer, Richard Scott. 'There goes the neighbourhood,' said the leading Traveller. 'I'm not a snob or anything but it will be velour tracksuits and puffa body-warmers on the washing line and rough girls in low-slung jeans. It will be GEORDETTES next, mark my words. I intend to call Sir Alex and other residents to an emergency meeting at the first opportunity. This will make you laugh. What do you call a chav in a box? Innit. What do you call a chav in a filing cabinet? Sorted. What's the first question at a chav quiz night? "What you lookin' at?"' Rooney has a mission to support the indigent sex workers of his native Liverpool, where a CCTV camera recorded his charitable efforts outside a brothel. 'I'll shag you for £50,' he shouted. Not all the prospective recipients of his bounty are as grateful as they might be. Curvy brunette Gina McCarrick told the *Sunday Mirror* that young Rooney has a face 'like a smacked arse'. Inexplicably, Rooney was voted most fanciable footballer in a survey of women fans carried out by research agency TNS Sport.

See also McLOUGHLIN, COLLEEN.

Root, Henry (1935–2005). Right-wing fishmonger who, in 1980, experienced a low glimmer of notoriety by writing facetious letters to busy people and thereafter organizing them into a spoof book, *The Henry Root Letters* (Weidenfeld & Nicolson, 1980). This laborious prank was taken to have been modelled on *The Life and Death of Rochester Sneath* (1974) by the ill-mannered Conservative politician Humphry Berkeley (1926–94). In fact it was a straight rip-off of a much funnier book, *The Lazlo Toth Letters* (1977) by the American comedian Don Novello.

See also BRYSON, DR KIT.

Ross, Jonathan (b.1959). Over-excited chat-show host with a mind like a bowel disease. He thinks quicker than you can flush the chain. Julian Clary meets Frank Skinner. One minute he's talking dirty to Liza Tarbuck, the next he's flirting with a Hollywood hunk. There's something unresolved here. Enforced shower-sex with four very large men in a top-security prison?

Ross, Paul (b.1955). Jonathan's less successful brother. Also a TV presenter, his career reached its zenith with *The Paul Ross Show* in 1997. Since then he has been reduced to scoffing 15 pork pies a day in a desperate bid to become eligible for *Celebrity Fit Club*.

Rossetti, Dante Gabriel. *See* MORRIS, JANE; SIDDAL, ELIZABETH ELEANOR.

Rushdie, Salman (b.1947). Party monster who lives off canapés. Invited everywhere for his flashbulb smile. His actress wife Padma Lakshmi tries to persuade him to get back to writing, but Salman is having none of it. 'I'm loving these,' he says, of the rose petals scattered around the washbasin of one West End nightclub. 'Small touches like this make all the difference to a party, don't you think?'

S

St George (early 4th century AD). It's hardly surprising that with a patron saint like George the English seldom show fire in the belly, pride in the shirt or turn Twickenham into a cauldron of emotion. For one thing, he was born in what is now Turkey, later becoming an officer in the Roman army. He became England's patron saint in the 16th century for reasons that have never been adequately explained. He is also the patron saint of Moscow and Portugal, where he is believed to have acquired property on the Algarve. He never slew a dragon, or if he did it was merely a large lizard, and he never visited England. An enlightening comparison can be made with St David (or St Dewi), the patron saint of Wales. Born *c.*520 near St Bride's Bay, Pembrokeshire, St David presided over two Welsh synods, at Brefi and the 'Lucus Victoriae' or Synod of Victory. He died in 601 as Bishop of Menevia, afterwards St David's. His feast day is 1 March. Small wonder that with such a patron saint the Welsh consistently show pride in the shirt. Which isn't to say that Gavin Henson, the conceited centre three-quarter, won't be hit as if by a wrecking-ball from outer space, his various parts being redistributed around the field, once Mike Tindall is fit enough to resume his duties in England's three-quarter line (*see also* LURCH, CHARLOTTE *and* PHILLIPS, ZARA).

St Valentine (*c.*1315–?). St Valentine has similarities with St Michael since they share common origins in the retailing business. The first Valentine (Mario) ran a chain of dry-goods outlets in 14th-century Siena, and with the fortune his early marketing strategies achieved he was able to bid successfully for canonization from Pope Pius VI (a pope remarkable by modern standards for having strangled most of his dinner guests and thrown their bodies into the Tiber). The marketing strategy employed today by the gift-card industry is in many respects identical to the original blueprint Valentine himself laid out in 1356.

San Lorenzo, the. Celebrity restaurant situated in Beauchamp Place, Knightsbridge, and run since 1963 by Mara Berni, a busy little Piedmontese. Originally a favourite rendezvous for 60s Celebrities such as Michael Caine, Mick Jagger and Anouska Hempel, it now relies on the continuing patronage of Liz Hurley, who gives acting lessons there on alternate Thursdays to friends like Posh Spice who have ambitions to repeat Liz's success in Tinsel Town (it has escaped their notice that Liz never achieved any success in Tinsel Town). There was great excitement in June 2005 when Guy Ritchie said he would be visiting the restaurant at lunchtime on the following Thursday. He would be looking for two girls to play Posh Tarts in his new film *Muff*. They all turned up – Victoria Beckham, Jennifer Ellison, Nancy Sorrell, Abi Titmuss, Tania Do-Nascimento, Lisa Snowden, Sophie Anderton, Dr David Starkey, Vicki Walberg (Miss UK). Ritchie said, 'I'll take those two there', and he pointed towards a couple of working girls (Dopey Linda and Fat Fiona) who had dropped in for a quick reviver between shifts at Chelsea Girl Escorts, situated in Beauchamp Place opposite the San Lorenzo. Dr Starkey later claimed that he would have been picked before Dopey Linda or Fat Fiona had he not been obliged to leave the audition half way through to take part in a lingerie shoot for Agent Provocateur.

San Marino. *See* MARINO, DAN; WORLD CUP 2006, ENGLAND'S PROSPECTS IN.

Sarpong, June (b.1976). Tireless TV presenter, born in Leytonstone of Ghanaian parentage. Has a laugh like Lauryn Hill being tickled and a quick, slick line in chat that always makes some sort of sense. In a nutshell, the friendly, sorted side of Yoof TV. Career lows: *Your Face or Mine?* with Jeff Brazier – TV so tacky you were in danger of sticking to it – and *Pop Beach*, an optimistic attempt to make Great Yarmouth into a Hawaiian jamboree. June, in a pink crochet cap and frayed blue togs, yelled 'Great Yarmouth, are you having fun?' Great Yarmouth's teeth collectively chattered in response. Career high: *T4* with Vernon Kay. What's next? She could end up presenting a lifestyle fashion show, *Sarpong's Sarongs*.

Sassy. Scrawny, no-neck American actress reduced to vibrator sex.

Science, the wonders of modern. A means of finding continued employment for Johnny VAUGHAN.

Scott-Lee, Lisa (b.1975). Wildly sexy singer, if you go in for squashy faces and too-tight stiletto straps. In 1997 Lisa left her home in Rhyl to answer an advert in *The Stage* calling for members of a new pop band that was to be called Steps. The novelty of a band starring both boys and girls proved popular and their album *Steptacular!* went platinum four times over. When that group folded Lisa won a solo record deal, and she continues to produce tunes that are popular with the gay community. She also has a lot of fun. 'I got cautioned for mooning in Dublin,' she giggles. 'I have this thing where I stick my bum out of the window the first time I visit a new country.' Perhaps she should be encouraged to visit Oman, where this offence might land her with 15 years in a confined space.

Sedative in Swiss psychiatric wards, music used as a. *See* CORRS, THE.

Seldom out of step with the crassest aspects of the contemporary sensibility. *See* FINNIGAN, JUDY.

September Celebrity *Faux Pas*

Roger Scruton (b.1947) rides illegally with the Quorn. At the first jump, fat women go over their horses' heads. A dismounted girl steps into a hole and is savaged by a badger. The fox explodes in a ball of fur and faeces. The moustachioed MFH sticks the fox's penis into the ear of the first pubescent girl to arrive at the kill. Weeping women cover their faces and shoot their broken horses. Hounds are rewarded with toy dogs and tropical birds. Only country people understand.

Michael Portillo returns from a holiday in Mexico sporting a ponytail.

Jeffrey Archer participates in a partridge shoot organized by Hugh Fearnley-Whittingstall. He wears plus fours in an attempt to reinforce his country identity, but fails to overcome his fear of cows, and refuses to cross fields. He claims another man's bird, slows partridges down with bird-lime, knocks them out of the sky with the butt of his 12-bore. Fearnley-Whittingstall shoots his dog for disciplinary reasons and hangs it in the pantry. Afraid that the dog may be on that night's menu, Archer returns to London in a hurry.

At the Notting Hill Carnival, **Cherie Blair** limbo dances competitively with John Prescott. **Michael Howard**, looking resolute, is asked the time by a bespectacled African student, hands over all his money and runs. **Prince Charles**, concerned that he will one day be hung by the heels from a lamppost by disaffected subjects, attends in Hawaiian shirt and open-toed sandals, fails to recognize **Prince Harry** in woolly wig smoking ganja with drug-crazed street thieves. Former home secretary **David Blunkett** hand-jives with heavy-footed community policemen. Blunkett's dog sniffs out stash of weed in Rastafarian church, grasses up congregation, drops record number of rungs on Celebrity *Faux Pas* ladder.

Selling suppositories in Boots. *See* SURREAL.

Sex and the City Lifestyle, living the. Three Cardiff-based fat girls get together for a night out and feel really zeitgeisty.

Sex Inspectors, The. 'Sounds like one for us, Kevin'.

See also ADULT CONTENT; CHANNEL 4; LYGO, KEVIN.

Sex therapist. A wizened matron from California instructing a semi-circle of jack-naked housewives in the use of orgasmic aids.

Sexy. Plain but noisy.

See also BUBBLY.

Shergar. Celebrity Horse. Rumoured to have ended up on a spit outside a kebab stall in Old Compton Street. Alternatively, lost in the MAZE AT LONGLEAT.

For other Celebrity Horses, *see* BUCEPHALUS; RED RUM.

Shooting Stars. See SURREAL.

Shortly to be photographed in a lesbian clinch. A former UK pop tottie who, having moved to LA, can't even get a walk-on part in *Desperate Housewives*.

See also SHORTLY TO BE PHOTOGRAPHED IN NOTHING-LEFT-TO-THE-IMAGINATION UNDIES.

Shortly to be photographed in nothing-left-to-the-imagination undies. A former UK pop tottie who has been photographed in a lesbian clinch and has appeared, to no avail, in *Desperate Housewives*.

Siddal, Elizabeth Eleanor (1834–62). Known to Siddal insiders as 'Guggums'. It was a roller-coaster life. One day you're a common-as-muck milliner's assistant, the next, you've been spotted by the Pre-Raphaelite Brotherhood and your painting's in the Royal Academy. How SURREAL is that? Being a tall, pouty stunner with coppery red hair must have helped, as Lucinda Hawksley points out in her biography, *Lizzie Siddal: The Tragedy of a Pre-Raphaelite Supermodel*. It was the look Holman Hunt was going for in his 1850 painting, *Converted British Family Sheltering a Missionary*. And in 1852, Sir John Everett Millais found her to be his perfect *Ophelia*. ('He was totally blown away when he saw her. I mean, like, *totally*,' said a Millais insider at the time.) But posing for this painting wreaked havoc with her health, since it required her to pose for days on end in a tub of cold water. Tubercular infection set tragic Lizzie on the slippery slope of laudanum abuse that eventually killed her.

Before her death she found time to marry bad boy Dante Gabriel Rossetti, the art world's Darren DAY. Exhausted by his many infidelities, she died of a laudanum overdose (a note pinned to her nightgown makes it clear that suicide was her intention). Rossetti was so racked with guilt that he buried many of his poems with her in Highgate Cemetery. As was his custom on such occasions, he retrieved these shortly afterwards.

Sincere regret, expressing. A soccer player who has glassed three doormen at the Wellington Club and now hopes to avoid a jail sentence by booking himself into a detox clinic. Alternatively, aristocratic crack addicts working the same scam. Sooner or later, the latter suffer disagreeable symptoms. When not stealing money from their sisters' handbags or looting their country seats for marketable ancestral treasures, aristocratic freebasers spend all their time maintaining the pipe, examining its ducts and gullies for impurities and bits to lick. They drink ammonia and search each other's eyeballs for maximum dilation. They crawl on the carpet searching for rocks. The women are frigid, the men impotent. They lose four stone in weight and attempts at intercourse are abandoned when their bones scrape together with a noise like Janet Street-Porter dragging her front teeth down a blackboard. Only when they get arrested with six ounces of cocaine in their underwear do they check into an addiction clinic in an attempt to impress the magistrate. As to what happens to less privileged crack abusers, who cares?

See also APOLOGIES.

Slanging-matches, the mother of all. A D-lister insults a C-lister and gets some B-list publicity. The Battle of the Boobs kicks off. Sexy Jodie MARSH from Brentwood, 32DD, squares up to legendary glamour girl JORDAN, 32FF.

Round 1. Stunning Jodie leads with a stiff left jab. 'Jordan's got no class. I've got more style in my little finger than Jordan's got in her fat arse.' Ouch!

Jordan wobbles, but she comes out fighting: 'Jodie's a big-nosed slapper.' Kerrump!

The *Daily Star* is behind scrumptious Jodie – her boobs are 100% real, they announce.

But raunchy Jordan, relaxing on a millionaire's yacht in Puerto Banus, takes time off from romping with best pal Jerri Byrne (32DD), to point out that gorgeous Jodie has saggy tits.

Sadly, these two girls have no idea how to have a real cat fight. If gorgeous Jodie had any skill at this game she'd respond to Jordan's claim that she's got a nose like a builder's elbow by claiming that she's never seen a builder's elbow. 'It's obvious that our backgrounds are very different,' she'd say. Then she'd slap her in the mouth.

Slater, Kat. *See* WALLACE, JESSIE.

Smillie, Carol (b.1961). Former topless model. Nose like a trigonometry problem. Still lives in Edinburgh, unaccountably known as the Athens of the North. A wet, miserable, Scotch-bastard place only made tolerable by a substantial heroin habit. She recently said, 'When I get home I take my make-up off and undergo the transformation from being Carol Smillie to being Mrs Knight.' Bad luck for Mr Knight. Carol falls off Celebrity *Faux Pas* Ladder.

Smith, Zadie (b. 1975). Cambridge-educated model of floral hair adornments and colourful headscarves. In an interview with a New York magazine in 2005, she proved herself to be a perceptive critic of UK celebrity culture. 'It's just general stupidity, madness, vulgarity, stupid TV shows, aspirational arseholes, money everywhere.' she said. A pity that popular pressure forced the statuesque beauty to issue a statement retracting this trenchant comment.

Snowden, Lisa (b.1974). Born Snawden, in Welwyn Garden City. Blessed with almost six feet of comfortable curves, Lisa has got your body. The body you deserve. The body that's inside you somewhere, if only you could reach that far. A body like Simon Carr's. Lisa also has a wonderful memory: 'I can remember my first bra,' she informed the *Daily Star*. She has graced adverts for Dove, Mercedes, Neutrogena, Lynx, Gossard, and nothing delights her more than putting on that Special K red leotard. It just makes her want to leap around and smile. After dating Dane Bowers and *CSI: Crime Scene*'s Gary Dourdan, she met George Clooney on the set of a Martini commercial. Although they have enjoyed happy times together, Lisa eventually lost out to her rival, Wilbur, Clooney's pot-bellied pet pig. If that's where Special K gets you, stick to Weetabix.

Soap opera stars, bald. Steve McFadden. Ross Kemp. Joan Collins.

Sorrell, Nancy (b.1981). Former lap dancer now married to the comedian Vic Reeves. In November 2004 she took part in *I'm A Celebrity, Get Me Out Of Here*, and was the first contestant to be evicted by public vote. Greeted by Ant and Dec, she trilled, 'I've so reached that stage when I want to bring out an album! EMI are really interested. They do Robbie Williams, you know. I'm looking at all the possibilities.'

'Sounds like one for us, Kevin.' *See* ADULT CONTENT; CHANNEL 4; LYGO, KEVIN.

Spake, Jeremy (b.1969). It's six years since the BBC's fly-on-the-wall series *Airport* first brought the plump, Russian-speaking baggage-handler into the nation's homes. Jeremy is as camp as Christmas, but, in spite of what viewers might think, he's a happily married man with two lovely children. Not, of course, that it would be of any consequence – in these politically correct times (*see* CLARKSON, JEREMY; LITTLEJOHN, RICHARD) – if he was as gay as a goose, which he isn't.

Stansfield, Lisa (b.1967). The Edith Piaf of Bolton. Lisa's traditional home-produced handbag-soul has given way at last to Trevor Horn's Big Pop. It suits her down to her Manolos. Her delivery is now enormous, especially on ballads. It's like being run over by a fudge juggernaut.

Star-studded salon opening. The *South Wales Mercury*'s 'Outstanding Launch Party of the Year Award' went to the opening in May 2004 of the Mark Jermin Hairdressing Salon at the Holiday Inn, Swansea. Among the Celebrities attending the occasion were:

☆ Charlie Brooks – *EastEnders*
☆ Adele Silva – *Emmerdale*
☆ Helen Adams's sister
☆ Ashley Campbell – *Mysti* – New BBC Saturday morning show
☆ Jessica Garlick – *Pop Idol*
☆ Hayley Evetts – *Pop Idol*
☆ Gina – *The Salon*
☆ Ricardo – *The Salon*
☆ Katherine Jenkins – New young Welsh opera star currently No. 1 in classical charts
☆ Adele Vellacott – Darren Day's ex
☆ Max Brown – *Hollyoakes*
☆ Lucinda Rhodes Flaherty – BBC Cavegirl – Harry's girlfriend
☆ Bonnie Tyler – Singer
☆ Lisa Jeynes – *Big Brother 4*
☆ Lucy Bolster
☆ Catherine Zeta-Jones' parents
☆ Lee Trundle – Swansea football team
☆ Roberto Martinez – Swansea football team
☆ Other unspecified players from Swansea football team

Stein, Rick (b.1945). Charmless cook. Educated in the independent sector, but he cranks his accent down through three sub-classes when appearing on television. He's the sort of man who goes everywhere with a common little dog, often called Chalky. Worse, he'd obviously prefer food to sex – perspiring with anticipation when confronted by a plate of Ragoût of Turbot and Scallops with Chicory, Fried Tarragon and Noilly Prat, rather as other men feel a softening in the loins when, in the course of researching a book on 15th-century madrigals for the Oxford University Press, they in-advertantly stumble into Jo Hicks's web site.

Sterne, Laurence (1713–68). Few authors become so famous that they are recognized. You could share a lift with Thomas Mann, offer your seat to Mrs Gaskell or stick your leg out and trip up Dorothy Wordsworth and be none the wiser. But Sterne sat for Joshua Reynolds in 1760, and the portrait of his beaky, naughty face was reprinted and disseminated so often and so widely that he became instantly recognizable. So when Sterne died and his body was stolen by gravediggers and sold to a Cambridge professor of anatomy, and the winding sheet was pulled back ready for the lecture in dissection to begin, bingo! Commotion and outrage from the students, who refused to dissect their favourite novelist, and insisted instead that he had a proper Christian burial. Who says being famous doesn't have some benefits?

Stevens, Rachel (b.1978). Cheerful pop star, lissom-limbed and glossy-lipped. She looks a bit like Mariah Carey before she went mad. Or Barbra Streisand after a particularly successful re-birthing ceremony. Born in North London, at 15 Rachel won a *Just 17* modelling competition. In 1999 she joined S-Club 7, with whom she had 12 top ten hits, released 5 albums and won two Brit Awards. Her solo career took off with the catchy single 'Sweet Dreams, My LA-Ex', originally written by Cathy Dennis for Britney Spears. (The eponymous LA-Ex is thought to be Justin Timberlake.) It's hoped that this enterprising pop poppet will get bigger and bigger (not literally – she's too fond of her Exerciser TM for that). Otherwise she'll just become another Geri Halliwell, and one's too many already.

Stiletto pants. According to fashionistas, they are the best thing since sliced bruschetta, darling. At last, the stiletto boot fuses with the trouser leg, in an effortless communion of elements. The brainchild of wonderful, wonderful Karl at Channers (*see* LAGERFELD, KARL). Simply the last word in trousers. Paris catwalks have seen nothing so thrilling since we had the inside-out coat last week.

Very edgy. Very now. And very hard to take off. Almost impossible, in fact. Like a pervert's wet suit. 'Give me a hand, will you, sweetie?'

Still more Celebrity Catchphrases.

'Whereof we cannot speak, thereof must we be silent' – Ludwig Wittgenstein.

'Get off the table, Mabel, the money's for the beer' – Wilfred Pickles.

Stock, thinking things over and taking. A Celebrity who has just been arrested with seven ounces of cocaine in their underwear.

Stone, Joss, properly **Joscelyn Stoker** (b.1986). Joss looks like a fresh-faced Devonian maiden, like your GCSE-age daughter's most attractive friend, but she sings like a 50-year-old survivor from the glory days of Motown. When she opens her mouth the surprise is like hearing Tess of the D'Urbervilles rapping. The daughter of a dried-fruit importer and a housewife, Joss is a bit hippy-dippy, the sort of girl who has flowers drawn in biro on her jeans and a nose piercing ('I can't get it out unless I pull really hard … and then it bleeds', she told the *The Times*). Her friends call her Joss Stick, which isn't an allusion to her shape. Joss isn't thin. She's comfortable. She endeared herself to the nation when, at the Band Aid recording session in December 2004, she said, 'Who the flip is Bob Gandalf, then?' Joss is also famous for having the biggest pair of lungs that can be healthy in a girl of her age. They produce a sound which is phenomenal, elemental, anthemic… and very very loud. She has sold 2 million albums, bellowed a live duet with Gladys Knight, belted out her songs on *Top of the Pops* and from every supermarket tannoy: 'Yeuhhh Haaad Meh, Yeuhhh Lawwwwst Meh…' Cut it out, Joss!

Strecker, Tania (b.1973). Once, a ravishing blonde TV presenter (*Beachmate*, *The Big Breakfast*). Now, a faintly haggard TV contestant (*Road Raja, Celebrity Wheelchair Challenge* – 'three Celebrities travel to Edinburgh without ever using their legs!'). Tania's slide down the Celebrity chute is thought to have been precipitated by gin and Robbie Williams, whom she dated for four months. She also made the mistake of claiming on Radio Five that her ex, Guy Ritchie, had been two-timing her with a pregnant Madonna. Tania was undergoing treatment with the AA at the time. In the final analysis, Tania simply doesn't deserve to be a Celebrity any more. She hasn't even mastered the art of one-upmanship. When Madonna introduced herself at the Mario Testino launch party with the words, 'I'm Madonna,' Tania replied, 'I know who the fuck you are.' She should have said, 'Oh really, and what do you do?'

Street-Porter, Janet, *née* **Bull** (b.1947). Tubular-limbed Olive Popeye look-alike. She says things about men that would carry a prison sentence in a civilized country. However, not to laugh appreciatively when she speaks would be as unkind as not to share the joke with a man who, on a formal occasion, has chosen to wear a false nose and humorous spectacles. Having agreed to appear *I'm a Celebrity, Get Me Out Of Here* in 2004, she said that she'd rather sleep with a cockroach than with any of the other participants. It is not obvious that the cockroach would have been comfortable with any such arrangement. Commissioned by the *Independent* to write about Greg Dyke's resignation from the BBC, she contributed a thousand words about herself. 'Like Greg, I don't bother with the niceties! You know J S-P!' No we don't, and we don't want to. That said, she has the merit at least of making Michael Winner seem self-effacing.

Street tuff. Posh making a tit of herself.

Stringfellow, Peter (b.1940). Night-club owner mentioned by Jacques Derrida in a paper discovered after the French philosopher's death in 2004. 'London, home of *la vie en gris,*' it starts. 'Slate skies. Thick crombies over old-style dancing-gowns in Piccadilly. Fat women going down on black ice. Paul Raymond's renowned Revuebar, where men with naval binoculars sit alone in cubicles. Slung up in the traction of his inhibitions, the Englishman in his cubicle is yet freer than the skipping Frenchman; he understands that the sharpest pleasures must have an edge of shame. Truly, *le vice français* is a limiting disregard for thrilling inhibition. I am reminded of this whenever I visit London. Emblems of *la vie en gris,* of what made England great, survive – Camilla Parker Bowles, Chris Tarrant, street derelicts huddled over heat vents in Piccadilly Circus, moth-eaten pageantry at the Cenotaph – but the dominating image is of a pot-bellied unashamed voluptuary in a powder-blue *cache-sexe* posing on a beach in the Caribbean with a woman forty years his junior. Is it a Port Said pimp? An Italian pandar? No. It is Peter Stringfellow, strip-show entrepreneur and enemy of *la vie en gris.* But here is a conundrum. Is he at one and the same time the furtive Anglo-Saxon voyeur and the tit-squeezing Gallic-style sexual extrovert? Achilles and the Tortoise in but a single form? A Zeno's Paradox *pour nos jours?*'

See also VIE EN GRIS, LA.

Stud muffin. 'An exceptionally successful and attractive person' (*Cassell's Dictionary of Slang,* 2005 edition).

See also TOTALLY FIT STUD MUFFINS.

Sugababes. Bully girls who produce great pop hits. Mutya Bueno (b.1985, face like thunder and thighs to match) and Keisha Buchanan (b.1984, Janet Jackson but without the charm) have been friends since school in Wembley and speak in their own personal code. They efficiently froze out former bandmate Siobhan Donaghy, who excused herself to go to the lavatory during an interview on their Japan tour and never came back. 'I hate her for running away and leaving us,' Mutya has said. 'Why couldn't she have had the guts to tell me to my face what her problem was?' Sibohan has since gone on to form her own group, Shanghai Nobody, and has been replaced with new Sugababe, the blonde, willowy Heidi Range (b.1983). Heidi is said to be doing as well as can be expected and hopes that some day soon Mutya and Keisha will start talking to her.

See also GROWING APART.

Surreal. An adjective used to describe any unexpected development. 'I mean, like, *hello!* Last week I was selling suppositories in Boots! Today I met Elton John! It's, like, totally surreal!'

See also LIKE; MADELY, RICHARD; VIC 'N' BOB; WORDS, CELEBRITIES' FAVOURITE.

Suspender belts, lower-class women cocaine and. *See* BOUGH, FRANK.

Sweeney, Claire (b.1972). Liverpudlian plebeian and professional smiler. Many of her smiles have a slightly forced quality, as if she's on stage and determined not to let the audience notice that she has sat on a pin. She started off singing and smiling at working men's clubs, aged 14, then starred in *Brookie*, then toured the world with P&O cruises singing Celine Dion songs in between calling bingo and smiling at incontinent tourists. She smiled on posters to indicate how comfortable she found the bras of Marks and Spencer. Smiled to indicate the joy the Lottery could bring. Smiled on *Celebrity Big Brother 2001* and smiled while murdering her husband as Roxie Hart in *Chicago*. Please, somebody take her away.

T

Tantric massage group. Common women taking their clothes off in the afternoon.

Taxi drivers, shameless. The modern Celeb has to think twice before hailing a black cab. They will be abused all the way to the Hammersmith roundabout ('So, Mr Bremner, how comes you're not funny any more?') and then criticized, all the way back to Hackney, for mean tipping ('Guess who I had in the back before you? Not what you'd call generous'). And that's only supposing they don't have sharp ears. If they do, the Celeb's conversation will appear on the gossip website Popbitch or similar. *Vide* the couple Kate Moss and Daniel Craig. Daniel – 'You're gorgeous.' Kate – 'I know that.'

Te Kanawa, Kiri (b.1948). Yodelling Samoan with a weakness for Broadway musicals. When they do Sondheim she's either sitting in the stalls with New York's A-list queers or cavorting on the stage. In the latter case, she looks like Clive James doing the lambada.

Television we deserve, the. In February 2005, the television critic Charlie Courtauld asked a Channel 4 executive what sort of programmes he was looking for. 'Programmes about interesting people,' replied the executive. 'You know – like kids with huge tumours on their faces.' It was a telling insight, Courtauld noted, into the sort of audience TV executives imagined they catered to. Particularly Channel 4 executives. 'According to them,' wrote

Courtauld, 'we want the freakishly unusual (*Little Lady Fauntleroy*), the ghoulish (*Anatomy for Beginners*), the nasty (*Cosmetic Surgery Live)* and the plain cruel (*Big Brother).* All these are served up for us in the name of "education". But these programmes are only educative in the way that 19th-century freak-show fans were educated when they went to poke, laugh or stare at the Elephant Man.'

See also CHANNEL 4; GREAT TELEVISION; LYGO, KEVIN.

Text messaging. A means of communication by which the views of hairdressers and bar staff are broadcast on Channel 4 News.

The Day My Boobs Went Bust! 'Sounds like one for us, Kevin.'

See also ADULT CONTENT; CHANNEL 4; JORDAN; LYGO, KEVIN.

There goes the neighbourhood. *See* ROONEY, WAYNE.

Thompson, Emma (b.1961). Unaffected luvvie. Expressions she uses on set to prove she's one of the chaps: 'Oh fuckity fuck!' 'Oh lorks! I've just come on!' 'Crikey Moses! My knickers have gone up my crack!'

Thornton, Kate (b.1979). TV frontperson. The suggestion that she resembles a punishment-block warder in a peak-time ITV prison drama is entirely without foundation.

Thoroughly Rococo seeing-to, Petsy getting a. *See* BONKING BORIS.

3am Girls, The *Daily Mirror*'s. Glamorous gossips, with the most sought after job in Wapping. Who wouldn't want to spend every night mopping sick off Natalia Imbruglia's chin in the hope she'll let slip a secret? Who wouldn't want to arrive at a party and have Mel C shout 'What are those sluts doing here?' For their services to Celebrity culture, they received five pages of coverage in *Vanity Fair* magazine and won a *What the Papers Say* award.

Titmuss, Abi (b.1976). Average-looking blonde seeking employment in the entertainment industry. Has own nurse's uniform and lots of experience in front of video cameras. Cynics thought it a bit fishy the way she dashed from the day job in casualty to be at the side of her undeserving ex, John Leslie, as he faced allegations of rape. And the cynics were right. Since standing by her man, Abi has shed several layers of clothes and landed a job with Richard and Judy. Sadly, her contract was cancelled following revelations that she and Leslie had enjoyed a four-way orgy. Oooh, matron. There is a widely circulating video of this event, in which Leslie points out that he paid for Abi's new breasts. Mmm, nice. What's to be done? They're very short of nurses in certain parts of Africa.

See also FOREPLAY, JOHN LESLIE'S IDEA OF; GODIVA, LADY; UNDIES, ABI IN HER.

Toad, Mr (b.1908). Amphibian suffering from road rage. On the advice of Carole Caplin, he lets off steam with the primal exclamation: 'Poop Poop!'

'Toilet', 'gift' and 'hospitality', the sort of man who would say. *See* COWELL, SIMON.

Totally fit stud muffins. *See* BEST, CALUM; DAY, DARREN; LURCH, CHARLOTTE (for Gavin Henson); WALLIAMS, DAVID; and *see also* STUD MUFFIN.

Tragically robbed of his own childhood by the pressures of performing. A paedophile with $500 million in the bank (and whose fans, crucially, might be readers of *The News of the World*).

Troubled TV presenter. Serial *frotteur*.

Tweedy, Cheryl (b.1983). Leader of the attack pack known as Girls Aloud. 'If we weren't doing this, we'd be on the checkout at Tesco,' she says. Plenty of time for that, of course. Prancing about in a leather bustier pretending to sing is not necessarily a job for life, love. Admittedly, Cheryl Tweedy does it with aplomb, and has won the support of Julie Burchill, who has dubbed her 'Chav princess supreme'. Her plump, oiled thighs and meticulously straightened head of hair may have won Burchill over, but to more discerning eyes Tweedy is clearly a nasty piece of work. In January 2003 she punched a 39-year-old part-time law student Sophie Amogbokpa in a nightclub toilet. The assault was motivated by a lollipop.

See also AUGUST CELEBRITY *FAUX PAS*.

Twenty-four hours in the life of Frank Bruno. The former boxer suffered from a damaging bout of confusion in 2003. This was unsurprising. One moment the *Sun* shrieked 'BONKERS BRUNO LOCKED UP'. The next, it cooed 'SAD BRUNO IN MENTAL HOME'. And lastly, the compassionate voices at the *Sun* announced, 'TIME AND SPACE TO HEAL! A FUND FOR FRANK!' As if the confused old fist-fighter didn't have enough on his plate already, trying to convince us that he's the little Italian jockey Frankie Dettori.

U

Undies, Abi in her. 'Sounds like one for us, Kevin.'

See also ADULT CONTENT; BACKLASH AGAINST ELITISM, THE; CHANNEL 4; GREAT TELEVISION; LYGO, KEVIN.

Up for it. Common young people happy to display their private parts on *V Graham Norton*. Alternatively, a *Big Bruv* contestant who has just been awarded a 1st class degree in the History of Fine Art (*see* JUBIN, SHELL).

V

Valance, Holly (b.1981). Cut-rate Kylie. Born Holly Vuckadinovic, she changed her name first to Holly Shagpile, then to Holly Doublebed, before settling on the winning formula and shooting to fame. She once said of her her pop hit 'Kiss Kiss': 'When it comes on the radio, I switch off.' Evidently she's a woman of taste. Currently in Hollywood, sifting the offers.

Vaughan, Johnny (b.1966). Hapless loudmouth who has not presented one successful programme for eight years – since the BBC spent £3m acquiring his services, in fact. He went to public school, but not a very good one (Uppingham). He then became a cocaine dealer, but not a very good one. His last customers were two detectives staying in a hotel off the M1. He offered a defence, but not a very good one. He claimed that he was testing the gear for someone else. 'Who?' asked the detectives. 'Someone I met in a Post Office queue', replied Vaughan. Johnny, of whom it has been said that he looks like a less attractive Jimmy Carr, now pollutes the airways with his inane breakfast show on Capital Radio.

Versace, Donatella (b.1955). Raddled camel who inherited overpriced frock emporium from her deceased brother Gianni in 1997. She was once refused entry to Splash, a New York discotheque, since the doorman insisted she must be a Donatella drag-queen impersonator. Her passport photo was taken by Steven Meisel. When a make-up artist once suggested that she go for a more natural look, she responded with horror, crying, 'No! More is more!'

Vic 'n' Bob. They're so totally surreal! 'Why are you sitting down, Vic? 'I'm having a crap, Bob.' Off the wall!

See also SURREAL.

Vie en gris, La. A coinage by the French philosopher, Jacques Derrida (1930–2004), characterizing the British – more accurately, the specifically English – way of life. It was first discovered in an uncompleted paper about the nightclub owner, Peter STRING-FELLOW, a man Derrida took to be the enemy of English reserve.

Derrida famously approved of 'the Englishman's inability to escape from the straitjacket of his inhibitions', comparing his failure in this regard favourably with what he dubs as *le vice français* – 'the skipping Frenchman's inability to understand that the sex act is more satisfying if accompanied by a dark edge of shame'.

Vivacious. Fat and plain.

Vivacious and popular. Fat, plain and noisy.

Vorderman, Carol (b.1962). A regularly irrigated, unavoidable presence on national television. You can't get away from her. She's all over the place, like a mad woman's breakfast. She recently bought one of those TV sets which becomes a mirror when you close it down. She couldn't tell whether it was on or off.

Wacky. Glasgow exhibitionist runs around *Big Bruv* compound in her knickers, is later squashed flat by Portugeezer in mud-wrestling contest. 'Sounds like one for us, Kevin.'

See also CHANNEL 4; LYGO, KEVIN.

Walberg, Vicki (b.1979). Former Miss UK who made her acting debut playing the part of Fern BRITTON's body in a Ryvita commercial.

Wallace, Jessie (b.1971). Enfield-based actress known for her portrayal of Kat Slater in *EastEnders*. Forever having pregnancy dramas in order to keep up the circulation of *Now, New, Hot, Heat, Closer, Woman's Own* and *Company*. After all, she is Walford East's answer to Courtney Cox. Jessie met her fiancé Dave Morgan at Chelmsford Magistrates Court, where he was a police officer and she was up on a drink-driving charge. (Marrying the man who arrests you is a romantic ritual widely practised in the North; *see* GEORDETTES.) Their relationship was rocked in 2004 when Winston Rollock, a builder and friend of Mr Dave Morgan, sold a nasty story to a downmarket Sunday newspaper. 'Winston is now an ex-friend,' commented Mr Morgan, who, since Jessie dumped him in 2004, is now an ex-fiancé.

Walliams, David (b.1971). Born Williams, he changed his name in order to qualify for Equity. A talented wally in programmes such as *Little Britain*, he is also a serial seducer of questionable taste,

and has been linked to Jayne Middlemiss, Patsy Kensit, Abi Titmuss and Denise Van Outen. He showed off his bachelor pad in a three-page spread in the interiors pages of the *Sunday Telegraph*. It features a curved leather banquette in cantaloupe, to match the custom-built cupboards. He is rumoured to receive visitors here wearing a mauve silk dressing-gown.

Water, Celebrity. Celebrities don't drink from the tap. The very least they expect is Fijian, filtered through the purest ecosystem known to man and thus fit to rehydrate the likes of Andy Peters and Maureen Lipman. Kabbalah water goes one better. Their literature reads: 'Over the millennia, ancient Kabbalists believed water to be the source of all cleansing. Before drinking, the sages would inject the water with special meditations to help activate the powers of cleansing. These waters have been imbued with those same meditations. We encourage our customers to write to us and share their personal experiences after drinking our water. Write to: CA 90035.'

Weatherspoons, micro-skirted Valkyries descend on. *See* GEORDETTES.

Weatherwomen, actresses, models, royal trollops, tarts, Ulrika, whatever. *See* CAPRICE; DO-NASCIMENTO, TANIA; LANGTRY, LILLIE; LAWLER, KATE; MARSH, JODIE; PARKER BOWLES, CAMILLA; RICE-DAVIES, MANDY; ROBINSON, MARY; SORRELL, NANCY.

Weddings, invented. Dale Winton and Nell McAndrew (2003). Cynical stunt pulled in order to shift a few extra copies of *OK!* magazine.

Weddings, mistaken. 'That was a total ugh. I was not in love at all. We got crazy in Las Vegas.'

Westbrook, Daniella (b.1973). Deformed addict dressed up in a baby-doll negligée. 'Sounds like one for us, Kevin.'

Wildlife on Two (8.30p.m.). 'Kate Humble explores the world of the macaw and reveals that there's more to these colourful parrots than meets the eye.' 'Doesn't sound like one for us, Kevin.'

William-of-Orange. *See* DUNCANFROMBLUE.

Williams, Robbie (b.1974). Born in Stoke, Robbie was a Take That puppy – plump-cheeked, big-eyed, full of beans. Then he left the group and become an up-for-it break-away lad. Parties, coke, boys, girls ('I am the only man who can say he's been in Take That and at least two members of the Spice Girls'). His first solo album, *Life Thru a Lens* flopped. Then came 'Angels', which was positively anthemic. The follow-up albums made Robbie a mega-star, a pin-up, a fat boy, a muscle-man, a rock god, whatever. He has Boris

Johnson bursting into tribute choruses of 'I Don't Want To Rock, DJ!' during interviews. Robbie is the clown of our age. His ebullience is never far from tears, his despair never far from comedy. The more megafamous he becomes, the more unhappy Robbie is. The artist Alison Jackson depicted him bouncing on a bed covered in £50 pound notes, weeping. John Updike has said that Celebrity is the mask that eats the face. To look at Robbie's face is to see both the mask and the rotting flesh beneath. He will

never go away, or become contented or domesticated. He will become Norma Desmond, but not so pretty.

Winchester By-pass, The. *See* POSITIONS, CELEBRITIES' FAVOURITE SEXUAL.

Winner, Michael (b.1935). Now to be seen in television commercials wearing a ballerina's tutu, or merging into the foreground at a Celebrity Funeral, Winner was formerly a film director. He made his mark with *Some Like It Cool* (1959), which was shot in a nudist camp. He later enjoyed a long collaboration with the boorish actor, Oliver Reed. Dubbed 'the hell raiser's hell-raiser', Reed, when drunk, liked either to be beaten up in pubs by members of the working class or to indulge in acts of unfocused exhibitionism – the latter aspect of his character guaranteeing him many appearances on Michael Parkinson's 'chat show'. In 1973 he stripped naked in a Madrid restaurant and dived into an aquarium. On that occasion he was beaten up by the Spanish police. If there was no one else to fight, he fought himself, once knocking himself out.

Winslet, Kate (b.1975). Clumsy British actress with an aversion to glamour. 'Y'know,' says Kate, talking to a Fox newscaster at the Oscars about her $5000 De La Renta dress, 'I really HATE this frock, I can't even bloody sit DOWN in it, God knows what happens when I want to go for a PEE. CHRIST!' The camera swivels away dramatically, taking in a quick shot of the Fox newscaster, who looks like she's sucked a lemon, before settling com-
fortably on petitely perfect Lara Flynn Boyle.
Winslet can still be heard off camera, bellowing over the red carpet, 'Where's the bangers and mash? I'm starving, Marvin!'

Winslet, born in Reading and trained in Maidenhead, first appeared on television in a Sugar Puffs advert, dancing with the Honey Monster. Next it was the role of Pandora in *Adrian Mole*: *The Musical*. She was making a pastrami sandwich in the deli where she worked on Saturdays when she heard she had won the lead role in *Heavenly Creatures*, a film which would lead on to *Titanic* and major stardom. It is not known whether she finished making the sandwich.

Winterson, Jeanette (b.1961). Flame-haired avatar of 20th-century fiction. Brave, briny and unbridled; the crack of light forcing itself through the establishment door... but that's enough of what she thinks she is. To the rest of us, she's a funny-looking novelist with a bit of a bob on herself. The adopted daughter of two Pentecostal evangelists, she was raised to be a missionary, and (though she rejected religion at 16 when her parents threw her out for lesbianism) she retains a zealot's enthusiasm for art and literature. And one author more than all others. When asked to nominate her ten best novels of all time, nine of the novels on her list were by herself. The tenth was by her cat.

Winton, Dale (b.1961). Sinister TV presenter with a face the colour of a tangerine. His mother was the tragic 60s starlet Sheree Winton, whose real name was Diana Fluck. The showbiz anecdote has it that the film actor, Stewart Granger, afraid that he might blurt this out at an awards ceremony, rehearsed his speech all day and, when the moment came, introduced her as 'Diana Clunt'. Winton is the three times winner of the AWARD FOR ORANGENESS SPONSORED BY TERRY'S CHOCOLATE ORANGE.

Wintour, Anna (b.1941). Skeletal British fashion editor of *American Vogue*. Amusingly dubbed Nuclear Wintour. When entering a dimly lit gallery, she prefers to tell the management to turn the lights up rather than remove her sunglasses. Asked who had been the major influence in her life, she immediately replied, 'Diana Vreeland, the greatest editor *Vogue* ever had. She was so uncompromising. Towards the end of her life she committed herself 100% to yellow. Everything had to be yellow. Yellow cushions, yellow sofas, yellow tables, yellow dresses, yellow carpets, yellow walls. She died of jaundice. They didn't find her body for three weeks.'

Women's lib. Sunday supplements now have 'Me and my vibrator' columns where the knitting patterns used to be.

Words, Celebrities' favourite. I, me, my, my latest book, my latest film, my column, my diet, my latest single, my knickers, my tits, my bum, my zip, my mum, my fly, my show, my mates, my great mates, my fans, my saving sense of humour, mad!, totally mad!, hey you guys, *so* last week, hilarious, what!, brilliant, focused, well barrelled, imagine!, Robbie! – you're *too* much!, pressure, yours truly, believe, would you believe, I don't believe it!, nude, starkers, just a laugh, just a giggle, truly a classic, I'm like 'how sad is that?', the public, the viewers, you at home, ordinary people, no way, my next guest, legend, great, all-time great, the man, the main man, charismatic, sexy, lovely, marvellous, how great is that?, of whom it's been said, and I quote, the size of Kent, anecdote, raconteur, my great mate Caine, relaxed, tanned, a big round of applause, the nation's heartstrings, LA, the Big Apple, the other side of the pond, royalty, royalties, charity, wisecrack, a classic wisecrack, tell me, tell us, tell the people at home, how did it feel, crying all the way to the bank, can't be bad, we should be so lucky, LIKE totally SURREAL.

Wordsworth, William (1770–1850). Total wazzer. 'Earth has not anything to show more fair...' But he hadn't seen Jo Hicks in a riot skirt.

World Cup 2006, England's prospects in. They'll struggle to beat San Marino. They'd struggle to beat Dan MARINO, and he's had two hip replacements and wears a surgical collar.

Worrall Thompson, Anthony (b.1956). Smug cook with a face like a crushed Bee Gee. 'Must rush. Anthony Worrall Thompson's on the telly. I never miss a show if he's in it.' You'll not hear that said. A mystery.

Wyatt, Petronella (b.1970). The *Spectator* reader's wet dream (*see* BONKING BORIS).

Yet more Celebrity catchphrases.
'We have nothing to fear but fear itself' – Franklin D. Roosevelt.
'Nice to see you, to see you nice' – Bruce Forsyth.

Yobs, Celebrity. *See* BARDSLEY, LIZZIE; EVANS, CHRIS; LITTLEJOHN, RICHARD; McKENZIE, KELVIN.

'You know J S-P!' *See* STREET-PORTER, JANET .

Young, Will (b.1981). Crooner. 'Must rush. I'm off to buy the new Will Young single.' You'll not hear that said.

Picture Credits

Every effort has been made to trace the source of these pictures. Should there be any unintentional omissions the publisher will be happy to include them in a future edition.

Rex Features p.10, p.13, p.29, p.31, p.41, p.47, p.73, p.81, p.93, p.104, p.113, p.120, p.129, p.133, p.139, p.140, p.153, p.183, p.187, p.210, p.213, p.226, p.230, p.234, p.239, p.242, p.252, p.255, p.259, p.260; Bridgeman Art Library p.132; Corbis p.172–3